The Clothes Have No Emperor

Also By DJ

A Fleeting Improvised Man

The Clothes Have No Emperor:

Conversations, the Art of No-Self

DJ
and
David Bruneau

The Clothes Have No Emperor Copyright © 2014 by DJ.

All rights reserved. Printed in North America. No part of this book may be used or reproduced in any manner whatsoever without written permission except in the case of brief quotations embodied in critical articles or reviews.

This book is a work of non-fiction though certain names, organizations or places have been altered to maintain anonymity.

For information contact www.afleetingimprovisedman.com

Book and Cover design by DJ

Canadian Cataloguing in Publication Data
****

ISBN: 978-0-9919954-2-4

First Edition: November 2014

Dedication

This book is dedicated to radical iconoclasts, awakenists and seekers of Truth who had the fortitude and great compassion after awakening to not remain silent. In particular Howard Beale who passionately urged us to- "God damn it folks-WAKE UP !"

CONTENTS

∞Chapter One∞ 1
   Introduction 1

∞Chapter 2∞ 7
   2012 7

∞Chapter 3∞ 23
   January 23

∞Chapter 4∞ 55
   February 55

∞Chapter 5∞ 111
   March 111

∞Chapter 6∞ 133
   April 133

∞Chapter 7∞ 161
   May 161

∞Chapter 8∞ 177
   June 177

∞Chapter 9∞ 187
   July 187

∞Chapter 10∞ 215
   August 215

∞Chapter 11∞ 251

September *251*

∞**Chapter 12**∞ **279**

October *279*

∞**Chapter 13**∞ **285**

November *285*

∞**Chapter 14**∞ **309**

December *309*

Afterword **337**

Acknowledgements

Edited by

Flora Salyers
Valerie Porter

The Clothes Have No Emperor:

Conversations, the Art of No-Self

∞ Chapter One ∞

Introduction

"Actually, DJ," came David's reply, "Serious spiritual seekers I presume." I tended to agree with his outlook. Yes, this book would likely appeal more to spiritual aspirants seeking Truth, Absolute Reality, the pure Beingness of nonduality, enlightenment, or simply the end of their world as they know it, than it would to those seekers greatly interested in self-help projects or spiritual materialism.

Earnest spiritual folk, those who aspire to wake up in their own lifetime as the Buddha famously did, are a relatively rare lot. I hope this outlook does not smack of spiritual elitism, for that is not my intent at all. In fact, I abhor such sentiment. It just seems that Truth-realization is not what most seekers are chasing.

Those seeking alignment with the non-false are discontent to merely engage in metaphysical banter, practice religious rites and rituals, or spend time considering yet more belief systems. When it comes to seeing through their own self-ignorance, they seek resolution as swiftly as possible. The proposition of being unable to discern the shit from the Shinola, as it were, was no longer tenable. They have to know for themselves just what the heck is really going on. Though, curiously, an American Tibetan Kagyu lineage monk once chastised me for having the audacity to want the "brass ring for myself."

That's the thing with seeking seriously: Ignorance will no longer suffice. I was not interested in acquiring a new lifestyle like that monk, a former Californian accountant, had. I desired Truth for its own sake, and I wanted it posthaste for, you see, once upon a time I numbered among the league of serious seekers extraordinaire. I was prepared to, and indeed eventually did, sacrifice everything in the pursuit of acquiring the "pearl" of inestimable value.

Curiously, I discovered that in order to gain everything I first had to lose it. It seems the ALL (True Nature, Self, Consciousness, Spirit, God, The Ineffable) usually reveals itself only when you have *nothing else left to lose, nor anything further to gain*. My previous book, *A Fleeting Improvised Man*, chronicled in detail how driven and resolute my desire to awaken became. The old school 60s catch-phrase, "That was a heavy trip man," sums up my journey pretty well. Heavy but rewarding. "Truth or bust" became my rallying cry. So, yeah, waking up to Reality is a serious enterprise indeed.

Considering this "serious seeker" business further, I asked myself if this book would have interested me back in the days when I was mired deeply in the throes of my spiritual quest. I concluded it likely would have, for I had relished similar material then. For example, the books of Christian mystic Bernadette Roberts, "truthist" Jac O'Keeffe's insightful awakening guide, Zen inspired audio chats by Adyashanti, and the enlightenment trilogy offerings of iconoclast Jed McKenna held my attention.

Like those straight-talking harbingers of Truth, I and fellow collaborator David similarly aspired to tell it like it was during the course of writing this book. This necessitated detailing the highs, as well as the lows, of the waking-up process with great candour. Find herein, then, an intimate and often humorous yearlong correspondence between two experienced and spiritually adept "friends of Truth."

In these pages you will discover various strategies the ego employs to reinforce its self-as-centre stance. By investigating the means by which the "I thought" arises moment to moment, you will discover how the dream state is maintained. If you desire peace of mind and holistic well-Beingness, the kind that neither arises nor falls away again, or if you would simply appreciate more clarity in your life, this book may well have something to offer you.

Most importantly, this guide may inspire you to give up seeking altogether. Perhaps you will sense the invitation to come to a full stop and relax as ultimate reality itself. I assure you this stateless state is readily available right here and now to anyone who is no longer interested in abiding as "endarkenment" a single minute longer.

Writing *The Clothes Have No Emperor: Conversations, The Art of No-Self* was to engage in satsang, a term increasingly employed these days in certain spiritual circles, which means to gather in the name of Truth or association (Sanga) with Being (sat) in Sanskrit. Truth-telling was indeed what David, a decade's long serious seeker, and I, a guy whose narrative simply came to a halt one day and never resumed, certainly aspired to do during the course of our exchange. In fact, we committed to meet each week via e-mail for a full years' worth of spiritually relevant investigation. Our dialogue often reflected how life lived itself when it lacked a centre. Centre, of course, here refers to the egoic sense of self. To be self-centred is to be human. That's quite normal. No-self or non-self is an entirely different way of moving in, or as, existence itself and our dialogue increasingly focused upon this singular subject as the months went by.

Seeing through the illusion of small s self was what spiritual luminaries, such as Buddha with his sutra on non-self, or Ramana Maharshi with his self-inquiry technique designed to illumine a Self that "knows not" were pointing to. To realize this was to see the world as it truly was. This kind of direct experience leads the way to liberation. "Discover the kingdom of heaven" for yourself, as the Bible extols us to do and then be amazed when "all else is added unto you."

In the final summation, that which discerns separation, other, distinction, or duality vanishes when the Great Realization unfolds. ONENESS reveals itself to itself. Unity is the One before a second, or alternatively the Zero before a one. No-thingness itself. Non-duality. This is what comes to the fore when the self is dropped. I recognize that's a bold statement to make. It must never be taken on faith alone. Investigate the pointers in this book for yourself. Do the inquiry. See what you come up with through your own shrewd observations and direct experience.

To wrap up this introduction I'd like to mention in brief how this project came to pass, for it will help elucidate the beginning of the next chapter. The conversation that ensues arose during the course of a regular e-mail chitchat session David and I had been carrying on for some months. David was also engaged in a separate exchange with Josh, one of his fellow bloggers from the K-centre (a spiritual lerning centre of sorts) website, and during the course of one somewhat tense back-and-forth, David requested my opinion.

Josh is a most interesting and well-meaning chap, but I often find his spiritual rhetoric perplexing to say the least. David terms Josh's outlook "curious." I have come to wonder if Josh is suffering from that malady the Zen Buddhists term "Zen sickness" or "emptiness sickness."

Zen sickness is an extreme form of nihilism whereby the egoic self, through some kind of spiritual practice, investigation or insight, comes to newly apprehend and then identify strongly with emptiness itself. Self has not been seen through entirely, nor wholly transcended, but rather merely reimagined as a newly discovered object of awareness. Where the

I/ego-sense was once the focus of identification, "apparent I" has now come to replace it.

Whatever or whomever these emptiness sufferers perceive themselves to be, it is now defined by lack of content. They dwell in a *hohlraum* (German for empty space) of sorts. There is still identification going on, but it is much more subtle in nature and has seemingly come to regard itself as the formless void of pure Beingness itself. This misapprehension consequently inspires certain non-dual practitioners or neo-advaitists as they sometimes refer to themselves, to proclaim over and over certain catch-phrases such as "there is no other," "everything is just happening," "all is illusory," things just happen to the "apparent self," and so on. These non-dualists deem seeking as a senseless pursuit for there is nothing to discover, nowhere to go, nothing to acquire, nor anyone to do it. There are just apparent happenings, apparent students and apparent teachers. In a sense all of this is true...but...and this is a huge but...from the view afforded here it is not quite the way they put it. In truth, just as they state, there is not two; but similarly nor is there One--at least not as an object of awareness.

The difference here is a case of, on the one hand, strongly identifying with the ALL, and on the other actually moving from or as pure Beingness itself. Those suffering from emptiness sickness have become fixated on the One whereas previously their identification lay entirely with the two, i.e., the ordinary dualistic state of affairs we call normal reality. For now I'll leave it at that.

I have often found a certain urgent, occasionally even bordering on strident, tone to Josh's blog delivery as well as those writings or talks given by certain other non-dualists he loves to cite. Though Josh would have it otherwise, I find this kind of talk inherently dualistic which is ironic as I am sure he would say his "apparent" outlook is bereft of any duality whatsoever. The fact that certain neo-advaitists dismissively admonish and perhaps even occasionally belittle those seekers who don't quite share their (apparent) outlook only serves to demonstrate to me that there is still a strong sense of self-identification going on. Paucity, lack, and the nihilism of the void defines their new outlook and boy, oh boy, do they ever want their audiences to appreciate this fact. I wonder who is driven so? I have observed Josh write one, sometimes even two, blog entries almost every single day for weeks on end. Why?

It's like they have discovered the other side of the duality/non-duality coin and feel compelled to share the good news. Some-thing has given way to the other side of the coin marked by no-thing, yet still identification persists. Duality's doubloon has yet to entirely disappear like the coin which vanishes from a stage magician's palm does (only to reappear in his other hand some moments later – but that is a spiritual twist best revealed later). Embodiment is incomplete. The realization that emptiness is fullness and fullness is emptiness I suspect has yet to dawn on folks like Josh.

Of course, I realize these musings are speculative. And ultimately I am a guy who claims to know nothing at all. I certainly wouldn't try to defend any of the conjectures I have just presented. And to be sure, I usually found Josh's blog offerings entertaining and informative. I also acknowledge it was Josh's postings that originally brought David and me together for this project. Gratitude then is extended to the "apparent Josh," whoever or whatever you may or may not be. Your writings were appreciated. Apparently.

∞Chapter 2∞

2012

21 Nov. 2012

To: DJ

    Today I (David) made a comment on the latest blog by Josh as follows, entitled something like, "The Story of the Apparent Me", on the K-Centre site and would welcome your (DJ's) response if you want to look at it.

    David

19 Nov. 2012 - 9:01 P.M.

    The Story of Me...Apparently

    Submitted by Josh to K-centre Website

    Featuring the writings of Tony Parsons, a well-known neo-advaita (non-duality) teacher:

    Practices like meditation can bring an apparent state of peace or silence. Self-inquiry can bring an apparently progressive experience of understanding and strengthened awareness. But for awareness to function it needs something apart for it to be aware of. Awareness simply feeds separation, and a state of detachment can arise and be mistaken for enlightenment. All of these states come and go within the story of me....

[Portion excised for the sake of brevity. DJ]

...progressive teachings of enlightenment which recommend methods such as meditation, self-enquiry, or the idea of recognition or surrender, are based on the mistaken belief of there being a self who can choose to do these things. Tony Parsons, July 2012

20 Nov. 2012 - 11:35 A.M.
To: Josh and K-centre Blog

Great quote that rings true and yet...how helpful is it to say there's no one with nothing to do?

David

20 Nov. 2012 - 12:07 P.M.
Submitted by Josh to K-centre blogs

From here there is/was never anything to do...there has never been a some "one" who could do anything.

"How helpful is it?"

For me it is/was an enormous relief!

I don't have to try and hold myself together or even believe that there is a separate consciousness inhabiting this body that can choose anything.

And better yet, there is a knowing that all of these somebodies are actually not responsible for any action either.

Taking this one step further, the work of Darryl Bailey clearly exposes the myth that there is even any person or form at all, including the so-called human form.

Every "thing" is actually un-form or motion.

From "Essence Revisited":

The mental agonies of life are wrapped around the idea that we're something separate from the movement of existence, a "me" owning and directing the thoughts, feelings, interests, urges, and actions.

The apparent karmic chain of personal responsibility is based on this concept and carries with it the burden of guilt or pride of accomplishment.

Realizing we're a movement of the larger happening of existence removes us from the karmic wheel of personal responsibility.

AND

As Sailor Bob Adams says..."The human being has never done anything...All is This, expressing itself.

Josh

21 Nov. 2012 - 1:34 P.M.
To: Josh and K-centre Blog

Some contemplation on the Tony Parsons quotes follows:

As there is no self to choose, or to "do" anything, then what is recommending meditation, self-inquiry, etc.? It can only be consciousness itself recommending practices and enjoying their benefits and the profound beauty and sense of significance of a deeper knowing of itself that may arise as well as the non-dual "not-knowing" that may "happen" in the midst of so-called practices or inquiries. It must also be consciousness alone that is seeing the uselessness or limited nature of "practices." According to Tony, the only thing to be attained is the realization that there is nothing to attain. How is this realization to happen? Some kind of inquiry is almost certainly required, and consciousness is sometimes recommending such as an expression of its own compassion and intelligence.

David

22 Nov. 2012 - 11:00 A.M.
To: David and K-centre Blog

Hmmm, thanks David,

From here there isn't any "consciousness" recommending anything.

What you seem to be putting forth here is a duality of sorts in that it alludes to a "consciousness" that wants or needs a deeper knowing of "it."

From here, there is not an "itself" that has use for recommending anything...this apparent play of existence is just happening without any direction of a "consciousness."

Having said that...there appears to be an urge in some apparent forms to do practices and others not...who knows how or why any of this apparent Play works. It's a mystery.

Peace, out
Josh

22 Nov. 2012 - 12:07 P.M.
To: Josh and K-centre Blog

It seems that duality is needed in order to experience anything or talk about what *is* in any way. Duality is not a mistake and is only an apparent duality; without it there is absolutely nothing to be said. If there is no consciousness then what is conceiving and writing those words? If you say it ultimately can't be defined and is a "mystery," I would agree with that.

    David

22 Nov. 2012 – 12:48 P.M.
To: David and K-centre Blog

A lesson from *A Course In Miracles* comes to mind...
"I give everything all of the meaning it has."
Josh

29 Nov. 2012 – 1:56 P.M.
To: Josh and K-centre Blog

It seems true at a certain level of thinking that I give everything all of the meaning it has and that this is a profound insight and truth. At the same time "I" have found that there are "meanings" given by consciousness or life itself that are not meaningful in the way the mind conceives of meaning. In the midst of silent awareness or presence where there is no movement of thought, something is sometimes revealed which is outside the conventional structures of the thinking mind and which is not in any way being made up by the "I" or thought, unless we say that the I is awareness or Intelligence itself. This "something" or no-thing has a significance that could not be denied in a thousand years...

    David

1 Dec. 2012 - 9:27 A.M.
To: David and K-centre Blog

From here the words *consciousness* or *awareness* or *presence* are totally meaningless labels.
There is only This, and It has no needs or meanings.
    Cheers, Josh

The entries above by Josh and David were the ones David asked me to consider and comment on back in late 2012. Herein follows my (DJ's) reply:

This is a topic which arises from time to time. As I recall, we once quickly broached it together. It's hard to succinctly state my position...oops, there goes the apparent me again, I mean the apparent me apparently taking a position, in this apparent email. LOL

The problem that often arises with Tony Parsons's nondual pointers is his Absolutist viewpoint. Yes, there is nowhere to go or anything to find or do. You are already THAT. In truth there are no teachers or students but a fat lot of good that will do you if you are still firmly entrenched in the relative. I can safely say that everybody who listens to Parsons is not abiding in the Absolute. Otherwise, why would they care to hear what he had to say? So I dare say that his audience is doing something, i.e., considering his words of wisdom. If there is truly nothing to do, why is he up there telling them this?

In reality the vast number of seekers in one way or another do lots of varied kinds of seeking stuff until they get exhausted of the whole thing...or don't.

It's little known – Parsons himself doesn't publicize it much – but apparently he was an Osho disciple. So I guess he did plenty of those things he now sees as useless.

Once again, from the absolute, they are useless but from the relative they would seem necessary...until they aren't. In my case I dreamed along quite happily until middle age, never caring to do otherwise. Then attention was turned towards certain spiritual practices which caused the appearance of insight and eventual awakening. Had that spiritual seeking never happened, I dare say I would still be merrily or miserably dreaming along right now. Doing nothing generally maintains the status quo, don't you think? I am putting this in a pragmatic rather than a philosophical way.

Until the players shuffle off the stage, it is still a play. And in the play things seem to be happening. When everything ceases that is an entirely different story.

As long as one is still in relative reality and things appear to be happening, then let's be honest—that is the way things appear to be. To try to convince ourselves otherwise is, as Randal Friend once said, "just bullshit." For me I can say meditation and contemplation worked wonders. Were they necessary? Can't say, but they did happen. And I did awaken, so they definitely weren't harmful. If grace is just an accident then surely they must have made me accident prone. How many of those who become Truth realized did so through "doing nothing"? Any? Apparently not Parsons.

Adyashanti says that the message these neo-advaitists love to proclaim is often a dangerous one. He points out that the ego loves to get a hold of it and use it to justify its own enduring ignorance. I remember he once said something along the lines of, "Trying to do something from the absolute viewpoint is ridiculous. Not trying to do anything from the egoic one is plainly idiotic."

I once met a guy who had not done anything for fourteen years after hearing this kind of message. I asked him if it helped. "Nope," he said, "I'm pretty much the same as I was 14 years ago."

The only way that doing nothing is going to help is if you follow that sentiment all the way- absolutely one hundred percent do nothing. Go all the way. Give up entirely but just entirely. Nirvana yourself. Cessation. That's what I am talking about, but this is not the kind of understanding seekers are attracted to. They'd rather sit on their arses and do nothing.

Did I ever meet Josh? I wish he would quote others less and instead reveal what he knows directly. Quoting others smacks of dogma and belief systems. Spirituality has nothing to do with what you believe and everything to do with who/what you are. Or aren't. Who cares what Sailor Bob has to say? Has doing nothing led to your own liberation? Isn't that the only thing that counts?

Glad to hear that you're doing something; dyad retreat was so rewarding. Like I said before, you are your own authority on this whole matter. If in an apparent world spiritual results are apparently unfolding for you, then I say great. How do we know it's great? Cause that is what is happening. It's all good. Have fun!

Love,
DJ

22 Nov. 2012
To: DJ

I'm enjoying your comments and perceptions as they agree with mine! But seriously, I very much appreciate the reflections and the questions.

I think it would be interesting if you were to put this answer - or most of it at least - in a comment on Josh's blog posting. It might shake him up a bit, although he seems to be pretty much entrenched in his "position" which he would probably claim is no position. It would also provide any readers with more alternatives to consider regarding this possibly misleading formula that there is nothing to do.

To add a little to what I said in my last email about not listening to the mind, my intention was to not believe in any thought in the area of telling me what I am. I then realized a bit later that no formula can be really alive but quickly becomes a dogmatic belief. More useful is to look at each thought as it arises and ask, "Is it true?" Seeing the truth or untruth of thought moment to moment is always alive and fresh and remains open-ended.

Love,
David

30 Nov. 2012
To: DJ

Hi,

Harvey (k-centre administrator) enjoyed your letter and wants to invite you, again, to be a blogger on the K-centre website.

We were discussing what would motivate us to criticize or question Josh's or anyone's concepts or understandings. Is it merely an egoic tendency to judge and to assert that we know better, or is it something else?

So far my exploration of the motivation question has proved interesting but not conclusive, i.e., still open for discovery. It does seem that there is a pure urge for the truth in a way that goes beyond personal considerations. In the case of Josh I sense that something is rotten in the state of Denmark and there is an urge to address this bad smell. "He" seems to be so slippery that in his own mind (so to speak) he fully believes in his avoidance of any challenge to his beliefs, which he would probably say are not beliefs. I wonder how he will respond to your letter. Ok, 'bye for now, David

1 Dec. 2012
To: David

You said, "…he (Josh) fully believes in his avoidance of any challenge to his beliefs."

Crudely put, it still comes down to beliefs. If there are any, then you ain't THAT. And if you are THAT, you most assuredly ain't. There is no THAT. There is no God. If one is quite certain that all is God, as Josh is, then there is still a viewpoint that knows this. There is still a subject and object relationship. It may not be recognized as such, but it is so. Objectification still exists. When the mind no longer moves towards thoughts, ideas, and opinions to inform itself as to whom or what it is, then what have you got?

In all honesty can the following, as Josh's reply suggests, actually be the case?

"…certainly no 'one' to help! Only God. And He/She/It appears to have a great sense of humour…no?"

Who is it that has taken the position that there is "no one to help"? Who "knows" that there is only God?

I've talked to you about the supposed "gap," as I like to put it, before. It is this gap that allows such ideas to be expressed. And they are only ideas or beliefs. This is not abiding as Truth realized.

As you know, Bernadette Roberts has a great narrative on "The No—Self." If you recall she puts it as such:

Egoic-Self or Self-centredness gives way to Non-egoic self or Divine/Spirit centeredness (with enough of a self to be aware of this) to pure No-Self. Life without any centre at all!

Have you ever been on the London Underground? You may recall the constant reminder to mind the gap. Josh might take note here. When this gap disappears, if it disappears, (for Bernadette Roberts points out that almost all Christian mystics never got to no-self) he will recognize that his utterings are misguided. That is not to say that he is presently being necessarily intellectually dishonest. I spent about a year hanging out in the no-egoic point of view. A decidedly marvellous, Divine or consciousness-as-all phase. Nice honeymoon, but it is over. The groom took off, and I'll be darned that the bride is nowhere to be found.

Until then, Josh will naturally hold firm to Josh's point of view, "There is only This expressing itself." Yet another wonderful point of view in myriad forms of expression. Life living itself in all its guises. Isn't it amazing? I once heard it said that the best trick ever pulled off was the Devil convincing humanity that he didn't exist. Well, I would say no, no. Not at all. It is rather you convincing yourself that you do! Now that is fucking amazing! Something out of nothing. Nothing out of something. Enough said.

Much Love,
DJ

PS: On the blog invitation. What do you think? I feel like declining. I so much more enjoy doing what we are doing together. The intimacy and aliveness of it is palpable. Few people read your blogs, less are spiritually mature enough to get what is being pointed at. Is that important? Nope.

I don't need affirmation, and debate is such a bore. Authentic inquiry and rooting out delusion is always welcome. Could we do something together other than blogging?

Maybe investigate a topic in brief once a week and see what we come up within a year. You choose a subject, next me. Could we actually find enough to investigate over fifty-two entries? Seems like that would be a lot to say about nothing. Could be fun. Maybe not. Could be illuminating. Maybe not. Of use to others? Maybe not. What say you fine man?

1 Dec. 2012
To: David

I see Josh is once again quoting others. It's quite amazing really how far the ego will go to convince itself that delusion is in fact the real meal deal. Here he uses Scott Kiloby to try to prop up his position...which Kiloby entirely negates any chance of with his final word: "But it is realized that what we are has nothing to do with a particular experience or dualistic conclusion."

Josh is very earnest and strident in his non-position taking. He says, "Kiloby resonates with me" at the same time insisting "there is only God." How does God resonate with anything? After all, it is entirely everything. For that matter how does God objectify itself even enough to recognize that "there is only me (God)"?

Josh would have us believe that "There is no Parsons..." whom he cites regularly. Why? Why quote him then? Another tact of his is, "I am the apparent guy who takes no position"... so is that clear? I am not a meditator. In fact there is no such thing as "meditation."

Of course, saying there is no such thing as meditation confirms the existence of the very thing you have just denied.

What he means to imply is that there is no meditation--- FOR ME. David, I am quite sure this is all very clear to you. Let's leave Josh to stew in his juices for a while, shall we? You give the guy enough rope and he will hang himself, eventually, one hopes. One way or another we never get out of this thing alive. Hope he succumbs quickly. For it is in the dying that living or life itself begins. Talk about rope; let's give Josh the final word. Taken from the opening of his last reply.

"This just popped up on my screen and there is resonance with this..."

If there is resonance, then a position has been taken. If there is a position taken, then who is it that conceives of this "resonance"? Who has decided to choose this quote above others? Who was moved to make any response at all? Who keeps writing blog after blog? Who is engaged in all of this positiontaking?

You and I both know that in nirvikalpa samadhi or 5-MeO all position taking is impossible. Those two examples (of course, not including awakening itself) are the best I can come up with to exemplify "Elvis has left the building." That is absolute no-self. But as we know, there is no one there to even know this. So from whence and how do Josh's thoughts arise if it is not possible to know anything when no one is home?

DJ

6 Dec. 2012
To: DJ

Hi,

I've been getting a kick out of your emails! I like the idea of meditating and communicating on various topics together and seeing what comes out. I just resigned from any further discourse with Josh – see his blog in response to my cartoon blog on the K-centre site "Are You a Lion or a Sheep?" and our following interaction. I got a bit riled up at the ridiculousness of his assertions. Tell me what you make of the exchange. Should we attempt to identify some topics or at least one to begin with? Do you have anything in mind?

David

10 Dec. 2012
To: David

I just checked the blog concerning the sheep/lion analogy, and I see you have made an entry. What a wonderful opportunity Josh afforded you for a clear insight to arise. You should thank him. You wrote in the body of your last email,

"I got a bit riled up at the ridiculousness of his assertions." David, are your assertions any less ridiculous? If so, describe how please.

This brings me to the topic for our first email inquiry. Can we start on 1 Jan. and continue for one year? Who knows, but we could try and see what transpires. Maybe the question or topic could be suggested each Monday.

Here is the first one

You said:

Talking about Truth seems to be a challenging endeavour. Some aspects can be clearly spoken of and then there is a point at which nothing can be accurately said: Words and concepts cannot reach the Truth.

This seems a good introduction for our correspondence about talking about the Truth for the next year. Is it even possible? Why bother if it is not. You say words and concepts fail yet also say, "Some aspects can be clearly spoken of." I wonder what these CLEAR aspects might be. This should be fun. Can you send me your reply 1 Jan. and I will follow-up?

Love,
DJ

1 Dec. 2012
To: DJ

Just a quick reply today...

What do you mean are my assertions any less ridiculous than Josh's! Whose side are you on anyway? Where's your loyalty? I like your idea about the inquiry exchange and will follow your suggestion if the world doesn't end on 21 Dec. *The End of Your World.* Hah

Will write soon,
David

12 Dec. 2012
To: David

You said, "What do you mean are my assertions any less ridiculous than Josh's? Whose side are you on anyway? Where's your loyalty?"

You are kidding right? Of course you are. Just a bit of light humour, right? If not then I hope the following is taken as a sincere attempt to answer your question.

If it does irk you even further, you might investigate this. Who is it that is being troubled?

Let me see...do you have ridiculous assertions...ridiculous thoughts, ridiculous notions? Hmmm. Short answer, YEP, or longer answer see below. Take your pick. By the way it is not personal. Mine, yours, his, hers: same, same. Like my first book so succinctly stated: "All beliefs are bullshit." No new info here. When the gurus and sages start to actually believe their own rhetoric, well that is when my alarm bells start going off like they did when I bumped into Josh.

It depends on viewpoint. More to the point, it depends if there is viewpoint. Is there viewpoint? Really? I mean when you are not pretending there is.

Full disclosure. This DJ character keeps repeating ad nauseam, "I don't believe anything I say, so why should you?" He's repeated it enough times. Maybe he is sincere. What could he mean by this? Perhaps absolute negation. Neti, neti (not this, not that) plain and simple.

As straight as I can put it, anything I think or say is nonsense. I heard a spiritual teacher put it well the other day as follows: The difference between you and me is that I know that I am full of bullshit, and you don't." I would add that what the teacher said is bullshit as well. And I am sure he would concur.

Like I said, I am dumb beyond belief. Literally beyond beliefs. What remains when you no longer use beliefs to inform yourself as to whom or what you are? You have said before that you realized you are "making it all up." So what, then, can be taken seriously? If you have never been able to find yourself anywhere ever at all, nada, then I wonder how such terms as ridiculous and astute presumptions even make sense.

In truth anything you say is neither astute nor ridiculous. Is it? As far as the TRUTH goes, anything I have to say about anything at all is irrelevant. What's being pointed to here is the difference between thinking about the TRUTH in a relativistic symbolic manner and actually Being it. Being That. Just BEING.

I can assure you that my assertions are just as ridiculous as any Josh makes, maybe more so, as he appears to be a very sensible guy, and I am just a fool. Truth is there is absolutely no truth in any of our assertions. There is absolutely no reality in any beliefs. They are laughably absurd. That came to me not as a belief I might add but simply as a direct realization that this was the way things actually were. But again, this is crap. Humorous the lengths the mind will go to convince itself it actually knows something.

That is why I was wondering if you could point out any assertions you made to Josh that were not ridiculous, i.e., which ones were inherently truthful. Beliefs only vary in degrees of delusion. In consensual reality some are deemed relatively normal, some hailing from the realm of cloud-cuckoo land. But I say they are all as wacky as can be. But heh, that's mind stuff for you. Lots of fun, and suffering, to be had there for sure.

These days it all seems very much like going to the theater. In Shakespeare's day the rabble would occasionally get worked up enough to boo the villain or cheer the hero, but it was all in good fun. Nobody really took it to be real. It's a tale, full of sound and fury, signifying nothing!

Whose side am I on? Well show me the line drawn in the sand, and I will stomp on over. Sand? I can't even find the bloody beach. It's all just ocean from the view here.

You know what I mean. Stop kidding around. Or don't...it's all good. Have fun.

What's it all about, Alfie? Consider these song lyrics, "Is it just for the moment we live? What's it all about when you sort it out, Alfie?"

http://www.youtube.com/watch?v=KoNtj27a6Rk

Much love,

DJ

PS

Dec 21. End of the world. We should all be so lucky. LOL

12 Dec. 2012
To: DJ

Guess we were writing each other at the same moment. Thanks for the song and the thoughts. It's fun that you took my words seriously enough to answer them but really didn't believe them either!

Love,

David

PS: Did you notice that Josh thanked me in two consecutive replies under the "Sheep or Lion" blog? You just never know...and what does it mean anyway, Alfie?

The Clothes Have No Emperor

∞ Chapter 3 ∞

January

4 Jan. 2013

To: DJ

Happy New Year to you, too!

    To pick up on one of the original questions we were going to discuss, i.e.,"What can be spoken of clearly?" I would say that there seem to be various truths about how the human mind functions that are probably true for everyone. For example, the "mind" has a strong tendency to create an image or representation of who we are. We can discuss what is meant by "mind" soon if we want. No problem so far, if it is understood that the representation is not the thing itself – not who or what we really are.

    However, it can be seen (if one looks) that the mind creates an attachment or a holding onto the self-image, which creates an experience of being an object in the world. This objective self-concept is then subject to the world, including the opinions of others, the offering or withholding of love and approval, and all the many uncertainties of life which can threaten the continued secure existence of the self-image or identity. The self-image probably always includes an image of the body, as the individual bodies are what give us the sense of being distinct entities.

    The mind thus creates identification with a body and an attachment to its continued life or existence. This inevitably brings with it, like a shadow, the fear of death, injury, disease, and so on. Perhaps more simply it could be said that the desire to be creates the fear of not being, or the desire for security creates insecurity. Which comes first? Which is cause and which effect may not be so obvious or easy to determine. Is it the desire for security that causes insecurity, or is it the insecurity of the human predicament which causes the desire for security? Would there be any sense of insecurity if the mind or thought didn't conceive things that way, didn't have within it a deep tendency to avoid or move away from the unknown and formless and to reach for the apparently graspable, the physical or thought forms that seem to offer some permanence and security?

So, I'm proposing that these kinds of psychological truths, and there would be many of them, can be explored through looking into the nature of ourselves, our thought processes, and how these thought processes (called "mind") create our reality. Within this arena the processes of thinking and experience can be examined through meditation or inquiry and clear insights will arise which have the power to weaken the hold of deluded thinking over our sense of self so that a different, more free and enjoyable sense of self (or no-self) can be known.

If these knowings are worthy goals, then this kind of talk and pointing could be said to be worthwhile if it leads to or at least orients someone to some direct seeing. Many of the spiritual teachings which emphasize self-knowledge and inward looking seem to focus largely on this area of experience. What this "knowing" is and its nature can be explored in more depth as we move along, and that may take us into the realms which are more difficult to talk about. So, I suspect we will be moving from the realm of what is knowable and describable— and is very useful to contemplate and understand through direct seeing—into the realm of the less definable but more open and unbounded, or even beyond such words and descriptions.

Considering your question about acceptance, I would say that for me it's not really about accepting anything in a positive sense. As you say, who will be doing the accepting? Most certainly it will be the mind, the ego, or self-concept that adds some good idea – especially if it sounds spiritually or psychologically appealing – to its store of beliefs in an attempt to shore up its fabricated structure.

What I meant is more that the resistance to the fact that all strategies of mind are ultimately useless falls away gradually or suddenly as inquiry deepens so that the fact can operate in consciousness to create an alignment of experience with the Truth. The acceptance would not be a mental gesture but more a surrendering of resistance and of the idea that there is anyone to resist or surrender. Make sense? As to what has so far been "accepted" in this way, I find I cannot (at least on a first look) measure the degree of acceptance or of surrender. I could attempt to make some evaluation (but don't feel drawn to do so) and then, beyond that, there would be the total not knowing of what might arise in the next moment to show that surrender is incomplete. And is surrendering even the issue at all? What really is surrender? Maybe a topic for future inquiry. I suspect you may have some interesting perspectives on this and some of the above contemplations, and I look forward to your feedback.

Be Well,
David

7 Jan 2013
To: David

Here are some comments on select snippets of your January 4th entry. The first excerpt which I will comment on reads:

> To pick up on one of the original questions we were going to discuss, i.e., "What can be spoken of clearly?" I would say that there seem to be various truths about how the human mind functions.

Yes, at the simple, base, gross level (and for purposes of insight haven't you found that this is the level that most interests us?) it would appear that the body/mind apparatus shares commonalities throughout all strata of humanity. When I started to investigate this area, I was astonished by how uncomplicated, programmed and conditioned my mind was. I seemed to be carrying out my daily routine using little more processing power than was available to an electronic watch or chip in a car engine. Very basic computer code really. A high school kid could write it.

So, yes, the predictable goings on of the mind can be spoken of quite clearly. But this is not speaking about the Truth is it? Rather, this kind of endeavor reveals that the human position is oriented towards reality in a fundamentally deluded manner. Isn't it the case that the best the conceptual mind can ever hope to discover is how misconceptions have arisen? It can discover "untruth" but will never know "what" is true as reality is not a position the ego takes or arrives at.

In this fashion I found that I could quite naturally reorient myself and move toward what is True by simply backing away from what is false. I couldn't see what was true, in fact never did, but I sure as hell could recognize a "dirty rotten stinker" when I smelled one. And that rotten odour that increasingly repulsed me turned out to be wafting up from my very own self! Never saw that one coming.

So to put it succinctly, yes we can speak clearly about matters of the mind and in doing so falsehood can be revealed, but all bets are off when it comes to speaking about the Truth.

I hold no truths. I am the Truth (or the impersonal Self, awareness, God or spirit - call it what you will...well kind of...). In fact that's all there really is (except when appearance, Samsara, Leela, momentarily seduces us with its beautiful charms).

I once was hell bent on discovering the ANSWER. Well, I'll be darned if I didn't discover that that was precisely what I was. But I digress...the point is there is no objective truth about THE TRUTH that can ever be enunciated. Right? We can speak later why this is the case but for now that's enough.

And is surrendering even the issue at all? What really is surrender?

I like Anthony de Mello's definition of enlightenment which goes "Enlightenment is 'absolute' cooperation with the inevitable." That is true surrender. You, the you who you take yourself to be, can never surrender in this fashion. It's not in your nature. But the ego sure as hell can be transcended. To awaken is to be surrendered.

Unfortunately, this is not an act of volition. I sense you catch my drift here as you seem to be saying something akin to this in your statement above. In a large part it is a mystery to me how it comes about. Some call it Grace. I would suggest that your well-articulated and accurate musings above on the nature of mind seemingly help predispose you to becoming "nirvanaed." You can't surrender, but if enlightenment is judged to be a kind of divine accident, then I reckon one can make themselves accident prone in just the manner you are doing above.

Here's hoping you become ever more the "accidental aspirant."

Break a leg,
DJ

9 Jan. 2013
To: DJ

Good Day DJ,

I found your feedback very much to the point and have no argument with any of it. The conversation can continue. So, what can be spoken of in terms of the goings on of the mind are truths with a small t which, as you say, show us the ways the mind is functioning to create separation from the truth of what is and what we truly are. This is very valuable in weakening the dominance of the egoic mind or consciousness over Being. It seems to be motivated to begin with, at least partly, by a desire for a better experience of life. There may also be a more subtle urge to know—and, even more deeply, to be—what is true beyond the creations of mind and mistaken ways of thinking and perceiving.

This pure urge for Truth is not motivated by personal concerns about relief from suffering or attaining a better experience of life, and I have found that such concerns spontaneously lose their potency as the self-investigation proceeds. The personal motivation may lose its strength partly because it is more and more fulfilled. As I see more and more deeply into the nature of my conditioned mind with its limitations, these limitations melt away and the sense of Being comes more to the foreground of experience.

Similarly, as the experience of living becomes more peaceful, loving, and full, there is less and less need to seek anything. But also as I look into myself (so to speak), the understanding comes that there is in fact no one to benefit from any improvement in my life and that the idea of a person which is created by thought is what actually limits my experience of what I truly am. The "I" that is seeking is nothing but a construct of thought; the whole endeavor of seeking anything for this "I" becomes empty of meaning. And yet the pure urge for Truth remains and becomes even stronger or more predominant, and so the investigation or inquiry into Truth or Reality becomes deeper and more fascinating in its own right and not for the purposes of any reward or attainment.

In the initial phases of inquiry into my true nature there is, as you say, a usefulness in making distinctions which separate out what I am not (e.g., my thoughts) from what is more true (i.e., the Awareness that notices the thoughts). This is not only conceptual but in my experience is a tangible knowing of different dimensions of reality. Awareness is known experientially to be "more" true or real than thoughts. The sense of living from and as awareness is different from living in identification with transient thoughts. Consciousness is increasingly (or perhaps, as apparently in some cases [like yours?] suddenly and completely) freed from involvement with the aspect of the thinking process that is full of contradictions and conflict and enjoys this greater freedom as a sense of relatively more happiness (or a kind of absolute happiness). At some point, the concern with personal happiness seems to pretty much fall away for the same reasons discussed above although again there seems to be a kind of spontaneous natural urge that remains, at least so far in my experience – a curious paradox which could be explored further.

My inquiry lately has been moving more and more into what seems like another dimension where it is seen at moments that to make any distinctions between awareness, thought, feeling, Beingness, and so on, is merely an arbitrary activity of the mind or thought. It is seen that these kinds of separations of one aspect of consciousness from another have ultimately no validity or reality from a larger or deeper perspective. Thoughts are arising from the same indescribable Mystery that awareness is an expression of and Being an experience of.

The distinctions between these are no longer valid in this dimensionless dimension where everything loses its form and becomes empty but not empty, nothing but not nothing, without qualities but the ground (or no-ground) from which all qualities arise, are known, and dissolve into. It has become exquisitely clear at moments that Truth is knowing nothing. When I become love, peace, or any quality of Being, I no longer know it. There is no longer any object of knowing, no longer any duality to create an experience of something. This may seem like a great loss, but in fact it is most profound (if any word can point to it) and is a direct realization of Truth. (Wow, I'm going out on a limb by making such an affirmative statement, but I trust you know of what I speak as you have referred to it in a number of ways in your last expression.)

As you said, "There is no objective truth about The Truth that can ever be enunciated." These moments of clear seeing do seem to leave a kind of knowing without needing concepts to describe it unless they are called forth while engaging in discussions like these.

There is much more in your writing that I could respond to, but I think this is good for now.

Happy travels,
David

14 Jan. 2013
To: David

I was thinking not so much about the details of our correspondence of late but rather the "flow" of it all. I use flow here very particularly. When "flow" is how things are operating, there seems to be very little discord and much less contrivance. Perhaps you would agree that spiritual discourse usually involves position taking, defensive posturing, debate and often hurt feelings, and ill will. It's kind of novel to see that this is not happening in our conversation. Really lovely isn't it? Not having to deal with beliefs and then having to defend them. Pretty much everything you have said was at one time or another my experience as well. And if it wasn't, well, you are simply relating your experience, so who am I to disagree? Quick answer—*Nemo* (Latin for no one or nobody).

I seem to find something satisfying in apprehending the Truth reflected back in this direction much like a "mirror brightly" might do. For some reason "that which is not me" rejoices in this. Steven Colbert coined the term "truthiness" which means:

> A quality characterizing a truth that a person claims to know intuitively, from the gut, or because it feels right without regard to evidence, logic, intellectual examination, or facts. *Wikipedia*

Maybe we could call what is transpiring between us a bit of the old truthiness. It's a novel experience to be sure. Not being moved to argue or disagree I mean. Of course, I am not talking here about avoidance of conflict. If there was a strong point of disagreement, as in "The Apparent Josh Story Thing," I will always pipe up in favour of the truth. But our conversation seems to be ridiculously easy going and enjoyable. It sure is great to "flow," isn't it?

Just moments before starting this letter I caught sight of the following on the net from Scott Kiloby which helps to explain what I am getting at. The timing couldn't have been better. He wrote:

Thought likes to conclude that its particular experience is "it." It looks for agreement in the world with those who mirror back its conclusion and disagreement with those who don't. The dualistic mind knows only for or against. Its subtle goal is to reinforce a "me" that is right in relation to the others that are wrong. This is how non-duality turns into fundamentalism.

Sooner or later it is realized that there is no single experience of life that is "it." This is arising as every experience and every dualistic conclusion. In this realization, the mind still does what it does. It plays in dualism. But it is realized that what we are has nothing to do with a particular experience or dualistic conclusion.

So I will now continue to play a bit in dualism, as Kiloby puts it, by bringing a few of your last points to the fore. You said in your last mail:

> This pure urge for Truth is not motivated by personal concerns about relief from suffering or attaining a better experience of life, and I have found that such concerns spontaneously lose their potency as the self-investigation proceeds.

Yes, the motivation here was very much as you describe. I like the way you put it: A "pure urge for Truth." As you say, this urge, which eventually became more like an overriding compulsion to figure out just what the hell was actually going on, was indeed "not motivated by personal concerns about relief from suffering or attaining a better experience of life." I would add that in the final estimation my egoic mind was not at all pleased with what was found, or more pointedly not found, but that was just too bad. As Chogyam Trungpa put it, "Enlightenment is ego's ultimate disappointment."

Of course, the ego learns to suck it all up since the results of no longer engaging in the dream state, i.e., the perceived eternal peace and joy, ain't half bad, but it's not the point, as you say. Additionally, if that is a seeker's motivation, if that is what they are chasing, then they will never find anything more than the briefest tastes of "it." As the enlightened ONES say, this kind of spiritual pursuit (seeking altered states and good vibes) is like a dog chasing its own tail. It is really paradoxical, isn't it?

For me the desire to know was as strong as a drowning man seeking his next breath of air, yet there was not a sense of grasping about it. This position is very counter-intuitive and hard to describe. It is a sort of "position less position," or the firmly entrenched position of no position. And, as you quite rightly say, was also not for the purposes of any reward or attainment. In my case there was certain desperation in the apparent seeking, yet not caring what the outcome might have been.

Meister Eckhart often points to a kind of requisite detachment if Spirit is to be found, as in:

> Know that when you seek anything of your own, you will never find God, because you do not seek God purely. You are seeking something along with God, and you are acting just as if you were to make a candle out of God in order to look for something with it. Once one finds the things one is looking for, one throws the candle away. This is what you are doing.

Throwing the candle away is to throw all concepts and position taking away and dwell, not "in" but "as" pure Beingness itself. This is your true nature. Well...kind of, and I see this is precisely what you are speaking of below.

As I look into myself (so to speak) the understanding comes that there is, in fact, no one to benefit from any improvement in my life.

"No one benefits"- that is quite an amazing realization isn't it, though as I alluded to previously wholly unsatisfactory to the little me. So be it.

... inquiry into Truth or Reality becomes deeper and more fascinating in its own right and not for the purposes of any reward or attainment.

Precisely! Truth for its own sake. Who would have thunk it? Why, no one of course. Doesn't the Absolute get a little thrill each time it reveals itself to itself? As you say, "the fascination" of "nothing at all." And what an immensity this emptiness turns out to be. And to think it was hidden in plain sight all along.

The sense of living from and as awareness is different from living in identification with transient thoughts.

Yes, I appreciate the distinction you make here. More and more it becomes not living "from" awareness but "as" pure awareness itself. Then ultimately even this distinction fades away. The gap inexorably closes between perceiver and perceived. Perhaps it is then recognized that there never was a gap to begin with. Not really.

Consciousness is increasingly (or perhaps, as apparently in some cases [like yours?], suddenly and completely) freed from involvement with the aspect of the thinking process that is full of contradictions and conflict and enjoys this greater freedom as a sense of relatively more happiness (or a kind of absolute happiness).

More happiness? Or perhaps it is that the state of dissatisfaction becomes ever more irrelevant with growing lucidity. The mind likes to spin it as a positive and to be sure it definitely feels like bliss and happiness to begin with, but later all that can be said is, just as the Buddha put it, "suffering has

ended." I don't recall him ever putting it forward as a positive – just a negation. That is my realization as well. It is a small distinction to be sure, but I want to bring it to your attention nevertheless.

At some point the concern with personal happiness seems to pretty much fall away for the same reasons discussed above although, again, there seems to be a kind of spontaneous natural urge that remains, at least so far in my experience - a curious paradox which could be explored further.

Paradox is our very nature!

...it is seen at moments that to make any distinctions between awareness, thought, feeling, Beingness, and so on, is merely an arbitrary activity of the mind or thought.

Yes, Yes - quite right! By God I think he's got it. Sooner or later it all becomes like this. Even walking down the street. No distinctions. Nothing. Or a seamless mass of indivisible every thingness. Most odd. Like another dimension. Bernadette Roberts uses exactly the same language. She calls popping into "no-self" to be like entering another dimension. In my experience even that distinction eventually subsides. Then what can be said? Nothing!

Truth is knowing nothing. When I become love, peace, or any quality of Being, I no longer know it. There is no longer any object of knowing, no longer any duality to create an experience of something.

Wow! I am astonished by the lucidity and clarity of that last part. That's it, indeed. No reason to continue this conversation. Enough said. But, heh, let's play some more just for the heck of it, shall we? Truth is indeed knowing nothing, and as you intimate, even that is not known. How ridiculously amusing, eh? Isn't it just the funniest thing ever? And amazing. To be alive, how fucking fantastic. I am in awe at every moment. Or maybe I am just awe itself. Or maybe I just am. Or am not. To be or not to be...hasn't that always been the eternal question about to erupt from your pursed lips? Isn't it the only one ever worth asking?

Well, Brother, it was so much fun responding to your letter. Please continue in whatever fashion you like. Always feel free to ask the "tough" questions if so moved.

Find below a letter sent out today to a Buddhist centre I wouldn't mind hooking up with. This is my introductory letter. Maybe I can be of service there. You might find it of interest.

Much love,
DJ

Hi Sensei,

Nice ring to that. That iconic honorific is particularly evocative for me, and I am glad to be using it once again. It has been several decades since I last spoke it. Wonderful memories come flooding back of my time spent studying sword arts in Tokyo under the direction of a marvelous Japanese gentleman who epitomized the warrior spirit of both the pen and the sword. It was also cast my way by students addressing me in the classroom during my time spent there. But enough of this waxing poetic, I shall get to the point directly.

My name is DJ, and I am a middle-aged Canadian male presently living in cooperative housing in lovely B.C. Canada. I am writing to you as a hankering to relocate has arisen and the suggested destination is your Cloud Mountain retreat centre. Why? Not sure. My life doesn't seem to operate much under motive and agenda these days. I could say I would like to be of service and probably have skills that your centre could utilize. I could also say I would like to meet a dharma teacher who actually knows what the hell he is talking about but doesn't "believe his own bullshit." About the "bullshit" part, I heard you say as much in one of your podcasts. Most impressive. I tell my spiritual buddy quite often much the same thing: "I don't believe anything I say, so why should you?"

I grew up on a farm in Ontario, have a degree in agricultural science and at one time was one of the biggest organic garlic farmers in Ontario. I mention this as I see garlic is one of your farm's enterprises. I also have a degree in film studies. Used to be a fairly proficient filmmaker. Have experience in sound editing such as recently cutting a commercial CD for a fairly well-known UK satsang teacher. Also a writer of sorts, survival skills expert, off the grid dabbler and other blah, blah, blah stuff which I now grow weary of enumerating for in actuality, I possess none of those skills or qualities. In truth I "am not," but that is not really the case either. Let me explain.

I could take the complete *Oxford Dictionary*, as well as all the encyclopedia sets of the world and throw them out the window while exclaiming, "none of that shit is me." Yet, I don't have a clue how to affirm to you who or what I am in the positive. Beingness, awareness, existence itself. That will have to do. In your podcasts I swear I hear the echoes of a "fellow traveller." What a rarity that is. And to think that dear Sensei is practically my neighbor. I guess I feel inclined to pop over for a spot of tea and a little chat.

Almost precisely five years ago I set out from Ontario to B.C. hell bent on determining the ultimate nature of reality and instead was surprised to discover "Self" – Not "myself" – but ineffable, impersonal Self (ONE) or absolute Non-Self if you prefer. Though in truth neither of those concepts quite cut it. How about life minus the Skandhas? Sort of. Awareness "awaring" itself? Maybe. Existence without a centre? Perhaps.

My teacher (Adyashanti, a Zen guy for fifteen years till he awoke even out of that tradition - perhaps you have heard of him - sometimes calls this "awakening." I don't claim this for myself. When the huge paradigm shattering shift occurred here, there was no one left to claim anything at all (though the remnants of my ego sure tried to for some time afterwards). The guy who was seeking just stopped one day. Seeker and seeking vanished into the moment (or perhaps the recognition arose that the guy seeking was never really present to begin with). Humpty Dumpty had his whopping great fall and never recovered, poor chap. I trust you know what I am talking about here.

I was "nirvanaed", "cessated." Things or no-things appeared or did not appear as they were or were not. Quietude became the norm (and of course still is, as this appears to be abiding wakefulness). Much later the analytical mind conceptually tried to figure out what the hell had actually transpired (much like Tolle sat on his park bench for two years cogitating over the matter).

One thing recognized was that my so-called life had in actuality been a marvellously contrived dream or play of sorts and I, the central character, had somehow been duped into buying into the whole charade as something other than it was, an illusion.

I discovered that my whole life had been spent dwelling in the "cinema of that which ain't transpiring." So, as it is that dream characters never actually awaken up and out of their dream lives to proclaim their lucidity, so too I cannot possibly claim anything along those lines either. Simply put, there was apparently once a guy that was dreaming away his life and this seems no longer to be the case.

I can assure you though that I am the "dumbest guy I know." I mean it. I don't seem to know anything save possibly one thing. In the aftermath of the final paradigm shift, many minutes later when the conceptual mind finally piped up, the first thought that arose was "Oh, my God, everything just is." Existence. Pure existence. "The One" without possibility of a second. Never ever could I have imagined this in an eternity of lives as it is simply beyond all imagination. I was gobsmacked! And it is really so simple once seen. Perhaps what has transpired here is existence has recognized itself. Maybe in a sense that is known. Besides this, man am I ever ONE big dumbass.

So perhaps you can appreciate why I say I don't know what is drawing me to your centre. Maybe we can find out together. To that end I propose a visit in February to take in a couple of weeks of your Jewel Ornament retreat. I would enjoy hearing your flavour of the dharma being spoken in person. I surely loved the material you presented in your podcasts. Listened to it all several times. Seems we "language" this stuff in a similar manner though, of course, you "dress" it up in Tibetan garb.

In 2008/2009 I stayed at a Canadian Buddhist centre in isolation and silent retreat meditating. Ostensibly Kagyu flavour though it was mostly self-guided. It turned out to be a perfect setting for realization to unfold though not for the reasons I had hoped. The teacher there was aloof, had little direct experience in Truth realization and employed less than skilful means when attempting to impart the dharma. Though, as I say, in the end it all turned out perfectly. All's well that ends well. And end well it did, indeed!

Cheers,

DJ

20 Jan. 2013
To: David

David,
Sent you a reply to this last week.
Wondering if you got it or I missed your response?
DJ

22 Jan. 2013
To: DJ
Hello DJ,

Coming back to your email and reading it again I find great delight in realizing the flow you spoke of and enjoying how it is all coming out. Your words are totally on track for this moment of "my" unfoldment and, as you say, act like a mirror to reflect the essence of what is being revealed.

Perhaps I can relate an "experience" from dyads last night which will communicate a "meaningful" response to your letter and an expression of what is current for "me." I was contemplating the question, What Am I? and when the instruction was given by my dyad partner to "Tell me what you are," awareness began to scan for something to report about what was present. Often lately when this takes place, there is a seeing that the only way I can conceive of being anything at all is if thought produces an image or conception. There is a seeing that any sense of an identity is purely invented by thought moment by moment and has no ultimate reality other than that. This has usually created a significant sense of freedom and joy when this kind of inquiry is taken up.

In retrospect I now see that there was perhaps always or almost always a subtle veil created by thought (but undetected because so automatic and "normal") which was limiting the true experience and significance of what this all means. This time as awareness scanned for a sense of what I am, there was a deeper sense of not being able to find anything. The question moved from, What am I? to Where am I? and, again, I could not locate myself in any place at all. The difference in this case was that the sense of nothingness or emptiness was so clear and evident and filled the space of awareness, although even space was seen to be non-existent. I was nothing in a more complete sense than usual and as you say it was thrilling in a way that is dependent on nothing outside itself: Consciousness being absolutely excited by its own presence without any content. There was a sense of complete fullness.

I sat quietly for a while this morning and the same essence of the knowing was present. Insights arose which confirmed and kind of filled out details of this truth, not as additions to some concept but more as an ever deeper recognition of the nature of This which unfolds freshly each moment. So I can say the insights were consistent with what had been seen and yet they arise as if for the first time and are not connected in a linear way. And can I say that This is not present this very moment? I think not.

I'm noticing that it's interesting to be writing these words into a space of listening (written to you) whom I trust already understands everything I'm attempting to communicate. It's different from explaining things to someone I think may or may not understand or may partially understand, and perhaps this accounts for some of the sense of flow in the communications. There is a kind of effortlessness that arises, a lack of struggle to express. You already know it, so it's more like a fun and interesting exercise to see what comes into form out of this emptiness that we are and out of which concepts are arising. Again, I sense the quiet thrill of consciousness exploring itself and playing in this way in the apparent duality. Great stuff!

I've started reading a book by Toni Packer called *The Silent Question: Meditating in the Stillness of Not-Knowing*. It was in the local library. I'm very much enjoying her way of putting things. Sometimes these days I feel I have no interest in reading any spiritual material or listening to teachers. It all seems so available and more fresh to just look directly at what is in each moment, reading the book of myself so to speak. And then I find myself picking up a book or watching an interview from time to time. No need to make any principle about it...

Towards the end of your letter you spoke about "the eternal question." I recently read a cult classic from the 70s; I believe it is called *The Hitchhiker's Guide to the Galaxy*. One of the few things I found of interest other than some moments of quirky humour was near the end of the book when a super computer named Deep Thought is given the task of coming up with the answer to the great Question of Life, the Universe, and Everything. It takes 7.5 million years to come up with the answer: 42. Of course, there is a great uproar. How can the answer be 42? When asked, the computer responds, "I think the problem, to be quite honest with you, is that you've never actually known what the question is." Maybe we could go into this more deeply in our next communication. One other gem from the same book you may find amusing and relevant is that the history of every major Galactic Civilization tends to pass through three distinct and recognizable phases, those of Survival, Inquiry, and Sophistication, otherwise known as the How, Why, and Where phases. For instance, the first phase is characterized by the question, How can we eat? The second by the question, Why do we eat?, and the third by the question, Where shall we have lunch?

Very Zen, don't you think? Body, mind, and then simple non-conceptual living, chopping wood and carrying water...

Be well,
David

24 Jan. 2013
To: David

Hello David,

Here are some thoughts on your previous letter.

There is a seeing that any sense of an identity is purely invented by thought moment by moment and has no ultimate reality other than that.

As you say one's identity is not inherently real. It is a mirage of the mind. You = thought. This brings to mind the question, Who are you without any story at all? Who are you when you don't think about yourself?

By wider abstraction, isn't it the case that all of seeming physical reality is manifested by way of thought as well? It seems to me that Leela/Samsara is really nothing more than the play of conception. Today I heard Adyashanti talk about the formless versus form and say "form is thought." At retreat I heard Jac O'Keeffe say that a tree was not there until she manifested it by way of conception. I once had a moment of clear understanding when it became apparent that the nature of our so-called reality was premised or formed through thought or information alone. That was its fundamental nature. While it certainly appears to be a tangible and seems to be constructed out of real "nuts and bolts," its actual nature is far more ephemeral than most suspect. Quantum physics is beginning to demonstrate this very thing. They tell us subatomic particles don't really "exist" as discrete entities, but as a wave of probability, until an observer notes them. This is not philosophy but has been scientifically demonstrated by the double slit experiment.

As Bill Hicks put it, "We are all one consciousness experiencing itself subjectively. There's no such thing as death, life is only a dream, and we're the imagination of ourselves." I remember you once said that you were "making it all up." Self, other, the birds and the bees: *thought* stuff or *the word made flesh*.

I was nothing...and as you say it was thrilling in a way that is dependent on nothing outside itself: Consciousness being absolutely excited by its own presence without any content.

Yep, I remember Plotinus once alluding to the fact that the best Spirit could ever do was to intuit itself. Perhaps this is the excitement you are referring to. ONE catching a glimpse of SELF.

There was a sense of complete fullness.

Exactly. How marvelous! Isn't it the fullest emptiness you could ever hope to bump into? Originally, this kind of experience scared the heck out of me. But that was only because I still had some capacity to reflect upon what was happening during meditation. This sense of dread passed over time. The mind grew ever more accustomed to relaxing into it all with no more need to reflect upon anything. Stillness became the norm. Then one day this experience became no longer state dependent, i.e., not only found during meditation. It became the norm. Or rather it always had been, but for the veil you spoke of, which makes things appear otherwise.

So, I can say the insights were consistent with what had been seen and yet they arise as if for the first time. And can I say that This is not present this very moment? I think not.

Yes, Yes, Yes...that which you are is indeed present at this very moment. In fact, it is the "moment" itself, for in the NOW you, the little you which you take yourself to be, is not. That is where the truth of it all lies. Now and now and now. No past. No future. I know you recognize temporal bound perception to be nothing more than a figment of the imagination because we have talked about the illusion of time previously. There has always been just the eternal. The rest is smoke and mirrors. You are already THAT. The seeker is the sought...blah, blah, blah...you've heard all this a million times. As you say, it is present at this very moment, for it is YOU. Somehow the trick is to naturally cease identification with the smoke and mirrors. No longer use "me" to inform yourself as to your identity but rather use "be." It is apparent that this reorientation is unfolding nicely for you.

I'm noticing that it's interesting to be writing these words into a space of listening (written to you) whom I trust already understands everything I'm attempting to communicate. It's different from explaining things to someone I think may or may not understand or may partially understand, and perhaps this accounts for some of the sense of flow in the communications.

This forum seems to have become "Monad's playhouse." Let's keep having fun and see what comes of it. I think a full year of weekly correspondence as proposed will pass quickly. The better part of a month is already over, and I feel there is

Chapter 3 | January

still so much more to explore with you. Yes, indeed, I have found this stuff almost impossible to relay to another unless it has also been their direct experience as well. How do you explain the ineffable to another—or even yourself?

I've started reading a book by Toni Packer called *The Silent Question: Meditating in the Stillness of Not-Knowing*. It was in the local library. I'm very much enjoying her way of putting things.

Yes. I discovered her a few years back. She has a natural elegance and straightforwardness to the way she puts things, and I recognized in her a certain quality that I also recognized in Adyashanti: An uncompromising stance of Truthfulness."

Sometimes these days I feel I have no interest in reading any spiritual material or listening to teachers. It all seems so available and more fresh to just look directly at what is in each moment, reading the book of myself so to speak.

That made me giggle aloud, "reading the book of myself" he says. How wonderful. That would make a good title.

And then I find myself picking up a book or watching an interview from time to time. No need to make any principle about it...

Yep, me too. I think the difference between now and when I was seeking, is that now I do it just for giggles. Also, some teachers have a way of expressing IT that has never occurred to me before and this elicits a kind of pleasure when I once again catch a glimpse of myself out of the corner of my I. Oops, meant to say "eye", but corner of my "I" works just the same. Meister Eckhart--"The eye through which I see God is the same eye through which God sees me; my eye and God's eye are one eye, one seeing, one knowing."

How can the answer be 42? When asked, the computer responds, "I think the problem, to be quite honest with you, is that you've never actually known what the question is."

I referenced that passage in the opening chapter of *A Fleeting Improvised Man* but cut it out in later drafts. Glad to see it again.

Known as the How, Why, and Where phases. For instance, the first phase is characterized by the question, How can we eat? The second by the question, Why do we eat? and the third by the question, Where shall we have lunch? Very Zen, don't you think? Body, mind, and then simple non-conceptual living, chopping wood and carrying water.

Very Zen, indeed. And as you say I found the humour in that book to my liking as well. I remember revisiting the entire Monty Python series just prior to my awakening. Just the kind of medicine to heal what ails you. I can't stress it enough. Have fun! In whatever venue or way that might be. Waking up seems to require both a wisdom as well as a heart-centred approach. I found humour, song and weepy movies to be wonderfully effective in openings of the heart. Perhaps you do as well or maybe something else tickles your bhakti centre.

"Knowing the right question to ask" is a great topic. I love your suggestion. I spent loads of time mulling this very topic over in several different ways. Let's see what you come up with. I will bring something to the table as well.

Have fun!

DJ

PS: Regarding the response to the letter I sent to the retreat centre, I thought my letter would reach Sensei, but I was mistaken. Sent it to the wrong person so now the cat is out of the bag by mistake. I have found it best not to share what I know with most spiritual folk unless I really know them and them, me. Oh well...what's done is done. I shall soon learn how it all will unfold as centre rep and I shall soon talk directly. Though spiritual people seem to be chasing so-called enlightenment, most seem to think it is only for special, faraway ethereal beings, Avatars, God-Men and the like. Of course, you and I are none of those things, nor was Buddha or Ramana, etc. Since I am just an ordinary guy who claims to be no longer asleep at the wheel, most spiritual types distrust me, hold me in low regard and usually treat me with mockery and disdain. You saw this yourself at your centre. Remember that woman who called me crazy? That's why I generally hesitate to speak up. I did not hesitate with Sensei as I take him to be a guy who "gets it." But just what the hell is IT...? Let's continue to explore and see if the spotlight of clarity can make it all a little less murky.

28 Jan. 2013
To: David

My inquiries to the spiritual retreat centre seem not to have worked out favorably. I offered to be of service, but the sales rep was not terribly interested.

He WAS, though, interested in extracting lots of cash from me. The two-week retreat I wanted to attend by way of introduction was going to cost $2,400, and he was not flexible on lowering that price. Seems like the centre caters to the moneyed class. He explained that I could not possibly contact Sensei directly because, after all, I was just a "nobody." He sure got that part right, bless his soul.

Find below my response to the question, Regarding truth realization, can the right question ever be asked?

If one poses a "right" question, then it follows that a "right" answer may eventually be forthcoming. If there is no correct answer ever to be had, then the whole premise would be moot, wouldn't it? Or would it? Could there be value in asking spiritual questions that never elicit any useful reply or even any reply whatsoever? The spiritually driven ego seems to be forever holding out the possibility that tomorrow the right question will finally be posed and at long last ALL will be revealed. Perhaps tomorrow will never arrive. Ever. In fact, David, if you get to tomorrow, please shoot me an email. Of course, we both know tomorrow never arrives. I will elaborate on all this in a bit, but first let's determine who is asking the question and to whom is it being addressed and proceed from there, ok?

Who is the asker? The little me or the big ONE? It must be some form of the little me as Mr. Biggy seems quite mute on all matters. I say some-form of the little guy as it is hard to exactly pin this sucker down. Just who exactly is "the little me"? Is it the neurotic one that is asking? Perhaps the wise one. Or the confused one, or the earnest one, or the depressed one. From whom, or where does the question emanate? Not really sure are we?

Many seekers may have discovered that their thoughts are arising spontaneously unbidden. I know you have, David. If there is no "questioner," then is a question ever really being posited? Who is asking the question? It might feel like "you" are conceiving of a question, but are you really? If you are, who is that? Who is this "you"?

Can a dream character ever ask a pertinent question so that it will actually elicit a meaningful spiritual realization? *Can't we expect dream questions to only reveal answers that tacitly continue to prop up the dream state?* Doesn't illusion just reveal more of itself? Isn't it the case that the dream must be transcended entirely if anything more than illusion is ever to be revealed? You can't rout out delusion by utilizing the very thing you seek to transcend. Or can you?

So how do we explain spiritual insight and great realizations? Don't they arise by themselves and take us by great surprise. Can it be said that "you" had anything to do with it? If you did, then who would that "you" be? I sure don't know.

Next up for consideration is the question, To whom is the query actually being addressed? The assumption would be some kind of entity, correct? An "answerer" if you will. I guess the short list would include the possibility of only self/little me or "other." Maybe investigating the format the question takes might be helpful in addressing this particular area of interest.

If the question takes the form of, How is it that I might be living in a dream state?, or Do I create my own thoughts?, or

Who/what am I?, it would seem that I would be addressing these questions to myself. At the later stages of my inquiry I realized it was somewhat strange to be asking such questions as I could not locate "myself" anywhere. Who was it that could respond, never mind relay any relevant information? Of course, earlier on such questions were very helpful in pointing out the illusory nature of self.

One kind of question I resisted asking were those that were distracting and time wasting in nature. The little me loved to get side tracked with how-many-angels-can-dance-on-the-head-of-a-pin type philosophical questions. For example, my ego was drawn to consider such irrelevant side-bars as, I wonder if the Dalai Lama is really enlightened because I heard him say by his own words that he wasn't?, or "Why do many Tibetan Buddhists eat meat?", or "Why are some famous spiritual teachers apparently such assholes?" Who cares?, came my reply. I would immediately move on with some pursuit more spiritually edifying. These kinds of juicy questions were beside the point as far as my own awakening was concerned. I came to see how the ego employed this kind of tactic to stay off the matter at hand. Namely, bringing about its demise.

Then there were the existential questions that seemed to be rhetorical in nature and were usually just thrown out into the ether without much hope of receiving a reply such as, why does realizing Buddha nature provoke so much fear in me? (This was just a temporary phase, thank God), "How can my long-held belief in reincarnation be accurate when now it seems to be just one more ridiculous idea?", or "Just what the hell is actually going on here?" I mean this waking up stuff is like something out of a science fiction movie. How can this actually be happening to me?

So how about it? Can the "right "question ever be asked? Again to whom is it being posed? Can we ever ask a teacher the question-of-all-questions? I certainly never found one. How about you?

Of course, undoubtedly there are better questions to ask as opposed to the real stinkers many seekers keep bringing forth, like those related to improving their lot in life or queries about how they might deal with the loss of a loved one for example. Fine questions for some other venue but not very appropriate for Truth realization.

I would suggest that any questions a seeker could ask that might ferret out delusion and misunderstanding regarding self would be the highest and best ones they could ever muster up. In practicality isn't it the case that this hardly ever happens? I used to imagine what relevant question I might ask my teacher if I ever met him. Even with great deliberation I found it a difficult prospect. In fact, I never came up with one that really satisfied me. You might agree that, in general, most seekers found at satsang rattle off the most trivial and banal crap imaginable. My God, there they are standing in front of someone they believe has a finger on the pulse of the Absolute and instead of asking the most spiritually edifying question ever they instead muster up something that just came to mind as they were sitting there in the audience or perhaps mention some cool "opening" they had last meditation. What a wasted opportunity. And if they can't formulate a relevant question, then at least that realization itself could be recognized. Mostly it seems they just ask any old question by way of introducing themselves to the teacher.

Sometimes, too, it seems like they are purposefully avoiding subject matters that might actually be of spiritual consequence. When given the opportunity to ask a spiritually relevant question they seem to consistently balk. Or maybe they subconsciously know that anything they might ask will be quite irrelevant, since going from me-ing to being doesn't involve the acquisition of new knowledge. Rather, it is a stance of "not-knowing" anything at all which reveals the true nature of things.

I remember asking you what question you asked Mooji when you finally got face to face with him. I was curious to hear your response, such is my longstanding fascination for this topic. Can you refresh my memory as to what you asked him? I remember it was a rather general kind of question, wasn't it? Something on the nature of self or some such, wasn't it? How about presently? What question, if any, would you pose to him now?

As far as revealing the illusory nature of the "I thought," the most pertinent question I ever employed was, Who/what am I? Despite doing this numerous times, I always came up with the same thing: Don't know. And, of course, in actuality, as far as Truth realization was concerned, I eventually found out there never was any answer to be had about anything at all. In the end no secret was divulged, no conundrum solved. But that is not the full story either.

Upon waking up, things were, in a sense, revealed to be as they actually were. There was a feeling of revelation and deja vu but not understanding. Several months after awakening occurred, my conceptual mind piped up one day in a rather mocking tone and said, *You was robbed, I say, robbed! You gave away everything and for what? You wanted to discover the ultimate nature of reality and in the end nothing was found. What does it all mean?*, it kept asking. *You big dummy*, my ego said, *you never did find the answer to your questions after all.*

How untrue. It was only when all questions ceased that the All revealed itself to itself. Seeker and seeking stopped only when the questions finally petered out. Nirvana. Cessation. The end to all questioning. The realization that I was already the very answer I had long been seeking. There is no answer ever to be had. David, you are the answer.

Love,
DJ

28 Jan. 2013
To: DJ

Hi DJ,

Wow, I'm amazed by the response from the Tibetan centre representative. Sometimes people— and especially ones we might think would be more open and inclusive—are perplexing. Or might we say that Consciousness sometimes seems to have a weird sense of humour or perhaps that all variety of experience and response is included in its expression! Or maybe we could say that it's all ultimately quite incomprehensible, and I did just say it!

I'll respond to your letter very soon...
David

28 Jan. 2013
To: David

Your quip was very apt and made me chuckle. Incomprehensible indeed! And funny...you bet! One piece of info I did not include is that the guy I talked to (I think, but not totally sure) never laid eyes on the email I thought I sent to Sensei. Thank goodness as it would have only made things worse. As it stands, I am an unknown entity, and it is his job to get me to pay up. Even volunteering there costs money. I looked at their board of directors. All professionals or captains of industry. All loyal to their root guru who is not Sensei but rather Namgyal Rinpoche, a Canadian teacher from Toronto who was a Kagyu Tibetan lineage holder. Sensei's teacher.

The guy on the phone, as well as others there, are teachers or vying to be teachers, though he said he was not awake but "awakening." It sounds like an old boy's network, and I suspect I would not be very welcome. Pity. The hermitage I lived at was also Kagyu and Namgyal was also that teacher's teacher.

The organization itself seems very much about power and control. Tibet was never a democracy but rather more akin to a theocracy with the Buddhists at the helm. The high lamas held all the power, and it seems this ethos has been exported. The American minions and the ones here in Canada often seem to be attracted to the baser elements of spiritual materialism. Still, I did detect a genuine spirit of truth telling regarding the teacher that interested me, at least in his podcasts.

The guy at the hermitage I lived in appeared to have no direct spiritual experience whatsoever. For him it was all about the allure of power and the respect his title, *Rinpoche*, afforded him; he got this title through what I regard to be a fake tulku recognition. Others in certain U.S. Buddhist centres are reported to support the same view as well. Apparently, he is thought to be a fraud by those American lamas and centres in the know. That fact was obvious to me. That was why I was so interested in meeting Sensei. Oh well...it's all a mystery, as you say.

Cheers,
DJ

29 Jan. 2013
To: DJ

Hi,

So, let's see what emerges as I read over your letter which I enjoyed greatly.

You pose the issue of who is asking the question, whatever the question may be, and I love the way you inquire into that. The Big One may be mute and not able to ask questions, but perhaps a capacity of mind which is not particularly identified with the little "me" can represent the silent undefinable whatever. Mooji calls this the "intellect of the Being." This is also the capacity which "chooses" Being over ego moment to moment and chooses not to believe the thoughts that are out of alignment with Truth. More than a choice, it is perhaps just pure seeing, which has an action of its own outside of any "doing" by the little me or separate ego.

But as I write this, I immediately sense trouble approaching as I imagine you asking, What is this Truth?", and "What does it mean to be aligned with it? I'm already in hot water!" Let me just say that something represents Consciousness in asking questions which can initiate useful inquiry into the nature of reality (and as you say, that something is hard to identify). One of these useful questions is, "Who is asking the question?"

For many years I considered myself to be on a spiritual path. My understanding seemed to be deepening and my experience becoming more peaceful, joyful, and loving. I saw that thoughts were just arising out of nothing and dissolving back into it and that self-images were just thoughts. And yet in a way that seems inexplicable now; there was never a deep questioning of the identity of the one who was on the path. "I" was on the path without really knowing what that "I" was or whether it actually existed. It seems strange now because it would seem that identity would naturally have been looked into in the practice of meditation and self-observation, and in a way it was. But then there came a point where the question, "Who or What am I?", took on a whole new dimension. I can't seem to pinpoint exactly when that happened, but it seemed to be about the time I started sitting in meditation with Claudio here in Victoria. He introduced me to the teachings of Ramesh Balsekar and the more profound aspects of Ramana Maharshi and Nisargadatta, among others.

I remember *Your Head In the Tiger's Mouth* (by Ramesh) having a particularly strong influence on my understanding. I remember one moment when I was sitting quietly at home and suddenly felt like I was waking up from a dream of myself, a dream that I existed and was living as a distinct entity separate from others. It was the sense of waking up from a dream into seeing that what had been dreamed was only a dream and in no way true to the awakened consciousness. I wouldn't say that it was a final or total awakening, but it certainly was a shift in perspective which in a significant sense was never forgotten or lost. After that, whenever I would hear myself or someone else speaking about their spiritual journey using words like 'My spiritual journey' with an energy of ownership or belief in the identity of that "I" or "my," it would just seem so obviously false and delusional. It then seemed that up to that point I had not actually been on the path at all but merely floundering around under the delusion that this "I" who was on the path was real; therefore, everything I was doing was, in fact, extremely misdirected, as were the same kinds of efforts by "others."

Chapter 3 | January

So, it seems that in this sense at least a question such as, "Who am I?, or What am I?" can turn the attention to investigating in a way that can dispel illusion, or at least a layer or two or many. If we assume that reality is desirable over illusion, then we could say these questions have value, at least at a certain stage of the so-called journey.

I just now reread your letter and find you have exhaustively dealt with many more subtle points in a way that absolutely delights something in me which I might call my truth register. There is so much that is directly to the point and to which I would totally give a stamp of approval, if that would have any meaning. You ask what question I asked Mooji when in front of him and of the perhaps half dozen times I've taken the opportunity to be in the "hot seat", or "electric chair" as he calls it. It was really only the very first time that I actually could come up with a question. The other times were essentially reporting on things that were going on for me or insights or realizations and just being open to any response he might have.

The question I asked was about my experience of everything dissolving into nothing and the sense that I couldn't say that something unchanging remained, even Awareness. His response was that Awareness didn't disappear but only the objects of awareness. An issue that you and I have explored on several occasions, I believe, and some interesting insights have arisen in contemplation of this subject with you and otherwise. One funny thing Mooji said was when I mentioned coming to the electric chair the previous day, he said, "The electric chair seems not to have worked" (as I was coming back again).

Normally, I just can't come up with any question that I can believe in and asking such questions as, "Who am I?" serves only to invite some deep looking and inquiry to which any "answer" can only be superficial and at the very most can point to the great Mystery. Any answer that can be conceived is still dependent on the duality of subject and object which has the capacity to generate a concept. This can be explored in one's own looking, and I love the way you have asked so many questions which could serve as points of contemplation for investigation so that perhaps the same conclusion you have reached at the end will be as glaringly and freshly in-the-moment obvious to me or others from personal experience, which seems to be the only valid way of "knowing" or "not-knowing."As Osho used to say, "Enough for today..."

Cheers,

David

The Clothes Have No Emperor
31 Jan. 2013
To: DJ

Good day, DJ,

Thoughts are arising to say a little more about the "right" question in life and maybe I'll get to it tomorrow or the next day - or maybe not. We'll see...

Cheers,

David

31 Jan. 2013
To: David

I encourage you to send them along posthaste, but like always, it is of no real consequence. In fact, I said those very words about my own musings to you in a letter I am soon to send off. What I write is of no import. I know I am definitely in trouble if I ever begin to believe my own bullshit. Point it out if I ever do.

Maybe what you are composing touches on some of the themes I am currently addressing. I am finding it quite challenging to put down in words the truth of the matter. I suspect it must be the same for you. Let's continue to be patient and see where we might be led, shall we?

Cheers,

DJ

∞Chapter 4∞

February

1 Feb. 2013
To: DJ

    Yes, it does seem to be challenging to write down anything absolutely true, and as soon as I write anything there tends to be a number of considerations that immediately question what has been expressed and reveal other angles to the issue. Such appears to be the limitation of the thinking mind when it comes to more and more subtle inquiries into the nature of reality. Still, it can be fun and useful to explore...And with your invitation I will indeed mention it if it seems you are starting to believe your own "BS" in a way that might compromise the living of the "answer" in an uncorrupted way. And immediately the question arises, "Can there really be a corrupted way of living?" Another topic perhaps. I also invite you to question my attempts at truthful expression.

    We seem to have agreed that the question, "Who or what am I?" may be the most useful one to ask. I wanted to back track a little to consider why this would be so, just to kind of fill in the blanks. In my experience I think the first serious question that came to me was,

"How can I be happy?" This was even before, "What is happiness?" because it's more basic to the human experience. I didn't want to spend time analyzing happiness; I just wanted some – or a lot – of it. It seems, looking around at people, that everyone wants to be happy. As we discussed before, this gets more subtle as one "evolves".

The normal response to the question, unless there is some strong conditioning or rare understanding otherwise, is to look to the external world for happiness. That is, getting the material goods and worldly status and the experiences delivered by them, including finding a good romantic partner and like-minded friends seems to be the focus of attention. Even the changing of consciousness with alcohol or drugs is aimed at improving the experience of socializing with others or connecting with a sexual partner, and so on. And so it goes on for the whole life unless something intervenes.

At a point in my development I realized (or the realization spontaneously arose) that my experience of the world was not just a matter of getting the objects of my desire lined up properly but was very much dependent on my own state of mind. This seemed like a huge revelation at the time and made sense of such pursuits as meditation and self-understanding.

The point that was added to the external search was the need to understand how I was at least partially creating my reality or experience of life by my own ways of thinking and reacting to the challenges of living. The question about happiness was becoming more inwardly directed and that seems to be how it continues to evolve. The issue becomes more to do with the "inner" reality and less to do with conditions in the outer world. It has become more and more clear how important it is to see what I am taking myself to be at any given moment, as what I am taking myself to be is determined by whatever beliefs about myself are holding sway and how those beliefs are shaping my experience.

For example, if I have a false idea about who I am then my experience of life will be distorted by that idea. Therefore, the question, "Who am I really?" or "What am I really?" The "who" question has generally become less interesting as the seeing happens that there is no person at all in the conventional sense and the "what" question seems to offer more fertile ground for a deeper investigation. Then, as you have suggested, even that question is seen to have no answer. It becomes about living the answer or being the answer: The non-dual realization of Truth. I still find the question a good one to contemplate so perhaps there is still a need to keep coming back to the awareness of the total simplicity of Being and/or there is a love of contemplating the nature of reality, and to do so there has to be a starting point that assumes there is at least a possibility of something to be discovered. I tend to agree with Mooji when he says that the most profound and enjoyable activity is the Self contemplating Itself. And that's what we're enjoying here! Also, it is my experience that discoveries happen spontaneously when resting in or as silence without any particular inquiring and that when a question is asked the way into the exploration is through the gateless gate of stillness.

   Love, David

   PS: I've now given you quite a volume of ideas to respond to. Oh, well...

2 Feb. 2013
To: David

   Thanks for sending off your newest insights so promptly. I love them! Will send new thoughts soon. Here is what I came up with. Enjoy.

   .. read over your letter - which I enjoyed greatly.

   Yep, I had the same response to yours. It was a joy to read and a bit of a surprise too, as I never heard you relate your awakening experience, *vis-a'-vis* your life-is-a-dream realization before. As well, I took your letter as an invitation to reflect a little further on the matter at hand. See below for further insight. As always, I offer it in the spirit of love and fraternity. It is simply what has popped up and is of no real importance. I pray you take everything I offer in this spirit...no real importance. After all, none of it is really True, is it? Just a bit of musing aloud is all...

   Here is the gist of what follows in totality below. I invite you to consider the following quote, "I knew that most people never see this reality because they attach to the material aspect of the world. Illusions of self and others fill their vision."
Buddha

   Investigate this wholeheartedly and see for yourself. Is it really the case that self and other exist? Can there really be an "asker" of questions or is this all premised on dualistic illusion as Buddha suggests it is. *Sapere aude*...dare to know. Why bother to read all the crap which I wrote below when instead you can find out the truth of the matter for yourself right here and now. And by the way, David—tag, you're it.

> You pose the issue of who is asking the question. The Big One may be mute and not able to ask questions, but perhaps a capacity of mind which is not particularly identified with the little "me" can represent the silent undefinable whatever. Mooji calls this the "intellect of the Being."

"Intellect of being" is what Mooji calls it, and you tell me this is a stand-in for the Absolute; very well then. As I rmember, J. Krishnamurti at times similarly referred to the "indefinable whatever" as "the intelligence" (hmmm...labeling something that is silent and indefinable by its very nature as any objective thing or quality seems suspect to me.) Perhaps you remember that I once brought up J.K.'s reference as a bit of a puzzle. *Intellect of Being* is similarly perplexing. Perhaps I just don't get it. That is a real possibility.

But I have to wonder about the use of the term intelligence. Intelligence as opposed to what? The experience here to date seems quite unable to entertain such descriptors as valid. It's like when a satsang teacher I once met said that waking up to reality was "finding the source." Source as opposed to what? Even if this inclination towards non-identification is not one's own waking reality, it is quite clear that this kind of labeling is entirely dualistic in nature.

This kind of symbolism is only that. The conceptual mind seems drawn to personify the ineffable with certain qualities, one obviously being "intelligence." But is this actually the case? Forget what these illumined folk say about it for a minute. Pay no attention to me either. Let's keep this real as I know you strive to always do and which the conclusion of your January 29 letter wonderfully demonstrates where you write, "personal experience, which seems to be the only valid way of 'knowing' or 'not-knowing.'"

So how about it then? When you have withdrawn so far that even the concept of your own existence can't possibly arise (by this I mean the "little you" you take yourself to be...or do you...?), tell me then about this "intelligence." Ascribe any quality to it if you can. Doesn't all of that arise later after the conceptual mind gets hold of things? In the moment, in the space between the thoughts, what can be said? How reliable are these after-THOUGHTS? Is it not the case that all thoughts are suspect? Of course, I include my own here as well.

For example, I conclude that since Mr. Biggy is the quietest guy you will ever bump into (indeed he has never uttered a single consonant), my mind spins the story that if a question is to be posed, then it must be emanating from the illusional small "I" persona figure as that is the only thing capable of jibber jabbering.

Who else could be asking it? But this is just a story I tell myself. This story is not taken to be real. It is not a position I have adopted. I wouldn't defend it. All thoughts are inherently untrustworthy.

Perhaps it is the case that "you" have recognized the illusionary nature of "you." At the same time undeniable TRUTHS have arisen, sometimes seemingly in response to certain questions and insight practices. The dualistic mind, therefore, concludes "if not A then B." If little me is an illusion and not to be trusted, then it must be that Big Me, or as you surmise, some kind of "stand-in" or divine Doppelganger, must be the one posing enlightened questions which in turn then must be generating spiritually edifying responses. After all, "There's gotta be somebody asking questions around here," doesn't there? Or does there?

In the spirit of full disclosure I have to admit that I don't really know where any questions or answers originate. In fact, there doesn't seem to be any centre to be had anywhere at all. So from whence could I conclude anything originated and to whence exactly would I conclude anything disappeared? There is no alpha and omega point as far as I can see.

In the relative world there is the appearance of comings and goings, but it is just that- simply appearance. I posited that it must be the little me asking such questions because Spirit is simply unable to. You posit it must be Spirit, or some such, since the little me can't possibly come up with spiritually relevant Qs and As due to its deluded nature. Both are possible, but it may be neither. Who knows? Who cares?

Would that "knower" be somebody like Mooji or J. K.? If they know how, do you know that they know? And more to the point what do you know? Do you know for a fact that there is an "intelligence of being?" Seriously, if I am missing something here I would like to be let in on the secret...

Don't take that last sentence too seriously. I recognize that we are both struggling in our attempts to describe the ineffable.

This is also the capacity which "chooses" Being over ego moment to moment and chooses not to believe the thoughts that are out of alignment with Truth.

I know you don't much support what you said above, but let me use it as a pointer. As there is the appearance that choices are made, it is natural to assume that there must then be a "chooser" somewhere, but is this actually the case? Is there a chooser who does indeed make choices, or is it rather simply the case that thoughts spontaneously arise by their own accord? Is there really any volition involved when it comes to decision making?

If there is indeed a wise "chooser," then why is it totally impossible to choose to have no thoughts whatsoever? If suffering is occurring why does this aligned-with-Truth-chooser-being not choose to have nice happy thoughts for the body/mind complex all the time and consequently do away with misery once and for all? Is choosing thoughts really the realm of Beingness itself? Does it really care what thoughts you have? Isn't this "divine intervention" just a fable your ego has spun for you? If this "intelligence" really cares what thoughts you have, please cite some evidence for this.

The overriding assumption has always been that thoughts are made by volition, and thus there must be a chooser but this is simply never the case. It is clear to me that I have never once managed to "make" a thought appear. I mean in the sense that a carpenter has foreknowledge or a plan before he makes or constructs a table into existence. Thoughts don't work this way do they? I never know beforehand what I am about to think, so how can I claim to be making or choosing thoughts? Isn't it the case that they just spontaneously pop into awareness unbidden?

This, then, is why it is impossible to make thoughts cease. Thoughts arise spontaneously all by themselves. "You" don't have anything to do with it. That's just the way things are. It is not within your capacity, never mind some nebulous, nondescript "wise one's" ability to choose anything at all.

To ascribe thoughts, the capacity to be more or less "aligned with truth," and then somehow entertain the possibility that an indefinable higher capacity or entity chooses said "right thoughts" is precisely as you stated "getting yourself in hot water." Scalding, I would say. Though some gurus may beg to differ, I suggest that there are no "good" thoughts or "bad "thoughts. As I said in my first book, "all thoughts are nonsense, utter bullshit. None are to be trusted. Whatever garb you try to cloth it in, this 'chooser' entity that you allude to does not exist." Like I have said before, "It is not so much that the "emperor has no clothes" but rather that the "clothes have no emperor." Or am I mistaken? Is there an "entity" found anywhere empowered to make choices? If so, I would like to know who that would be.

Let me just say that something represents Consciousness in asking questions which can initiate useful inquiry into the nature of reality (and as you say, that something is hard to identify). One of these useful questions is, "Who is asking the question?"

Considering the immediately above, when you say "something represents Consciousness" I would say this is getting closer to the heart of it. Here you are being quite vague but not vague enough by half. Absolute indefinability is the only way we can speak about the ineffable if we are being honest about it. Jac O'Keefe kept pounding this point into me again and again when I first met her. I am forever grateful for her dogged determination in not straying from this path. Whatever adjective I might have chosen to describe IT, she clearly pointed out that this was pure folly. This message was just what I needed to hear and apparently was the whole reason I journeyed to Costa Rica.

REASON FOR GOING TO COSTA RICA, HA! HA! DJ, YOU GREAT BIG FOOL. YOU ARE JUST TELLING YOURSELF ANOTHER STORY.

Yep, but that is no reason for getting in the way of a good yarn is it? To continue if you please...oh, yes, well...where was I?

Don't you just hate a spoilsport that ruins a perfectly good tale by introducing a little reality into it? And that, David, is precisely how awakening is fostered, just keep interrupting the story enough with a little clarity, and I guarantee you will awaken.

So to continue...well, a few weeks after visiting Jac, in fact while attending Unmani's retreat, where the message given was essentially the same one, I came to this direct realization myself. True nature cannot be objectified.

Chapter 4 / February

I take it that what you are pointing to above is the inherent intuitive sense of "truthiness" that insight fosters or that capacity which rises to the fore which recognizes "that which is false." I concur that this is my experience as well. Something does seem to recognize the Truth. It seems though that while, on the one hand, you are pointing out the nebulous quality-less ill-defined nature of the Absolute (for you refer to it only as a "something" with no definable qualities) that is symbolic (a stand in or "representation" as you point out) for that which you already are (you call it consciousness), you also wonder if it is the question "asker." Well, let's see.

How can some undefined "something" that is "nothing" ask or direct anything? And why would it even bother? This question doesn't seem to make any sense. Perhaps you would agree that you can't have your cake and eat it too. If you are speaking here of an indefinable "nothingness," then how can it choose things and ask questions? If it is indeed a "something," then describe its qualities. In whose voice are these questions being posed? Does it speak loudly or with little more than a hoarse whisper? Does it sound jocular or very serious when it pipes up? You get what I am pointing to here.

In a manner of speaking I can attest to you that you are already THAT. That— "THAT's all folks!" That, THAT is that. There can be no more or less of THAT. There really is nothing to solve here. THAT has nary a care in the world. It simply is. THAT is all there really is. This is to say that THAT is not anything at all.

So while it may appear to the mind that some force is interested in and personally guiding the awakening process, in actuality this could not be further from the truth. This is no more the case than it would be to say that the North Pole is personally interested in which direction your compass needle points. In reality it doesn't actually care which way your boat is headed. To crash on a dreaded shoal or make landfall in a deep water port is of no consequence to it. Magnetic North just is. That's its nature.

In the distant past magnetic lodestone was used as a navigation aid. Seafarers believed it to be imbued with magical properties. In Plutarch's mystical writings lodestone was referred to as the "bone" or "core" of the Gods. Of course, this is how myths are created. Story telling—that's what we seem to do best. The gods never actually serve any function in ship navigation or your awakening. The only one that cares which direction you are headed, is you. It's a complete mystery to me why awakening occurs in the first place. Only my mind could come up with a story about it.

This is not to say Spirit does not rejoice in revealing itself to itself. It's simply very quiet about the whole affair. "Mute" as I put it. Not because it doesn't want to pipe up but rather because volition or any action is quite impossible. No qualities can be ascribed to the absolute. It just is. Or isn't.

The sense of waking up from a dream into seeing that what had been dreamed was only a dream and in no way true to the awakened consciousness. I wouldn't say that it was a final or total awakening but it certainly was a shift in perspective which in a significant sense was never forgotten or lost.

Nice! Same thing here. Pretty much like you describe it. One shot deal, wasn't it? It seems unlikely that a realization of this magnitude needs to be repeated.

Just as you relate, I knew that there was still a way to go up the "pathless path" or down the "holeless" rabbit hole until the issue was resolved. At the same time, it was quite apparent that though I knew I was dreaming the whole story up, this knowledge did not negate the fact that I was still totally enmeshed in the dream state. Most odd.

A certain lucidity was engendered in that moment. The feeling was akin to how it felt to be in a lucid dream. I knew it was all "make believe" (good definition of "make believe" is *The American Dream*, since you gotta make yourself dream it to believe it) while immersed in the dream, yet it appeared to be as real as real can get. All I could do during that part of my journey was stay as alert and lucid as possible moment to moment and let things proceed as they might. Meditation was most rewarding in this capacity. Perhaps that is how it is for you too. Not doing anything, but just entirely one hundred percent nothing at all. And being lucidly aware that that is what is going on all the time: Nothing. Or better still, just being pure awareness itself. Works wonders. I trust you know what I am alluding to here.

And then one day I spontaneously "fell awake." Fell up and out of it all. Isn't that how you actually awaken from your own nocturnally induced reveries? Quite naturally with no apparent action of your own. Neat, eh? One day simply fall awake. Up and out of it all. Couldn't be simpler.

Cheers, DJ

PS: An afterthought. During my spiritual journey when I finally got really serious, I quite quickly recognized that I was just as ignorant as those silly sailors were with their "magical" lodestones. Here I mean where it really counts, i.e., not knowing my own true nature. In this milieu I wasn't even an "also ran." I was like that "agony of defeat skier" who never even got his name up on the board. Just totally out of the race.

If I couldn't recognize something as simple as who/what I was, then what else could I know for certain about anything?

So in the end it became a kind of demolition project. Not building up ego but rather tearing the whole fucking playhouse down. To cease egoic identification enough to eventually see once and for all that it never really existed in the first place. How did I stop building the edifice I call me? How did I disempower my empire of shit? By simply noticing what actually was. Coming to see that all my beliefs were unfounded. Every last one of them. The more closely I cared to peer into the miasma, the more deluded I realized I was. This is just an honest appraisal of fact. And it is not to say that I am any less deluded now. Now…? Now I just AM…or am NOT. Delusion doesn't figure into the equation one way or another. I came to see that we are all terribly confused. Humanity is in a very real sense insane. And by the way that would include you, dear David. Thought you were exempt, didn't you?

I was irrelevant and inconsequential. Truly. Hard to believe it, but I discovered that the world would somehow continue ticking along perfectly smoothly without me. Though everything seemed to revolve entirely around me, as I trust it does for you, I realized I was not special (or nothing special in "particular" as the whole ball of wax itself is pretty darn marvellous). The ego forever seeks the reassurance and the acknowledgement of others in order to bolster and validate its feelings of accomplishment and "unique status." *Oh look, look at me. Aren't I ever so clever and accomplished?* It continually craves to affirm and have reflected back to itself. It's all pretty sick really…and not true. It became shockingly clear to me how "wrong" I was about everything.

That's the price of admission if you want to play the game of "Me." Accept duality and the complete ignorance it entails. After all, how incredibly dumbed-down do you have to get in order to play a game of tag with yourself? Oh, and by the way David—tag, you're it.

Love, DJ

7 Feb. 2013
To: David

Below is the newest installment of "nothing ever happens"…and I report it!

In my experience I think the first serious question that came to me was, How can I be happy?" This was even before, "What is happiness?" because it's more basic to the human experience. I didn't want to spend time analyzing happiness; I just wanted some—or a lot—of it.

"I just wanted some—or a lot—of it." I couldn't help but burst out laughing reading that one. So very accurate. Do you remember when I was hanging out with the "New Thought" folks during my investigation of what made "spiritual people" tick? I rarely presented my point of view during my time spent with them but once did proffer Buddha's main tenet, "life entails suffering." They had apparently never been exposed to the fact that "life is inherently unsatisfying." That happiness is fleeting at best.

Well, the frumpy matriarch of the group, who looked ever so much like an aging British Prime Minister Thatcher, corrected me. "Oh no," she said. "Nope." She was, she assured me, happy indeed. A bit incredulous I asked her, "So you are telling me that you are always happy?" "Oh, yes," she confirmed. "It just seems that I could use a wee bit more from time to time (laughing)...but I'm not suffering, oh, no, not me."

I didn't then go on to point out that she had just confirmed the very thing she believed she was refuting. She clearly admitted that she never quite reached a high enough level of happiness to be one hundred percent truly satisfied. Satiated here infers the state of "being happy." This was precisely what Buddha had proposed. We never get satiated. Couldn't she hear the alarm bells ringing? Didn't anyone in the room note the klaxon call to awaken? Oh well, they seemed to be deep sleepers. No need to try to further trouse them. I just sat back in my chair and slipped again back into glorious silent emptiness.

As you very well know David, she, you, indeed everybody, will always be compelled to seek "more." This fact is quite apparent, but its ramifications are profound, and I appreciate that this is what you are pointing to. Our appetite for happiness is clearly insatiable. I love the Buddhist hungry ghost concept. That ghoul whose sensual cravings never cease.

This was the state of affairs "Mrs. Thatcher" was actually firmly entrenched in, though her ego was doing a brilliant job of persuading her otherwise. My existence, and by this I mean the "little me" I take myself to be, depends on this ruse for its very survival. It seems that our relentless quest to keep adding "onto ourselves" is a great strategy to prevent our true natures from ever being noticed. It's the case of forever "becoming," never "became." Never arriving to stop to find the "here and now."

This eternal moment, of course, can't not have been present all along. It's just that everyone is stuck in a virtual reality of their own creation which takes place in the so-called "past and future." In other words nobody is home; they are all out at the cinema of that which ain't transpiring. When the theatre finally closes its doors, "Beingness" spontaneously blossoms. You have always been home. The perpetual seeking never allows you to drop into the moment to discover this. Just stop, I say. Stop!

"Oh, dear, but what would I be without my story," some might well ask. Precisely. Our true nature is simply realizing what has always been. How is it possible to be other than that? This question of course makes no sense. But for a time it may "appear" otherwise. Constantly being unfulfilled is one sure sign that reality is still being kept at bay. Finding your true nature is like discovering that that lost wedding band you were so earnestly searching for had in fact been tucked away in your own breast pocket all along. Let me tell you that when that is discovered, for a second there you feel kinda foolish for getting all worked up over "nothing!"

As you pointed out, what a revelation to discover that perpetual seeking is a mugs game. Isn't it often the case that the simplest realizations are the most profound ones? I sure found that to be the case. That's probably one reason why Adyashanti resonated so much for me. I find him very adept at pointing out the profundity that often lies in the obvious.

When I say "obvious," of course, this turns out to be the case only when the point is grokked personally and deeply. Then you wonder how it was overlooked for so long. "My God...it's so, well...obvious, isn't it?" I would exclaim so after hearing one of Adya's better pointers. Like I had known it all along which of course I had. Just needed a little reminder was all.

At a point in my development I realized (or the realization spontaneously arose) that my experience of the world was not just a matter of getting the objects of my desire lined up properly but was very much dependent on my own state of mind. This seemed like a huge revelation.

Indeed, hugely revelatory. Again, simple but profound. When you see t-shirts or bumper stickers emblazoned with such moronic nonsense as, "He who dies with the most toys wins," your message runs entirely in the face of this kind of conditioning. "How glorious and rewarding it is to be materially enriched." That is the message we are bombarded with. Wealth, we are told, equates with personal satisfaction. Remember the long running TV show devoted entirely to that very theme: *Lifestyles of the Rich and Famous*? Does it get any clearer than that? But does anyone ever stop to check out if materialism is ultimately satisfying? Few indeed.

What a revelation to discover that the state of the world is not entirely object dependent. In fact, waking up to reality requires you to contravene almost everything you have ever learned or been told to believe in. The more engaged in the truth game I was, the more I came to expect the unexpected. Things became not stranger than I imagined, but stranger than I ever could have imagined. I would suggest that when things finally make no sense at all, it is then that you are really on to something. If it all looks utterly hopeless, even better! Ask Tolle about that one, he'll tell you.

The point that was added to the external search was the need to understand how I was at least partially creating my reality or experience of life by my own ways of thinking and reacting to the challenges of living.

Above you say that you are "partially creating your own reality." I think I see what you are pointing to there, but correct me if I am mistaken. Do you mean we automatically objectify everything, since this is how reality pops into focus for us? Though we assume subject/object relationships, the emphasis is almost entirely on the objects themselves, which are presumed to be exclusively "out there" somewhere. Then increasing lucidity or clarity of being sort of causes a change in focus to occur, almost like the focal length of a long camera lens changes from far to near. You have possessed this huge perceptual "lens" which was always capable of focusing from up-close micro to way out in the distance macro range but for some reason you always kept it firmly locked on what's "way out in front of you." You could only see what was on the horizon but nothing that was hidden right under your very own nose.

Would you say that you are still "partially" creating your reality now? I would propose that it can be nobody else but "I" who manifests the whole darn spectacle into existence. Do you catch my drift here? If you are the sole perceiver and arbiter of everything that apparently comes your way, who else but you is making it all up? If you look at reality this way, which is just realizing all of the innate abilities the "reality lens" has always offered, I think you can see what I am alluding to here. Who is it that makes the grass green? I mean really, really, really…could it be you?

The question about happiness was becoming more inwardly directed and that seems to be how it continues to evolve. The issue becomes more to do with the "inner" reality and less to do with conditions in the outer world.

Can you tell me a bit more about this "inner reality" thing? Can you elaborate on the concept of inner versus outer,

please? How does that distinction arise for you? I am not saying that this is, or is not the case. I am just curious, in a practical way, how it unfolds for you. How is it that the two separate "realities" appear to you as discretely different experiences? What tips you off that they are different in nature? What is this inner experience like? Is the "witnesser" of these two realities the same in both cases? Love to hear your impression about this.

It has become more and more clear how important it is to see what I am taking myself to be at any given moment, as what I am taking myself to be is determined by whatever beliefs about myself are holding sway and how those beliefs are shaping my experience. If I have a false idea about who I am, then my experience of life will be distorted by that idea.

Yes, I couldn't agree with the sentiment above more. When you state "how important it is to see what I am taking myself to be at any given moment" that, too, was certainly a cornerstone of my own awakening process. Some call it "awareness practice," others "mindfulness." Terminology is unimportant here, but it is interesting to note how this fundamental technique runs through many different spiritual schools.

You say "false idea about who I am" etc... I agree that to recognize how delusion arises in all its guises is paramount, but is it the case that there is anything else but Maya or illusion? You say, "if I have a false idea." This "if" (not "when I have a false idea" as in all ideas are inherently false always and forever) implies that there are sometimes "non-false" ideas as well. I would be most interested to hear several of these "true ideas" or non-false beliefs. What can you tell me that is not false? What is true? A few examples here would be most illuminating. Please send it to me in the form of, "I know that such and such is inherently true." And just for kicks tell me who this "I" is which purports to be able to discern the true from the false. When you say "false idea about who I am," I would translate that as "less deluded idea about who I am." For me, ideas always carry with them lesser or greater degrees of delusion. But none are ultimately "false," because that implies some are ultimately true. Which none are. Or am I incorrect? This is not a trivial quibble over semantics. What I am pointing to here goes directly to the heart of the matter.

I tend to agree with Mooji when he says that the most profound and enjoyable activity is the Self contemplating Itself. And that's what we're enjoying here! Also, it is my experience that discoveries happen spontaneously when resting in or as silence without any particular inquiring and that when a question is asked the way into the exploration is through the gateless gate of stillness.

I wholeheartedly agree with Mooji. Indeed, it is great fun to talk about "nothing." Though not always easy, is it? People sometimes dismissively refer to those drawn to spiritualty and meditation practice as being mere "navel gazers," don't they? But the actual dictionary definition of the term is, "Excessive introspection, self-absorption, or concentration on a single issue." The definition belies the serious nature of the enterprise. It's dammed hard work sometimes. If those ignoramuses chose to call me a navel gazer, then so be it. They have absolutely no idea what they are talking about.

It's such a paradox. On the one hand, I realize what I already am couldn't be simpler; yet, on the other, I recall that the first two weeks spent in silent retreat were the single most difficult undertaking I had ever engaged in up to that point. A half a year before that I had spent four months in absolute seclusion, but at least I didn't have the flipping meditation to contend with. Originally, I found meditating anything but relaxing. To maintain moment to moment awareness was darn near impossible. Now it's the way things just naturally are. It's the talking about it that seems trying at times, though often quite enjoyable as well. Once again, another paradox. In fact paradox seems to be my very nature. Well then... as you say, David...

"That's enough for now."

Hey wait a minute...that ain't the truth...How can that be enough? I never get enough. Never! LOL

Thanks for sharing. Like always, I very much anticipate your next reply.

Much love,
DJ

7 Feb. 2013
To: DJ

Hello DJ,

I just received your second outpouring today, but think I will respond to this first one below first. I think maybe you got involved in deconstructing or challenging some assertions which I wasn't actually making in the first place. So, there may have been some degree of misunderstanding in the communications. However, it doesn't seem to matter really as there's certainly no harm in any case in questioning what is said and reaching for a "truthy" response. The conceiving of a self seems to continue in sometimes subtle ways and to keep looking into its truth or lack thereof is a "necessary" activity. To say no more inquiry is needed could be a statement of supreme arrogance. It seems that the inquiry eats itself up at certain points and naturally falls away—until it arises again.

You question the validity of giving any descriptive term to what is, such as Intelligence or the "Intellect of the Being." I agree that to do so is an exercise in duality, conceptualization, but without thought and duality nothing can be said or needs to be said. However, is not the very engagement in conversation and inquiry as we are doing an exercise in duality? Are we not accepting duality as a means to discuss the indescribable which, as you suggest, cannot ultimately be spoken of at all? The invitation to see beyond duality is crucial in this investigation, is the essence of it, and must be looked into with total involvement. At the same time how do we then talk about any of this at all? It seems that the helpful thing is to be as clear as possible where the usefulness of thought and duality ceases, what its limitations are, and to also see beyond those limits, if in fact there is any "thing" to be seen. And our explorations seem to bring us to the fact that there is "no thing" to be seen and "no one" to see or not see "it." Mooji (to bring him in again) calls it a "non-phenomenal seeing."

You question whether there is any such entity as the "intellect of the Being" or "intelligence." I think my sense of it is that these are not entities in any sense but are more like activities or functions. As I understand it, brain researchers have looked for a controller which is directing the brain's activities and have not been able to find any such entity or point of control. There seems to be "nobody home," and yet, it can't be said that there is no brain activity (when the brain is active). In the same way there may be no identifiable entity who is being intelligent, but something we can call "intelligence" (or any other word we agree on) is nevertheless functioning. This seems to be a significant aspect of the great Mystery, that "deeds are done, actions take place, but there is no doer thereof," as the Buddha apparently said. I notice here that even the term "the" Buddha gives the mistaken idea that there was or is an entity, a noun, a thing called the Buddha rather that a pure functioning of Consciousness or whatever we are calling it. And, again, the word Consciousness is a noun and implies that there is a thing rather than a movement or flow or functioning. And then, as we go further into the investigation we come to a point of realizing no qualities or definitions can be the absolute truth.

You ask, Intelligence as opposed to what? Good question! Only in duality would there be more and less intelligent actions...I just sat with that for a few moments and had a "wow" experience where everything just fell away...The last word is Silence. This seems to be the view from which you have communicated for the most part, and at the same time, I suspect you would agree that any viewpoint, once it becomes a point of view, is also not true. The idea that there is a self is seen to be untrue, but then if the idea that there is "no self" is adopted, one has just picked up another concept which would then lead to all sorts of assertions or denials, such as the assertion that there is nothing (in the conventional sense). We both "know" that the "no thing" is not at all nothing. It's just nothing that can be defined. You seemed to think that I was arguing for the existence of a self of some kind, perhaps a higher kind of self or a more subtle self, but this was not my intention. Anyway, as you say, the only authority is our own direct experience, and you continue to invite the return again and again to the only knowing that has any real and practical value. So, let's keep looking...

You question the concept of some force which has an interest in the direction life as us takes. My first response is that in my experience so far there does seem to be a kind of force which can meet the arising of thought and emotion and not be drawn into their stories. If there is nothing to counter the flow or momentum of the egoic mind, then identification with a concept of self will have its way and suffering will be the eventual result. When there is a seeing through or insight into the nature of mind activity or "self-ing" there also seems to be a more or less strong force associated with the seeing. Maybe this is what Nisargadatta called "earnestness"—which he said was the most essential quality for a seeker.

This force, as I experience it, is not an entity but a functioning of understanding or "intelligence," perhaps what Mooji is calling "the intellect of the being." Clear seeing mixed with an energy of urgency or perhaps "passion." This just arises spontaneously at certain moments, perhaps when it is needed, or perhaps it can't be described in any linear fashion. I have a sense it is one with the urge for true freedom, which also is not created by "me" but arises from and as an expression of a process or movement which goes on beneath our conscious awareness.

I find it interesting to consider David Bohm's idea of the Implicate Order and the Explicate Order, where the real action is happening in the invisible realm, then appearing as some manifestation of that implicate realm into form and then returning to the formless dimension at some point. With thought, for instance, it's moment by moment. But you seem to be questioning whether there is any "order" at all as to how life unfolds. Contemplating my own experience what comes up is that sometimes I experience a kind of order and force of direction, and sometimes I've experienced a flow of appearance and disappearance with apparently no purpose or direction. It seems both can be true and, as they are just conceptions arising in the moment, neither can be claimed to be ultimately "the Truth." The final word is silence or not-knowing...

So, those are some attempts to wrestle with reality in the ring of duality. Are we still on track with our intention to discuss matters of practical significance to the ending of suffering? I have been finding enjoyment and "value" in the exercise as insights have arisen during the process of contemplating and communicating these things.

Enough for today...David

Feb 12, 2013
To: DJ

Hello DJ,

I'm sitting down to see what response can come to the second exposition you have sent recently. I sense an emotional tone in my body-mind that is not completely peaceful, and the mind says maybe I should wait for a time when I feel more in harmony and contentment. But then that would seem to be in contradiction to the very principles we are exploring as it would be based on a belief that what is showing up as a phenomenon has some significant meaning or relevance to what is true, and that it should be given weight and importance. Plus, it would be quite limiting if I had to wait to feel good before doing anything! Perhaps this feeling can be included in the totality of what is here and be part of the inquiry, without either rejecting it or giving it undue importance.

So, one helpful attitude seems to be to just allow things to be exactly as they are and to simply be present with what is here as thought-feeling. I can meditate on what's here and perhaps learn something about it, gain some insight which will have its own action within my consciousness. This would be limited by any sense of wanting to change what's here or go beyond it or such strategies of mind, so noticing anything like that at play would be part of the meditation.

Another thing I can "do" immediately is to ask if there is present an idea of an entity who is experiencing this state of body-mind and who is separate from it (as an observer). Who or what is experiencing this? As I engage with this question, there is a shift in "my" consciousness such that the subject and object of inquiry seem to dissolve and only a sense of spaciousness remains. And then I notice that maybe a hint of that felt sense is still lingering, but now it's floating in a space of emptiness which is full of a sense of Being. The experience has shifted from focus on emotional content to a more expanded and profound sense of Beingness. The Nothing that is not nothing... Within this spaciousness there is a process or an awareness at "work" which dissolves immediately whatever arises as thought or feeling.

Now the thought arises that thoughts will continue to arise nevertheless (or will they?). They will arise until they don't. Then, they will arise when they will. It seems no final statement can be made at this point...That was an interesting little contemplation.

So, onward to responding to your letter. Actually, I'm reminded of a thought that came after the end of my last writing. I had asked if we were still on track with the practical issue of what will bring an end to suffering. It came to me that we are still very much on track when discussing if the "me" actually exists, which seems to be the main thrust of our questions and sharings. There is the Zen master's response to the question, Why are we unhappy? We are unhappy, he says, because we are concerned 99 percent of the time with ourselves, but there isn't one (a self). So when we're exploring this question of the existence or non-existence of a self, we seem to be right in line with what Zen, as practical an approach to life as any perhaps, considers important.

I enjoyed your story about "Mrs. Thatcher" and your exploration of how we are always seeking for more. I've noticed in the last few days myself how strongly this seeking is conditioned into my modus operandi. In so many ways, obvious and subtle, the mind is wanting to "get" something for "me." Awareness reveals that this is self-defeating as, to confirm the Zen insight, there is no stable me that is present to benefit from whatever is obtained! The "me" is just a thought which is arising one moment and dissolving the next, constantly shifting like sand. And even sand has substance, unlike the "me". The me is made out of nothingness or the mysterious invisible whatever which is not nothing but is not something which can be held on to or made secure. Only when this is seen and there is a spontaneous stopping, as you suggest, does the consciousness come to rest as the Emptiness in which there is no lack and, therefore, nothing to be sought. I suspect you would agree that this stopping cannot be willfully done in any meaningful way. And then (in my case at least) the seeking just arises by itself again, though perhaps with less strength and more permeable to being seen through and exposed as the futile endeavor it is. It can also be seen that this self-seeking is not love and is thus the impediment to the expression of that energy or whatever we call it that can set us and the world right, or perhaps more our vision of ourselves (our no-selves) and the world as a first and most significant "step."

You asked about my statement that I realized I was at least partially creating my reality and wondered if I still hold the same view. I meant that at that time I at least saw that I was participating in the manner I was experiencing reality. Now I would say that I am one hundred percent creating my reality in that everything I experience is filtered through my perceptive apparatus and has only the reality that I give it. But then, what is the "I" that is doing this? Well, it appears to be nothing but the Whole or the Whatever doing whatever it does, arising as experience moment by moment, including the experience of a "me." So, in that sense I am zero percent creating my reality. Ah, the divine paradox again! What is more true and sublime than the paradox and the ultimate impossibility of knowing anything absolutely through the thinking mind? The most absolute knowing that has ever come my way was at the same time the knowing that nothing can ultimately be known. Another beautiful paradox...

As for the distinction between inner and outer reality, I no longer hold this to be of any meaning. And indeed, as you suggest, if the two are given any reality, then what about that which witnesses both? The ultimate witness is not two things but one awareness. And, as Rupert Spira explores so well, even the distinction between awareness and the objects of awareness (reality) breaks down when looked into in terms of actual experience. All that's left is the knowing itself. And then what is the nature or substance of that knowing?

Enough for today...David

15 Feb. 2013
To: DJ

Hey DJ,

Here's a link: http://www.rebprotocol.net/somasig.pdf

A friend sent me this link and referred me especially to the bottom of page 18 and to the text following, but the whole article may be of interest. I've so far only read a little of it.

I find that I look forward to your postings to our conversation and have been looking for your latest for the past few days. Patience...

Lately, I've been sometimes quite aware of the "me" sense, sometimes quite subtle, and the discomfort it creates in the space of Being. This seems to arouse me to look carefully at what's going on, which often results in some relief from that centre of me-ness. It is apparent that the Whatever, expressing as mind, is still moving as the experience of a separate self to a greater or lesser degree, and no final liberation has taken place. Does it ever? There is the concept of final enlightenment or transcendence of ego and separateness, but I'm a little suspicious as to its veracity. And yet the question only has meaning to the dualistic mind, does it not? And, as you suggested, that which witnesses dualism is not itself dualistic. That seems to be beyond concepts of enlightenment or ignorance. But that is only authentically, experientially true from the place of non-dual witnessing (or beyond witnessing as subject and object), not from the perspective of the dualistic mind. Maybe I'm rambling here. I'm always attempting to express something of that which seems to ultimately defy explanation, but there seems to be an urge to try anyway and maybe, with any luck, to die trying! But then, who will die?

And so it goes...David

18 Feb. 2013
To: David

Hi David,
The following is rather lengthy. I apologize and request your forbearance. It may appear that I have a lot to say about "nothing," but today I present the heart of the matter as "I" see it and this obviously was no easy task. I promise to be less verbose next time. Honest I do. ☺ You pointed to the theme I address today in your last letter, so I thought I would take it as an invitation to delve deeply into the notion of no-self, not-self or non-self. By way of introduction I present the following.

Just received an email from a seeking friend whom I haven't spoken to in a long time. The following bit she wrote made me chuckle:

You know my original plan was to go to India (I announced that at the Jac retreat in June of 2011) but for a few reasons delayed the trip - now I am not so sure if I will go given my aversion to GROUPS and DOGMA...Have to keep my eye on the prize. Even if it is, in a sense, the BOOBY prize :-). At least, that's what an old friend told me once on the coast of Costa Rica.

"Booby prize"—forgot I said that. Perhaps I borrowed it from Jed McKenna. Strikes me as quite funny. Echoes of what Buddha said about waking up only to discover, "I have attained nothing." So true. Nothing extrinsically valuable is received...how disappointing. But, of course, that is only the little me's appraisal of the situation. I can't say that nothing has happened since astounding transformation has seemingly occurred, but at the same time nothing has been added unto me either. So why not booby prize? The prize which isn't a prize. The "prizeless prize," won by "nobody." That last line makes me realize again why non-spiritual folks upon hearing such gibberish must often shake their heads in disdain and exclaim, "Hey Mildred, the loonies are at it again." It must seem like utter non-sense to them. Precisely. If it makes sense, it ain't REAL.

A housekeeping note.

I recall several spiritually immature seekers from the so-called past who got quite perturbed at me by my frequent use of the expression "in my experience." This was seen as egotistical or arrogant. I suspect it was an affront to their egos since who else could pass such judgment? If I state "this is what I (apparently) know," it simply is the case, and I like to affirm that what I am talking about is my own direct experience. Not mere philosophical postulating or recitation of others' ideas. I guess they got bent out of shape 'cause they recognized this behaviour was precisely what they were frequently engaging in. I think this tactic helps keep us both honest. Do you agree? Though now that it is pointed out, I probably will feel less inclined to do so.

Of course, I could be yet another in a long line of deluded power-seeking spiritual miscreants so full of their own hubris that they are utterly blinded to their own narcissism. Maybe so. However, as I pointed out above, I suspect this may not be the case here as this enlightenment gig didn't pan out so well for my ego. More confusion than ever and nobody cares much about what I have to say. Where is the inflated sense of self-worth in that? I sure wish I could get me some pay back for all my friggin' hard work, but alas there is none forthcoming. Of course, no self = no pay back. Still, one never knows. I could be bullshitting you, or simply be quite confused. Fortunately, if this indeed were the case, it would have nothing to do with anyone else's ability to awaken in this lifetime. Oh, and considering what my teacher's teacher said, "Only the big phonies never make it," I think you know quite well which side of the spiritual fence I lay on here. Anyhow,

Chapter 4 / February

now I'd like to move on and respond to parts of your previous letter.

Regarding your reconsideration of the question you posed previously, "Are we still on track with the practical issue of what will bring an end to suffering?" I was pleased to see you write:

> It came to me that we are still very much on track when discussing if the "me" actually exists, which seems to be the main thrust of our questions and sharings. So, when we're exploring this question of the existence or non-existence of a self, we seem to be right in line with what Zen, as practical an approach to life as any perhaps, considers important.

I wasn't quite sure if that question was intended to be merely a "checking in" or if you were subtly implying that my writing was meandering all over the place and irrelevant...which, of course, it is. What could I write that is not irrelevant? Don't these emails continuously skirt the issue at hand? Still, we are compelled to try. I was pleased to see that you feel we are still on track but, more importantly, "why" we are still on track.

I think you are discovering that I am pretty much a one-trick pony kind of Dharma prognosticator, and I suspect my take on Truth realization is not always quite your bag. Mooji's message of discovering what it is that is "aware" or discovering "the one that is aware," as well as self-inquiry utilizing the Who/What am I? question is, I suspect, more to your liking, though of course I am not at all suggesting you are limited to just this. Or perhaps I am mistaken altogether? Of course, it is of no consequence. I should note that I found Mooji's pointer, as well as the same message proffered by other teachers regarding "awareness," to be terrifically useful at a certain point in my journey. For some reason I just like to emphasis or point to lack, i.e., lack of self, rather than point to gain, i.e., discovering awareness.

I confess these days I pretty much can't help but say the same thing over and over again but in a slightly different form. I'm always, though, taking care to direct attention to the same realization. Namely, just as you wrote above, "There is no inherent self" found anywhere (that would include the "one" that is aware which Mooji instructs us to find). Self, quite simply, "is not." So, of course, if this not-self isn't simply an abstract conceptual ideation but rather is an absolutely lived reality from moment to moment, it then follows that suffering will naturally cease by its own accord. Only "sufferers" can suffer. No self, no suffer. That is why I direct attention towards disempowering the presumed "I" enough to cause it to eventually evaporate, rather than focus attention on ways to alleviate suffering through "right thought." That endeavour is quite simply pointless.

So, yes, we do seem to be right on track here. *When you throw the baby out with the bath water, suffering is rendered irrelevant, or more precisely not even possible.* Many misunderstand this point. You don't rid yourself of suffering by adjusting the way you think. It's more the case that you rid yourself of thinking by adjusting the way you suffer. No story believed in, no suffering capable of being self-manifested. Absolutely come to know that the story of yourself is just that, and you will see that there is nothing to adjust at all. On the journey I discovered lots of paths up the mountain, but they all eventually converged at the same place. The summit less summit. Non-self.

Read the truncated version of the Zen teaching poem below and tell me how it makes you feel. Confused? Nothing? (Are those dead words for you?) Resistance? Are you at this moment anything other than "not-two"? I bet in actuality you feel you are. How is that? Why do distinctions keep arising for you like "outer" versus inner experience or "being on track" versus off track or labelling "intelligence of being" versus ???, or desirable thoughts arising versus less worthy ones, or the quote now which you just wrote in this letter: "expression of that energy or whatever we call it that can set us and the world right." I know we all struggle with words but perhaps there is something more significant going on when you keep making these kinds of distinctions.

Perhaps if you consider an excerpt of Zen/Chan master Seng-Ts'an's poem below and then check out the reality of it for yourself, you can come to see that there has never been anyone to "set right," nor world to "improve." Reality, things as they really are, has never suggested that this is necessary, or even possible. Only your thoughts inform you otherwise. Have you ever entertained the possibility that they cannot be trusted or relied upon to reflect TRUTH as it actually IS? Since we want to keep on track and engage in practical, real world investigation here, I thought I would quote someone who is very succinct and points directly to the heart of the matter. I just read the following poem today for the first time and marveled at how well Seng-Ts'an laid out the essence of Zen. Seems even more direct than the *Tao Te Ching* though I have omitted several verses for the sake of a little more brevity. If you care to read the whole thing, it's freely available on the web.

If only I could write so well about "nothing" myself. I apologize for my clumsy attempts which are so evident in the face of this great "cloud water" master's work. Nonetheless, his description of actual lived experience of his life and mine are not different. I would be quite happy to let "Verses of the "Faith Mind" stand as a testament to universal truth realization and say no more on the subject. Everything you will ever see me say will be but a feeble attempt to convey what is contained in those short verses below. I was pretty pleased to have just stumbled across them today, how about you? Here is an excerpt:

The Great Way is not difficult for those not attached to preferences. When neither love nor hate arises, all is clear and undisguised. Separate by the smallest amount, however, and you are as far from it as heaven is from earth.

If you wish to know the truth, then hold to no opinions for or against anything. To set up what you like against what you dislike is the disease of the mind.

...cease to cherish opinions.

...don't attach even to a trace of this and that, of right and wrong...

The arising of other gives rise to self; giving rise to self generates others. Know these seeming two as facets of the One Fundamental Reality...

...If the mind makes no discriminations, the ten thousand things are as they are, of single essence... When all things are seen without differentiation, the One Self-essence is everywhere revealed. No comparisons or analogies are possible in this causeless, relation-less state of just this One.

When movement stops, there is no movement—and when no movement, there is no stopping. When such dualities cease to exist, Oneness itself cannot exist. To this ultimate state no law or description applies.

...All is empty, clear, self-illuminating, with no need to exert the mind. Here, thinking, feeling, understanding, and imagination are of no value. In this world "as it really is" there is neither self nor other-than-self.

To know this Reality directly is possible only through practicing non-duality. When you live this non-separation, all things manifest the One, and nothing is excluded. Whoever comes to enlightenment, no matter when or where, Realizes personally this fundamental Source.

This Dharma-truth has nothing to do with big or small, with time and space. Here a single thought is as ten thousand years. Not here, not there—but everywhere always right before your eyes.
Infinitely large and infinitely small: no difference, for definitions are irrelevant and no boundaries can be discerned...

Chapter 4 / February

> Words! Words! The Way is beyond language, for in it there is no yesterday, no tomorrow, no today.
>
> By Seng-Ts'an, Third Zen Patriarch from "Verses on 'Faith Mind'" as translated by Richard Clarke, "Faith Mind."

So we find that the poem ends with the realization that "The Way is beyond language," while the Tao Te Ching begins with the same reminder. It must be a significant point. In fact, it is crucial. It is pointing out the difference between thinking about reality (which of course is the sole realm of normal human egoic existence [I doubt cats suffer much from existential angst]) and Being Reality or existence itself. No thoughts. No symbolic language required to mediate your reality. No more abstractions. No more mind stuff continually projecting a virtual recreation of existence. What happens is a cutting out of the middle man so to speak. Immediacy is born upon awakening, such that reality no longer objectifies itself. This realization is quite different from having an experience of "oneness." In that case the experience ends and you immediately fall back into egoic self-identification. That's the steady state, that's the "original sin" you were conditioned to accept after birth. It's digital. On or off. Awake or asleep. There is nothing in between despite stories seekers tell themselves about how much more awake they are now than previously. Krishnamurti concurs when he says, "It is not something that you reach step-by-step as if you were climbing a ladder. Enlightenment is not in the hands of time."

For me all this was only recognized in retrospect, after the dream ended once and for all. So I conclude that anyone reading these words of wisdom—mine, yours, some Zen guy's—will quite probably find them for the most part useless and irrelevant. When I was in the trance state, this kind of pointing was not my lived experience. Now that it is quite evident how things really are, of what use are these pointers? Again, "Words, words - the way is beyond language."

David, I remember when I started to get a sound conceptual appreciation (but limited only to that) of this stuff and thinking, "these enlightened guys have forgotten how it was." It's all very well to talk as they do when you eventually "get it," but what am I to make of their admonishments and esoteric pointers in light of my present self-identified state? Don't they remember how it was? Can't they express the dharma in practical ways that make sense and reflect how my life actually transpires (and yes I see the irony as I guess my pointers make just as little sense). I felt some teachers were pretty much out of touch with reality. Of course, in retrospect I recognize it was I who was totally out to lunch. But only just totally.

I don't know what to say except that what Seng-Ts'an points to is exactly the way things are when the "I" is not resisting what IS. Seng-Ts'an is talking about "lived reality," not that phony sham existence seekers accept while checked into the cinema of that which ain't transpiring. That has nothing to do with LIFE. But again, prior to the "little me" dropping away, Seng-Ts'an's descriptions of what it is like to live life without a centre seems remote and not very applicable to one's own reality save for a bit of philosophical conceptualization or mystical speculation. In short, I bet most would find these nonsensical verses of no practical benefit, so why pretend otherwise? Still the perennial question begs to be answered: "How can I awaken in this lifetime?"

What seemed to work for me was striving to discern the false nature of self and then endeavouring to no longer identify with it. Is that not what Seng-Ts'an is actually pointing to if one cares to look? That's not to say it is easy. How can self disown itself? How can thinking mind think itself out of existence? Here meditation seemed useful for there was nothing to think about at all while engaging in this practice.

I have an idea. How about you reconsider what I wrote previously (find immediately below), in conjunction with the Seng-Ts'an verses (particularly his theme about a self which is constantly moved to make distinctions), and tell me what you come up with:

You say, "false idea about who I am" etc... I agree that to recognize how delusion arises in all its guises is paramount. But is it the case that there is anything else but Maya or illusion? You say, "If I have a false idea." This "if" (not "when I have a false idea" as in all ideas are inherently false always and forever) implies that there are sometimes "non-false" ideas as well. I would be most interested to hear several of these "true ideas" or non-false beliefs. What can you tell me that is not false? What is true? A few examples here would be most illuminating. Please send it to me in the form of, "I know that, such and such is inherently true." And just for kicks tell me who this "I" is which purports to be able to discern the true from the false. When you say "false idea about who I am," I would translate that as "less deluded idea about who I am." For me ideas always carry with them lesser or greater degrees of delusion. But none are ultimately "false," because that implies some are ultimately true. Which none are. There is no true or false. Or am I incorrect? This is not a trivial quibble over semantics. What I am pointing to here goes directly to the heart of the matter.

If you elect to provide me with examples of a "true idea," would the following which you wrote be among them—"the knowing that nothing can ultimately be known." Is that idea actually true? Or is it more the case that nothing can be said at all? If all ideas collapse in the face of Reality, why does it still feel like some ideas are false and some true? I would say because distinction is still alive and well for you, David, and I suspect you would agree. There is no problem admitting that, is there? As far as David apprehends and relates to reality, would it be incorrect to say that you actually do "apprehend and relate to reality" and part of that process would include making distinctions? Preference - and resistance - is still very evident, right? No problem in admitting you have a "thinking problem." (Of course, as mentioned above, there really is no problem, just an apparent one. Again, no-self = no problem). And I would suggest that part of the solution might lie in first recognizing that it actually exists. Remember I once quipped about the need for a TA (Thinkers Anonymous) association. At one time I sure could have used it.

I recall being really astonished at how the story of DJ manifested itself through compulsively referring to the past and future, while simultaneously having a never-ending dialogue about how everything shouldn't be as it was. It was one thing for me to pay lip service to this recognition but quite another to see how ridiculously absurd it was for me to attempt to manipulate and control reality in such an insane manner. It then became a much smaller matter to see how everything was relative to everything else with no absolute right or wrong position to be found. Distinctions were only a product of my own imagination. They weren't inherently real. I found there was no way to verify anything I believed in. Therefore, why believe in anything at all? That included all of my long-held and cherished opinions like power brokers are an evil scourge, environmentalists are humanity's hope for the future, eating meat is bad (or good as some Tibetan Buddhists would have it), reincarnation is a reality. What nonsense!

And that was that. The story could no longer sustain Itself. There was no more fuel for the egoic fire, no more juice to sustain the charade. The story of me just finally went away. This waking up business is not much more complicated than that. It requires but one solitary sacrifice, you. You have to shuffle off the stage and go home. But that ain't such a bad bargain to strike when you think about it. When did you ever chance across a better deal than getting something for nothing? That is what you are being invited to see here. How nothing appears as something (you). That's all.

Much love, DJ

PS: I invite you to please let this letter sink in and settle a wee bit before responding. Maybe read it over a few times. Bring it home with you and compose a response offline over the course of a few days. I really would value a thoughtful reply on this no-self theme from a guy such as yourself with decades of experience on the mat, so to speak. If you see things differently, here is your forum to speak up. I am certainly not seeking confirmation, just the truth. David, tell me what you absolutely know. I would love to hear it.

19 Feb. 2013
To: DJ

Good day, DJ,

At your request I will restrain myself from answering your February 18 letter for a few days at the least and will read it over several times before then. At the same time I would ask you to read over my last three letters as it seems you have not read them, or if you have read them, you have very selectively chosen to focus only on certain words and to ignore other ones that were even right beside them and were corrections or being given more weight. The letters were sent on Feb. 7, 12, and 15. The Feb. 12 letter was corrected in a few places and resent with a request to ignore the first one. I don't feel you responded to my explanation of the "intellect of Being" idea but merely mentioned it again in a disparaging manner. Anyway, perhaps a rereading would reveal something to you of the possible contradictions and dualistic thinking in your own expression and the nature of your seemingly selective interpretations. Is there some agenda hiding in your letter? I have plenty to say about it but will, as I say, refrain from the knee-jerk reaction and be with it for a while. That way, it will definitely have value as a subject (or is it an object?) for self-revealing awareness.

Cheers, David

23 Feb. 2013
To: David

I throw this out as a general introductory question. I asked myself this kind of thing several times along the path and found it helpful so now direct it your way... do you want to exist as joy, freedom, and ease, or do you want to be right? How important is it to you that others be wrong? Remember, there are seven billion of us. Wow, that seems like a never-ending stream of potential misery. And the great thing about truth realization is the discovery that there was never wrong or right to begin with so nothing needs to be changed. Resistance is futile...you are never gettin' outta this thing alive, so why not sit back and be joy itself for a while?

You said:

1. I don't feel you responded to my explanation of the "intellect of Being" idea but merely mentioned it again in a disparaging manner.

Okay, I will provide a comprehensive comment below just as you have requested. I don't generally engage in this kind of THOUGHT-full analysis as I find it such a bore. Further, you probably won't much appreciate the results.

2. Anyway, perhaps a rereading would reveal something to you of the possible contradictions and dualistic thinking in your own expression and the nature of your seemingly selective interpretations. Is there some agenda hiding in your letter?

So considering "...possible contradictions and dualistic thinking..."

I fully expect you will be able to find whatever you are seeking, but just what is that, precisely, David? If it is dualistic thinking, and selective interpretations you are after, then being the clever boy you are, you will surely discover them by the bucket full, but why waste time on such folly? If waking up in your lifetime is truly what you seek, why devote your attention to how others act? Maybe your time would be better spent routing out your own delusion and leave others to their own devices. As the Beatles said, "Let it be, let it be, let it be, oh let it be..."Just sayin'...

I find it quite telling, and it speaks directly to the heart of the matter here, that out of all the things you could have chosen to pick from my last letter (which I thought might have been very relevant material vis-a'-vis truth realization pointers) to immediately comment on, those two points above were it. Do you happen to see any significance here yourself? I mean that was an awfully long diatribe I subjected you to...really, really...those two points you bring up are what got you all fired up immediately? Didn't Seng-Ts'an's klaxon call to awaken stir your heart? Didn't his poem, long esteemed by truth seekers throughout the centuries for its richly evocative and beautifully articulated pointers, turn awareness in on itself even if only for a moment?

Before I jump into my comment on your point of "intelligence of being" proper, I present the following observation which may shed light on what I say subsequently. You have an interesting way of making a point, which doesn't strike me as a point at all. Here is an example taken from your last letter.

> Whatever, expressing as mind, is still moving as the experience of a separate self to a greater or lesser degree, and no final liberation has taken place. Does it ever? There is the concept of final enlightenment or transcendence of ego and separateness, but I'm a little suspicious as to its veracity. And yet the question only has meaning to the dualistic mind, does it not? And, as you suggested, that which witnesses dualism is not itself dualistic. That seems to be beyond concepts of enlightenment or ignorance. But that is only authentically, experientially true from the place of non-dual witnessing (or beyond witnessing as subject and object), not from the perspective of the dualistic mind.

What exactly is your point here? Well, there isn't one "exactly" is there? Would you not agree that it reads more like a stream of consciousness observation rather than a question or clear pointer? There is no precise stance offered (which by the way is fine); so, what part do you want me to comment on, acknowledge or request further elaboration about?

Where should I start? Which discrete point? Or which combination of thoughts? Or would you prefer all of them be addressed in totality which of course is time consuming, especially if requested for all future letters. It may be quite clear to you, but please forgive my ignorance because it sure is not apparent to me.

Maybe in your future letters you could put an asterisk beside each point you feel needs my utmost acknowledgement. That sounds time consuming because it would be pretty much the whole thing, wouldn't it? After all, everything we say is so very important, and should not be ignored, right? And while you are at it, perhaps you should instruct me ahead of time as to what points I should bring up in response to your own ideas. Wouldn't it be so much nicer if I could present to you exactly the ideas you would like to most hear? Maybe you could append a little sidebar to each of your letters suggesting good talking points and ways I should address them. That would be perfect. Then, reality would correspond to exactly how you would like to see it unfold.

Of course, I have just resorted to the absurd above, and I do apologize, but it was in order to stress a point. Hasn't it become apparent to you how your ego pretty much wants reality to unfold precisely in the fashion described above? Isn't it true that you believe the world would be a whole lot better place if everyone, all seven billion of us, could just subscribe to your way of thinking? Isn't it quite astonishing how all of us always get it so wrong for so long, while you alone are the sole beacon of sanity in a world gone mad. That's certainly the way I saw it. Seven billion people in the world, and I could argue with each and every one of them yet never once be wrong. Pretty sick, eh? How about you?

Or maybe, just maybe, you could let everything be as it is. Did you happen to notice the large amount of points that you did not address vis-a'-vis my own writing? Did you happen to notice that you were very selective in which ones you addressed and which ones you entirely overlooked? In particular, you were seemingly very careful to skip over several key points that I made repeatedly through the course of several letters. And here is the thing— my mind might inform me that you should not be doing this, but, and here is where reality always holds sway, you quite clearly are ignoring certain points (or so my mind may inform me), so whom am I to argue with reality. So I just don't give two hoots about it at all. Why argue with the way things are? I just ignore the ramblings of a confused ego if and when it happens to pop up (which rarely does happen these days since no reaction is forthcoming anyhow). So now, I will look at the first point you cited above. I know I promised to make my next letter short, but you have requested a thorough analysis, and I aim to please.

First, to be clear, the point regarding "intellect of being" was included in the newest letter as but one example in a much larger point being made regarding your (and all those experiencing normal egoic reality) propensity to make distinctions. I think it is most significant that you want to stress how I "didn't get you." Doesn't this confirm my point? Aren't you driven to make distinctions, and aren't you making one now? Who cares if I am making a distinction about your making a distinction? My state of being is irrelevant to your own awakening. And if you now say, "Aha, DJ is making a further distinction here," who cares? How does it improve your state of confusion to make a distinction about my making a distinction about your making a distinction?

Quite obviously you are wasting yet more time and energy on further distinction making. Maybe this is why some old Zen guy suggests that making distinctions, abiding in duality, is a sure recipe for discomfort. And did you happen to recognize that he was addressing you, David, at the time. He didn't say go check out what the other guy was doing. 'Cause obviously you'd have to engage in more dualistic thought and position taking to find out. Are you starting to see how this actually works?

You feel I misunderstood you or even worse have ignored you entirely. (Ouch! Oscar Wilde delightfully points out how affronted the ego can get by this kind of treatment. "There is only one thing in the world worse than being talked about, and that is not being talked about.") You say I have erred by making a wrong supposition and further slighted you by not admitting this fact. To whom is this so important? Why not take a look and see how this kind of position taking will always lead to suffering. Why are you resisting the fact that we may not concur at certain times or ignore each other's points entirely at others? Who cares? No, I mean, really, who is the one that cares here? And why? I once looked into this and could find no good reason for always demanding that others see things the way I did. I never could find the reason why it irked me so when they didn't, which by the way was almost always. How about you? Do you feel better for trying to correct the error of my ways? On the other hand, do you feel better when you remain silent on matters that bug you and then have the pressure intolerably build up? Could there be another way entirely? Yep, and it gets to the heart of spirituality, and it is what I keep pointing to.

You say "disparaging" manner...how so? That seems a pretty strong accusation (and position) to make. Reading the material directly, how was it that you found me, and I now quote the dictionary here, "speaking of someone in a slighting or disrespectful way; belittling manner?" Seems like I have

Chapter 4 / February

gotten your hackles up a bit. Seems like that has happened several times before between us.

So you have invited me to revisit your position (and, yes, it seems pretty apparent that a position has been taken, but by whom I wouldn't have a clue) concerning the "intellect of being" and how it exists but is not an entity per se, or rather there is no doer, or more pointedly, this intelligence is nothing at all but maybe is more precisely seen as silence itself...(scratching head?) I quote you now on "intellect of Being" or "The intelligence ""I think my sense of it is that these are not entities in any sense but are more like activities or functions."

This sounds suspicious to me and here is why. Labeling an entity or "being" which possesses intellect or intelligence and then denying its very existence seems nonsensical. For God's sake, why call it a "being" to begin with? And how are functions or activities intelligent? A function of a car's motor is to provide motive power. Is that intelligent? A function of a heart is to beat. Intelligent? A function of brain synapse activity is to convey electrical discharge among others things — is that intelligent? So, I am sitting here dumbfounded as I wonder how a function or activity can be intelligent.

Intellect is defined as, "The power of knowing as distinguished from the power to feel and to will." I always thought that intelligence or intellect was ascribed to a living being and it was that entity that was deemed intelligent, i.e., that chimp seems pretty intelligent, or that guy is of normal intelligence. Functions are devoid of intellect. One function of the brain is to take raw heat sensing data provided by the finger tips and create a subjective experience out of it. This function is not inherently intelligent. It, by itself, lacks the power "to know." But Jane (whoever that being is) is considered intelligent for not sticking her hands in the fire. So if Mooji or Krishnamurti say that Spirit possesses intellect, or that "intelligence of being" exists, then I take them at their word. Problem is there is no Spiritual entity that exhibits these properties.

Explain to me how "nothing" is intelligent? My sense, unlike yours, is that there is not one function or activity of my brain that is by itself inherently intelligent. I have never heard someone describe biological activities or functions as being capable of expressing intelligence in and of themselves. So, I respectfully beg to differ. Of course, you are now free to counter my counter argument. And so it goes… for countless lifetimes. That is the plain, honest, simple, truth perpetually ignored in favour of this non-sense. No thank you.

As I understand it, brain researchers have looked for a controller which is directing the brain activities and have not been able to find any such entity or point of control.

If by a "controller" you mean the thing that perceives itself to be in control, and for a human that would be the "me sense" or "I," then you are entirely mistaken here. An "entity" in its truest sense has been found. In fact, you may recall I mentioned such a fact in my book. A part of the brain called the anterior insular cortex has been identified by scientist as the centre responsible for self-awareness. In fact, they said it provided the human condition with its ability to answer the question, "And how do I feel now?" It's not a CPU per se, but rather the bit of grey matter that allows you to feel like "a you." And this "me" quite certainly perceives itself as an entity. So I suggest that an entity exists, unlike your proposal.

There seems to be "nobody home," and yet it can't be said that there is no brain activity (when the brain is active). In the same way there may be no identifiable entity being intelligent, but something we can call "intelligence" (or any other word we agree on) is nevertheless functioning. This seems to be a significant aspect of the great Mystery, that "deeds are done, actions take place, but there is no doer thereof," as the Buddha apparently said.

Buddha may have "apparently" said this, but in actuality he most certainly did not. In fact, Ramesh Balsekar said it in

Chapter 4 / FEBRUARY

conversation once, and I gather other advaita teachers have had occasion to continue to erroneously misquote it. Balsekar both misquoted the original passage and made the wrong attribution as well. The quote actually reads, "There is no doer but the deed. There is no experiencer but the experience. Constituent parts alone roll on. This is the true and correct view."

It comes from an immense work called the *Visuddhimagga*, or *Path of Purification*, written by Buddhaghosa, a monk from Sri Lanka writing in the Sixteenth Century. I find the Balsekar misquote, as well as the original, not very helpful; indeed, it is pretty inaccurate as far as actual truth telling goes.

For example, consider its implications. If deeds are done but there is no doer, then I guess suffering happens but there is no sufferer. This seems like an absurd proposition to make. Buddha in actuality would never say such a thing, and I will address this in a moment. And if he did, I could care less because it would fly in the face of my actual experience. Common sense shows that a sufferer suffers. That's how our language and actual experience works. Some entity, "somebody," owns suffering, right? Rocks don't suffer, but people do. Personhood = experience of suffering. No person = no suffering. I can assure you that in order for experience to be perceived there has to be an experiencer present. Is it not the case, David, that if you no longer have the ability to appeal to any of your thoughts, ideas, or feelings (no mental or physical sensory input), either through meditation or via some other means, then you, the you who is the experiencer, quite simply is not. If you disagree, then how does one explain the effects of anaesthesia? You go away for a while, thus no pain is experienced. And if I take a sledge hammer and whack you upside the head when you are not under the effects of anaesthesia, won't you feel it?

Experience = something perceived by an experiencer. No experience = nothing perceived by no one. Since when did you ever find experience to be had but no experiencer to be present? Are you capable of experiencing the No-Thing? How about the corollary—can no-thing/no-self actually have an experience? But this is precisely what you have proposed. I propose it might better serve you in this discourse to stick with what you actually know. Leave the quotes to others who don't know better. That's my take on it. As far as Buddha is concerned, I believe he would not express such a view either.

If there were deeds without a doer, then the doer would be absolved of all responsibility for what he or she has done, is doing or will do. The individual could claim there is only the deed but no doer, only phenomena flowing on. This would mean that there would also be no responsibility for the results of what we did. No "right" action possible. There is the doer, the doing, and the done, namely, the results. All three go together for none can stand alone. The doer arises in accordance with the dependent arising of the doing and the done. This is not necessarily my viewpoint, but it is in accordance with Buddha's. That is why it is so obvious he would have never said those words though you still may think otherwise. Furthermore, you will notice that Buddhaghosa said: "No other view than this is right." This is fervently absolutist in nature. The Buddha expressed concern about those who claim, "This is true, all else is false," so he surely would have never uttered those words. At least not on a good day.

I notice here that even the term "the" Buddha gives the mistaken idea that there was or is an entity, a noun, a thing called the Buddha rather that a pure functioning of Consciousness or whatever we are calling it.

And, again, the word *consciousness* is a noun and implies that there is a thing rather than a movement or flow or functioning. And then, as we go further into the investigation, we come to a point of realizing no qualities or definitions can be the absolute truth. You say, Intelligence as opposed to what? Good question! Only in duality would there be more and less intelligent actions...I just sat with that for a few moments and had a "wow" experience where everything just fell away...The last word is Silence. This seems to be the view from which you have communicated for the most part, and at the same time, I suspect you would agree that any viewpoint, once it becomes a point of view, is also not true. The idea that there is a self is seen to be untrue, but then if the idea that there is "no self" is adopted, one has just picked up another concept which would then lead to all sorts of assertions or denials, such as the assertion that there is nothing (in the conventional sense). We both "know" that the "no thing" is not at all nothing. It's just nothing that can be defined.

You seemed to think that I was arguing for the existence of a self of some kind, perhaps a higher kind of self or a more subtle self, but this was not my intention.

The conclusion you offer above requires me to back-track and mention how it all began. If you recall, I asked, Who was it that was the "question asker?" I suggested it must be the little me since "nothing" was mute. You said au contraire, that while "The Big One" may in fact be mute and not able to ask questions, perhaps a capacity of mind was available which was not particularly identified with the little "me," and it could represent or stand in for the silent indefinable whole whatever. Mooji calls this the "intellect of Being," you informed me.

I then pointed out that if "wholeness" is whole, which of course is undeniably the case both by definition and actual experience, how could it be a fragment of mind? If the absolute can't be added unto, how can there be a piece of mind or function that represents everything that is. Isn't everything that is, indivisible by definition?

You then went on to suggest how your position was tenable which has already been revisited above. Your point was that the mystery was somehow objectifying itself as some part of your human experience. That was your first proposition which you took some time and effort to substantiate.

Then, you moved on to assert that Buddha is not an entity, noun, or thing but a "functioning of consciousness." Very well. Next, you point out that it follows that no qualities can be ascribed to this no-thing, which would include intelligence or intellect. Finally, you conclude that the last word is Silence. This, then, totally negates your original supposition that there is a capacity of mind that represents "intelligence of being." That, of course, was my original pointer from the very start.

What seems to me to be most significant here is the fact that you originally held that Being was intelligent and tried in some ways early on to support this idea. I think this first inclination was the truest, as far as David's life actually is lived, the way you actually relate to reality. The rest that follows is after the fact conceptual repositioning. Thinking "right thoughts" as it were. Arriving at the right answer. Or maybe you drop into stillness for a moment, but this is not a steady state. After a while again, David arises to take centre stage and confusion again reigns supreme. Is this not how it works?

Can you not see that the ego's propensity to make distinctions and hold positions is the raw material out of which you manifest yourself? That's the important thing to recognize at every moment, not whether you get the "right" answer. Seeing through the delusion of "me" is brought about by moment to moment lived awareness. What I am talking about is waking up to see the way things actually are which is neither wrong nor right. You find out that there is no side of the fence to sit on. Therein lays the freedom that you doubt exists. "Being" is none other than absolute freedom. Don't think but rather "be" at every moment. Don't think about this proposition. Realize it. At first this may appear to be a struggle. Soon a carefree ease will take over as you abandon yourself to the natural state of things. What you are seeking is so very, very simple. David, "tag" you are it. Or make distinctions and hold positions and play an entirely different game. The choice has always been yours to make. Cheers, DJ

25 Feb. 2013
To: DJ

Hello DJ,

Chapter 4 / February

You recommended that I wait a few days before replying to your previous email, so I sent a very short reply to say that I would do so and invited you to review the previous writings in the meantime. I didn't respond to your many points because I was taking those few days, which turned into more than a few, to be with what had arisen, but now you have accused me of ignoring those very good points because I have not yet responded to them. And yes, there definitely were reactions to your letter, which is precisely why it was a good idea to take some time before answering. And now you have added so much more that should be responded to. I must say, it's pretty overwhelming.

You seem to have just launched into another round of criticisms and sarcasm, part of which is to say it shouldn't bother me at all. My next letter would have agreed with many of the points you have made but you seem again to have assumed that I was holding onto a position of opposition because I hadn't yet replied. And did we ever agree that you are my teacher and have permission to speak in such a nasty manner supposedly for my benefit? I would have thought that allowing each other some space—or, if you prefer (as you may say there is no "each other"), allowing the inquiry some space—would be more conducive to fruitful investigation. I suspect you will say that it is only my deluded perception which experiences this aspect of your expression as nasty. Please, if you wish to continue with these discussions, let's not pile on any more but see if we can work with what we have already put out there in our last few letters and possibly come back to a place of respectful conversation, which again you will perhaps say is mere defensiveness on my part.

Maybe it's dualistic and not very enlightened, but it seems to me only practical and an expression of skillful means that our conversations be held within an atmosphere of kindness and tentative exploration where there is space to think and feel in the moment towards a useful seeing and not be under pressure to have the exact correct words and understanding all the time. Of course, ultimately it's not about any of that but just about the Truth, and nothing else really matters. But in practice, I don't think you'll find many people, if any, very open to aggressive assertions and "pointers," unless they are disciples of Andrew Cohen. They would have to be already enlightened to not react to such ways of communicating, and is not, at least part, of the point of the communication to invite "enlightenment" for those who have not yet realized it? You have made various comments about my letters which just don't seem supported by the facts of the situation, and then you tell me that any rebuttal is just my reactive ignorance. What a Catch 22!

It's just like all the spiritual groups that say any disagreement with their dogmas or practices is only the ego's unwillingness to surrender. How can one argue with that? Damned if you do, damned if you don't. Of course, ultimately the only way out is to drop the "ego" all together - or see its insubstantiality, to "step out" of all this (so to speak: "who" will step out? etc.) so that none of it matters. That was where it was all coming to. There was some seeing that your expression was (intended or not) perfect in exposing unconscious concepts or unconscious aspects of what has become conscious to a certain depth but plainly not all the way through. There is no usefulness in defending myself. It's curious though that you yourself appear to be doing the very same thing in your last letter, and it seems to be a very human thing to do. There seems to be a tendency to quickly find fault before questioning what the other is really meaning to say. For example, with Mooji's way of talking about something which he is most likely not in any fundamental disagreement with you about, is this not trying to be "right?"

So, it seems like this may take a little unwinding. Are you up for it? I'm still game, but I'm not promising I'll be speaking from full enlightenment (as you would no doubt not expect either) and will probably make many mistakes. As you seem to suggest, is it not all mistakes? But why the nastiness in pointing to it and making it personal to me, as in "you" said this and "you" said that, as if it's some fault of a somebody? Isn't that way of speaking reinforcing the idea of a separate I, a doer? And yet it seems hard to avoid. I only should have the right to speak in such a deluded manner as I am the one wallowing in Maya. (This is only slightly sarcastic, and I own up to that element and acknowledge that in another sense it is not at all sarcastic and may be absolutely "true" [Please note the quotation marks!]).

I do agree we should speak as much as possible from our own experience and not from 'boring" thinking, but that also doesn't seem like any guarantee of ultimate veracity. I think our own experience has to be questioned continuously. But maybe you are making the distinction between our experience and what we actually know for sure, which I did intend to answer soon...

I'm coming to the end of this weird little communication probably full of nonsense and letting it subside for now. I will write more in response to the previous letters when moved and expect you will do the same when and if moved.....

Cheers, David

25 Feb. 2013

Chapter 4 / February

To: David

You said,
>So, it seems like this may take a little unwinding. Are you up for it?

Of course.

If you could address the part I drew your attention to awhile back, that would be great.

I see you are distressed but my intention is not one of malice. I regret you are uncomfortable, but it seems unavoidable.

And, yes, you are damned if you do and damned if you don't. That is a great pointer. So of course there is no alternative but...???

Cheers,
DJ

26 Feb. 2013
To: DJ

>Could you just remind me which item you mean that I should attend to first just so I'm clear on that...?
>David

26 Feb. 2013
To: David

The first chunk below was from several letters ago, and I brought it back again more recently. So, if you could take a crack at it, that would be welcome.

I also direct your attention to the second chunk as it centers on the Zen poem and distinction making, so is kind of related to the first bit. Could you have a crack at it as well?

Cheers, DJ

PS I have an idea. How about reconsidering what I wrote previously (find immediately below), in conjunction with the Seng-Ts'an verses (particularly his theme about a self constantly moved to make distinctions), and tell me what you come up with.

You say "false idea about who I am" etc... I agree that to recognize how delusion arises in all its guises is paramount, but is it the case that there is anything else but Maya or illusion? You say, "If I have a false idea." This "if" (not "when I have a false idea" as in all ideas are inherently false always and forever), implies that there are sometimes "non-false" ideas as well. I would be most interested to hear several of these "true ideas" or non-false beliefs. What can you tell me that is not false? What is true? A few examples here would be most illuminating. Please send it to me in the form of, "I know that such and such is inherently true." And just for kicks tell me who this "I" is which purports to be able to discern the true from the false. When you say, "False idea about who I am," I would translate that as "less deluded idea about who I am." For me ideas always carry with them lesser or greater degrees of delusion. But none are ultimately "false," because that implies some are ultimately true. None are. There is no true or false. Or am I incorrect? This is not a trivial quibble over semantics. What I am pointing to here goes directly to the heart of the matter.

Also perhaps if you consider the Patriarch's poem and then check out the reality of it for yourself you can come to see that there has never been anyone to "set right," nor world to "improve." Reality, things as they really are, has never suggested that this is necessary, or even possible. Only your thoughts inform you otherwise. Have you ever entertained the possibility that they cannot be trusted or relied upon to reflect TRUTH as it actually IS? Since we want to keep on track and engage in practical, real world investigation here, I thought I

would quote someone who is very succinct and points directly to the heart of the matter.
Love,
DJ

27 Feb. 2013
To: DJ

Hello DJ,

When I spoke of false ideas about who I am, I was relating more to how things unfolded for me many years ago very early on in my "seeking," but you took it to be current. Also, my words about setting us right and so on were revised in the next words to say something like "or more like setting our vision of ourselves and the world right" which included for me the seeing that there is no entity present as a solid self and implies a change or shift in our relationship or non-relationship to the world. I can't seem to find the letter where I wrote that, so I don't know exactly what I said, but it wasn't left as the idea you quoted. I think perhaps you were being too picky, and were you not thereby implying that there is a better way to express, better words to be used? Then you say that no words or ideas can express the truth.

Anyway, I can put that aside and respond simply to your question. There are no true ideas or concepts or beliefs. The truth of what I am, or what is, is not graspable by the mind, by thought, by any idea. We have discussed this numerous times, and I was surprised that you made such a big deal of my words which you thought were saying otherwise.

If there are no true or false ideas, as you say, then what makes the "Faith Mind" poem any truer than anything else? Just that its concepts are good pointers? I've come across it before a few times as well as other writings that seem as direct as some Dzogchen verses, for example, and probably many other teachings. But even the "Faith Mind" poem contains dualities and distinctions, telling us, "Do not remain in a dualistic state; avoid such easy habits carefully," "Do not seek for the truth" (as opposed to seeking), and so on. You make a distinction in implying that the "Faith Mind" poem is more accurate an expression than other ones. Our language itself is dualistic and all spiritual teachers speak in ways that could sound dualistic if we want to interpret them that way. I think just as much to the point were your pointings to the fact that even Seng-Ts'an's words are pretty much useless unless one has already had a direct experience of their meaning. No matter what anybody says, their words are not the truth: The truth is beyond words and ideas. Words can be provocations to look at the functioning of the "ego" mind, and in this way they may serve a useful purpose, even though they contain distinctions and dualities. It can't be otherwise, can it? Teachers generally don't seem to have a problem with using dualistic words and concepts and making distinctions while attempting to be as close to non-dualism as possible. If the suggestion to avoid making distinctions were followed all the way, then the distinction between distinction and non-distinction cannot be made. Again, all ideas fall down as ultimately meaningless. What use is any of it? Wayne Liquorman said hearing the non-dual teachings from Ramesh made his life easier. He, as the rest of us, had to penetrate to the meaning within the teachings.

I had an interesting experience the other night which I'd like to relate, but my time is running out for today.

Bye for now, David

27 Feb. 2013
To: David

You said,

"There are no true ideas or concepts or beliefs. The truth of what I am - or what is - is not graspable by the mind, by thought, by any idea."

Nice and straight forward answer just as you said, very fine indeed. And just to be crystal clear, this is actually how daily life presents itself to you. David does not find one position is right and another wrong since he finds all concepts to be untrue. No need to favour one point of view over another as all ideas are false? David can't seriously entertain any distinctions since all beliefs are inherently untrue? Even this very question is rendered irrelevant by your inability to make distinctions of any sort, so it is obviously some kind of trick question. For all intents and purposes you don't know anything at all. Anything you say is irrelevant. Anything you be-

lieve is of no consequence. This is actually how life unfolds moment to moment, correct? You said that in the past, position taking was possible but no longer, right? I just want to understand you correctly and wonder, *How, then, is it that I have offended you several times during the course of this correspondence given the fact that you don't believe anything your mind projects? I truly wonder how it is that I have managed to belittle and slight you.* Maybe, as you said above, I have misunderstood you or been too picky, but I wonder what leads you to believe this, and it is clear that you do believe this, yet at the same time you refute any possibility that this could be so as you say no beliefs are found to be true. I think you can appreciate the nature of my confusion here. It is genuine, and I certainly don't want to displease you again. What I am presenting here is not confusion over semantics. Could you elaborate a little further in the spirit of this wonderful investigation into truth? And hopefully you will find additional time to share your interesting experience.

Love, DJ

28 Feb. 2013
To: DJ

The insight or clear seeing happens sometimes, and almost always when inquiry is consciously engaged, that when it comes to the essence of who or what I am, no thought or concept can accurately describe it. This certainly does NOT mean that the mind no longer reacts or makes discriminations. The mind still functions much of the time in duality. The insights work invisibly and do whatever they do, changes are felt in the way life is experienced, but exactly how they work and what the results are, I have apparently no control over whatsoever. To set up any ideal about how my behaviour "should" be is a recipe for even further conflict on top of the initial layer of conflict potentially produced spontaneously by the thinking mind. And this happens anyway, by itself.

A sense of being unfairly treated arises; an urge to defend arises. "This" mind has not stopped creating these things and there's no way of knowing if it ever will or even should. The meditations and contemplations do whatever they do in consciousness, and who can say that it should be otherwise? That would be making distinctions and judgments according to some belief. Even if you say something is, so for you it doesn't mean it is so or should be so for me. I certainly do believe sometimes what my mind projects and other times not. The strength of the identification with mind becomes less-and-less. When a reaction is triggered it's a "good" thing because it reveals where there is attachment and preference and the seeing of the mechanism is liberating.

Does that liberation mean that there can no longer be any emotional or psychological reactions? Some seem to suggest that this is the final outcome or the only outcome worth anything, but I'm afraid the absolutist perspective that says it's one or the other, on or off, awake or asleep, just doesn't seem true in my experience—and is probably not helpful. Most teachers I've heard don't seem to subscribe to such a black and white understanding. For example, Adyashanti speaks constantly about the fact that even after powerful awakenings there is still a possibly long process of integration necessary where the still active tendencies of mind and emotion must be seen through again and again or at deeper and deeper levels. That seems more factual in my experience. But maybe it's not the case for you. Those teachers also say sometimes that they don't see any difference between ignorance and enlightenment; there is only true nature, Buddha nature, or Self, whether there are thoughts or not, reactions or not. But I'm not saying that's how I see things most of the time by any means.

The experience I had a few nights ago seems relevant to the discussion. I went to a dyad meeting feeling stirred up from our email interactions and in the first dyad quickly felt the most authentic place to be contemplating from (so to speak) was the state of reactivity. That's where the juice was, and that's why my responses to you were focused on that rather than appreciation of the "Faith Mind" poem or otherwise comments you had made. Why pretend something "spiritual" is of interest when the body-mind is experiencing an intensity of human emotions and perceptions? Much more "real" to be with that, explore what that is about. All judgments about my state fell away and there was only the feeling of righteous anger and the awareness of it. There was no sense that I shouldn't be that way. In that acceptance there was a sense of fullness and a presence which had no sense of suffering in it. Happy versus right wasn't even an issue. There was no unhappiness, just the pure feeling and sense of presence. I was at that point amazed to realize that within the experience was a sense of emptiness. The experience was of thought-feeling-sensation and nothingness at the same time, with no difference between them and no need to make any difference.

From there an inquiry began to look more into the reactive quality of the mind. Instantly, it was seen that reactions arise from the mind's (or thought's) fear of emptiness. The mind resists the nothingness and moves into reactive states of whatever kind. That insight shifted my state so that there was a sense of being in touch with, or one with, that which is beyond mind and cannot be described. The first knowing of anything that the mind could experience of that arose in the forms of love, beauty, preciousness, significance, and then subsided into not-knowing again and again. It was clear that the source of those beautiful qualities was the unknowable and that engagement or involvement with the qualities themselves, in the sense of wanting to perpetuate them or expand the experience, was to move into the realm of duality and conflict. And yet as long as there was presence, being fully there, there seemed to be no possibility of moving into "problems." In fact there was no such thing as problems.

It's getting difficult to write of this and still feel that it is an accurate account as the words begin to fail and the awareness arises that dualistic concepts may be coming in as the thinking mind tries to make sense of it all. Perhaps especially as I'm aware that I'm speaking to a listener with a razor-like perception which will probably cut to shreds anything that has the smell of duality. Perhaps duality in expression can't be avoided, but it seems that words spoken by someone who is directly experiencing the truth beyond the words have a potency to them, even if the words could be more "correct." Sometimes it seems to me it doesn't matter if they are completely accurate, as they never can be anyway (as we've discussed), but they can be powerfully inviting an inquiry into Truth, as does perhaps the "Faith Mind" poem. Maybe you have felt in some of my writings, or all of them perhaps, that the words were lacking in that potency or ring of truth, and with that I at the moment have no argument. Your questions as to the living reality of "no concepts" are very much to the point and have stimulated some useful inquiry part of which is a clearer acknowledgement of the still remaining separation between what is seen in moments of clarity and how it is lived or not lived in daily life. As I say, in my understanding the results of this are impossible to predict or control.

Enough for now, David

The Clothes Have No Emperor

∞ Chapter 5 ∞

March

1 Mar. 2013
To: David

David,
    Thanks for being so truthful. Thanks for letting your guard down and dropping the pretenses. Truth is beauty, so of course I find your lovely, alive words charming beyond compare. And to be clear, it's not that wacky DJ character that is so grateful. It's YOU. And you know it. It can't be denied. YOU love to catch a glimpse of yourself. And you keep proving this in moments of clarity, like in Dyad. Then and there you honour yourself. The sacred utters a sigh of relief on those occasions and there seems to be such amazing gratitude, correct? I encourage you to stay truthful to yourself. Don't concern yourself with how authentic your spiritual persona may appear to others. It's just another unconvincing threadbare guise in a litany you possess. Untruth does not stand a chance if you orient yourself in the opposite direction like you are doing here in this letter. I am going to add a few more comments to your letter over the weekend but wanted to send this off now.

I have an intuition that we have gotten over a hurdle here in this correspondence. I see less conflict in the future, though I expect you may still get a little PO'd from time to time with my silly banter. Thanks for keeping it real and continuing to engage in this investigation. You probably don't recall, but I once said I was the "best friend" you ever had. The significance of this statement may not have been apparent at the time, but what I was driving at was the fact that, as far as spiritual matters are concerned, I will never shy away from telling you how it really is. But rest assured any motivations I might have only stem from an inability to not tell the truth. And that is the easy part!

Cheers,
DJ

2 Mar. 2013
To: DJ

Hi DJ,

I'm glad that you had some enjoyment from my sharing, and I agree that great gratitude arises when I catch a glimpse of myself or another, which as you suggest is really the same thing

Some of the comments in my letter about how it is for me I later thought it over and wanted to add that what is true for me concerning aspects of the "journey" of self-discovery (the journey by no one to nowhere) is only what is appearing as the experience of the moment, shaped by the limitations of my own consciousness (to speak that way for the moment). For example, statements of others that may appear absolutist may not seem so when my consciousness opens to a way of knowing or experiencing that was not previously available to me. So, all that is changeable. What does not seem changeable is the fact that Truth is beyond concepts and description.

You say that you suspect I may still get a little PO'd from time to time with your silly banter. I wouldn't generally call it silly banter at all but sometimes wonder if you are purposefully attempting to provoke me in order to see if you get a reaction, which then proves that I am still ignorant. Then you can be the teacher, which you seem to enjoy. Or maybe there are aspects of your personality that are less than fully awake and are looking for ways to sneak out and assert their own rightness or superiority. It's possible, is it not? I'm not accusing you of anything here and am not claiming any certainty about such things. It may be, as you say, that the only motivation is your inability to speak anything but the truth. Anyway, I don't feel a conflict around it at the moment. And in the bigger picture it could be said it is all Consciousness unfolding as it will and does with nobody doing anything and, if taken in an open way, is all for our enlightenment (although there is ultimately no one to be enlightened). Or is it just the Leela, without any purpose? Again, concepts fall short and we (I) really don't know anything. I'll be watching to see if you have a reaction! As for a next topic, I was thinking there are still so many points in our previous letters that haven't been addressed that I'm sure there is plenty of material for exploration. Maybe if I just review the last few emails, I'll find some interesting subject or subjects to investigate and then you can respond. As I said at the beginning of our interchange, most of my expression is in the moment, is indeed often stream-of-consciousness, as you said, and does not need any response necessarily unless you feel moved. You can respond or initiate as you feel inclined. For me it is not a process of student asking teacher for an answer to my questions; it's more a spontaneous, possibly fun, and possibly insightful sharing of whatever arises as we go. Is that your sense of it, or is it otherwise?

    Cheers

    David

5 Mar. 2013
To: David

Enjoyed your letter thanks. See comments below.

...sometimes wonder if you are purposefully attempting to provoke me in order to see if you get a reaction, which then proves that I am still ignorant.

I could never prove that you were ignorant. That would be impossible. But you sure can do so yourself, and I trust you welcome such occasions whenever they present themselves. I believe you said as much in your last letter.

Then you can be the teacher,

Well, just like you I have teaching in my background so it comes naturally. I don't consider what I am doing here teaching per se as I don't think you can teach anyone to be what they already are. But I do see your point. The format I use seems akin to teaching in that I stress discernment. This format helps me to be as clear as possible so, yes, I do enjoy that. I aspire to be as clear and as insightful as possible. Ultimately, it truly is silly banter, and I know I am doomed to fail, but I aim to do so as eloquently as possible. Are you simply noting that I appear to enjoy myself, or are you requesting I frame the material in some other manner?

> Or maybe there are aspects of your personality that are less than fully awake and are looking for ways to sneak out and assert their own rightness or superiority. It's possible, is it not?

That is possible. One could fall back into the trance anytime, but of course they could not recognize this until out of it again. You say personalities "that are less than fully awake," but, as I said before, you are either fully entranced in the dream or not. This is my direct experience. There are no half measures here. Where do I lie? Who knows? Of course, it seems quite apparent to me that the dream has ceased for innumerable reasons I have noted but, again, who really knows? I don't know anything, so really can't say. And, of course, my state of being is ultimately of no concern to your own awakening, as I said before, so you should be pleased to keep that in mind.

And it would be particularly deluded if what was at stake was my "rightness and superiority" in this correspondence and not rather trying to discern the truth from the delusion. I asked you before to give me examples of how I was belittling you, but none were forthcoming. Can you please do so and also a few examples demonstrating my superior attitude which would also be most welcome. I guess they would be similar examples, eh?

For me it is not a process of student asking teacher for an answer to my questions; it's more a spontaneous, possibly fun, and possibly insightful sharing of whatever arises as we go. Is that your sense of it, or is it otherwise?

However it unfolds, is just perfect. Is it the same for you as well?

Cheers

DJ

5 Mar. 2013
To: DJ

Hello DJ,

I see you have sent me an email, but before opening it I want to express something. At this point I want to thank you for all that has transpired between us.

Last night at dyads the inquiry led to an experience of great gratitude for this whole process and unfolding, of which you have been a significant aspect. As you pointed out recently, it is not the character DJ that is the object of the gratitude but the Whole, of which DJ is an aspect or expression and not separate from. Actually, the gratitude has no object towards which it is directed and at the same time it includes all apparent objects or "people" who have shown up as participants in this grand unfolding which seems to get more subtle, profound, and rich while at the same time becoming more empty of specifics to fixate on or attach to, or resist, for that matter. And it is also not the character David who is the expresser of the feeling, but again is the wholeness expressing itself as an aspect of itself called David. This you have already said, but I affirm it to be the case in my own experience.

No more time at the moment but I will write further.

Love,

David

6 Mar. 2013
To: David

Gratitude. That's it. Well done. But as you point out true spirituality has no subject/object dichotomy involved in it. There is just a huge feeling that may at times almost bring you to your knees as you recognize "all is well." So there is no "well doer" is there? Just a sense that things are fine. Innate wellness. Or the conceptual mind may want to call it unconditional love. As you have surely discovered, this kind of love puzzles the mind at first, since it has no source or point of origin. The tender heart opens and an unfamiliar kind of weeping might ensue which is neither one of grief nor happiness, and, of course, there is a sense of recognition as well. And silence...and a lot more and a lot less. Along with gratitude you may have also sensed a kind of "welcoming." Maybe a feeling of homecoming. Welcome home. So I say YOU are WELCOME. Literally that is it. You, what you really are, is, and has always been, pure "welcoming" itself. No position taken, no distinction made, no opposition to what is. ALL IS WELCOME. That's how it really is and one finds those three words synonymous with each other.

DJ

12 Mar. 2013
To: DJ

Hello DJ,

You have captured the essence of my experience of gratitude and added further aspects which I can certainly agree with. There is a joy in reading words that communicate that energy of direct knowing.In some way I seem to have been struck slightly dumb and have been finding expression of what's going on pushed into the background by the predominant sense of silent Beingness or Indescribability. Insights and clear seeings continue to arise and subside with no need to remember any of them. There comes a sense of surrendering and letting go with nobody doing it, just a moment by moment melting into the Emptiness which is not empty by any means. Sometimes something is said which flows from the silence and seems not

Chapter 5 / March

separate from it, and is one with the essence of what is experienced. In that case the words seem to be able to carry the energy or reality of truth, of that which is beyond description. At the same time there is the awareness that the words and concepts are not themselves the truth at all.

I wonder if that is close to what you mean when you say you can't help speaking the truth and have no other intention. You have asked in a previous letter (and discussions) if I "have ever entertained the possibility that thoughts cannot be trusted or relied upon to reflect TRUTH as it actually IS." And we have agreed that no concepts, ideas, or thoughts are true: Truth is beyond all conceiving. And yet you have said that you can speak only the truth. And you have suggested that the "Faith Mind" poem "seems even more direct than the *Tao Te Ching*. There seems to be some contradiction here which could be more than academic and could have very practical significance in the way we communicate with each other.

If it is assumed that the concepts one is using are accurate representations of Truth, then it seems that easily leads to a kind of rigidity or fundamentalism, and one can end up endlessly arguing about the relative correctness of concepts. That seems to be often what passes for spiritual discussion or inquiry. So, I'm wondering, as I say, if this contradiction is resolved or dissolved by what I've expressed above, and I suspect that it is.

In another writing you have said, "What could I write that is not irelevant? Don't these emails continuously skirt the issue at hand? Still, we are compelled to try." And you have said in conversation a number of times that everything you say is BS. I'm not sure how important these wonderings are, but it's what's arising at the moment, and it may be significant. Any comment?

At this point I don't feel much interest in trotting out the examples of where you have spoken in "belittling" ways. Either it's BS, or it's a kind of truth, but what matters is what is revealed to me in meeting and being touched by your expression. (I'm aware of the dualistic concepts here, but that's how the conventional language is structured it seems). If you want me to do the exercise I can make the effort, but the issue seems to have become a non-issue at this point, and perhaps it is just as well left. If the same perception arises again in our communication, perhaps I can mention it at the time - when it's fresher.

Perhaps you have some juicy topic we could explore, or I can see what comes up in the next days.

Love, David

13 Mar. 2013
To: DJ

Hi, I was thinking today that we had already discussed the question of what can be accurately said about truth in our very first interchange a few months ago. However, maybe you have something to add at this point, and I'm still interested in any such arisings that are the updated "now" version, so to speak.
Cheers,
David

13 Mar. 2013
To: David

David you just sent an email with this: "I was thinking today that we had already discussed the question of what can be accurately said about truth." I actually touch on this below.
Cheers,
DJ

PS: I see Josh is now writing daily and sometimes even twice a day. That's a lot of conceptual mind chatter to be produced from a "no doer." I wonder why he seems compelled to do, or not do, so.

In some way I seem to have been struck slightly dumb and have been finding expression of what's going on pushed into the background by the predominant sense of silent Beingness or Indescribability.

There really are no words or concepts that improve the silence are there? The silence of the heart. It's palpable, isn't it? And the feeling is so indescribably exquisite. At times it actually feels like your heart may burst forth from your chest with divine love. You come more and more to experience relaxation as your nature. Resistance no longer attracts you. All is well. All is welcome.

> Insights and clear seeings continue to arise and subside with no need to remember any of them.

That is very significant in my estimation. Few would understand why. I remember this as an important turning point in my journey. The conditioned urge to recall and reflect and find significance in concepts subsides. Increasing ease and joy replaces the reflexive mind. I remember a clear choice being presented—I could either concentrate on remembering these cool insights or just be. Beingness is clearly blossoming in you, my friend.

> ...what you mean when you say you can't help speaking the truth and have no other intention. You have asked in a previous letter (and discussions) if I "have ever entertained the possibility that thoughts cannot be trusted or relied upon to reflect TRUTH as it actually IS." And we have agreed that no concepts, ideas, or thoughts are true: Truth is beyond all conceiving. And yet you have said that you can speak only the truth.

Not exactly. The distinction here lies between saying, "I can't help but speak the truth" and "I speak only truth." I believe I said the former but not the latter. When I say, as far as spiritual pointers go, that I can't help but speak the truth, what I am referring to here is truth realization vis-a'-vis lack of choice. You may recall Krishnamurti referred to it as choice less awareness. I don't have the capability to choose where identification lies (does anyone...really?). There quite simply is no identification. So what erupts from my lips can't be helped. Things are the way they are. I no longer resist this fact. To be clearer, I would not say that I "speak only the truth" but rather I "am the truth" in the way Christ supposedly put it, "I am the way, the truth, and the life. No one comes to the Father except through me." Like I said before, I never discovered the answer to it all. Instead, I found out I was the answer all along. And I would add that in not being able to do anything other than speak in a natural truthful manner I tend not to sugar coat what I say. It is so much easier this way. It is always exceedingly easy to tell the truth. It's the resistance, obfuscation and denial that is such a pain in the ass.

And you have suggested that the "Faith Mind" poem "seems even more direct than the *Tao Te Ching*." There seems to be some contradiction here which could be more than academic and could have very practical significance in the way we communicate with each other. If it is assumed that the concepts one is using are accurate representations of Truth...

Contradictions? Perhaps, but none are apparent to me. The "Faith Mind" poem is significantly shorter, less poetic, and more direct and from my viewpoint more practical regarding truth realization than the *Tao Te Ching* is. That's just the way I see it, but I would never feel moved to defend this non-viewpoint. I love both works. In fact, I took a university course devoted to nothing else but Lao Tzu's master work. For decades I would claim to be a Taoist at heart. Perhaps you would agree that certain pointers are more alive, clear and insightful than others. That is all I said about the "Faith Mind" poem. Adyashanti and others like to refer to it from time to time. I loved it when I stumbled upon it just like I love to hear your "alive words." But I certainly never mistook the poem for the moon. I know it is just a finger pointing. But a marvelous one none the less. For you, not so much I gathered, eh?

At this point I don't feel much interest in trotting out the examples of where you have spoken in "belittling" ways. Either it's BS or it's a kind of truth, but what matters is what is revealed to me in meeting and being touched by your expression.

If this feeling arises again perhaps you could momentarily distance yourself from it and examine it to see if it is actually the case or not. Just as I said previously that I could never "prove your ignorance," so too I wonder how it is that I could belittle you or diminish your stature in any way. Whatever I do or don't do is not your business. I am irrelevant. You are in fact untouchable.

And even more significantly, whose stature is at stake here? Certainly not Spirit's. You can't add unto nor diminish that sucker one bit. So why get so stirred up by the perceived slights the little me projects into the awareness field? It's just imaginal, isn't it? It's what the ego does, this pointing out of slights and insults, but to perceive it as real must be an indicator of where identification predominantly lays. One tactic I employed to alleviate this problem was to continually laugh at myself. Not in a cruel, but rather, in a tender way, as one does when a baby has a temper tantrum or hissy fit. My ego was seen to be just naively acting in a conditioned unaware pattern. It didn't know better. The more I learned how the "house builder" came to operate, the more ridiculously funny I found the whole affair. Perhaps you could take yourself less seriously from time to time and see what comes of it. Take the whole darn shooting match with a grain of salt, and then you will be really amazed.

DJ

15 Mar. 2013

To: DJ

Regarding our friend Josh, he said in one blog something like he has reached the end of the search and feels motivated to share with others. Skepticism arises on reading such words...

I'll be busy for the weekend at the K centre so won't write for a few days at least. I appreciate your responses below and expect to say something in answer. On the issue of feeling slighted it is, as you say, pretty obvious when considered in a non-reactive way that it can't be anything but the ego or little me that can feel attacked or criticized and that has a need to defend itself. That's the bottom line it would seem.

Cheers

David

20 Mar. 2013

To: DJ

Good day to you. I found your explanation about being the truth versus speaking the truth very interesting and to the point.

As Truth is beyond all conceptualizing, any words spoken will only be more or less accurate approximations or representations of it but never the no-thing itself. The "silent Heart" (if we are to use some concept) expresses itself as certain fragrances (such as a sense of love or joy) and through words that have a potentially powerful impact on the apparent listener, including the listener who is speaking the words! At such times the words seem to emanate from the Emptiness without any preplanning but more as a tracking of how the formless truth is expressing through the organism, an often surprising revelation of the way it really is, as closely as words can say it. As you suggest regarding the "Faith Mind" poem, the words can be very direct and relatively to the point. But it also seems that the impact is very much dependent on the listener's state of receptivity and just where they are situated in their process of unfolding. Maybe there are numerous factors which determine the impact of any expression of truth on a particular listener.

Wow, it's interesting to engage in this exercise of considering Truth because I become aware while writing of how easily the thinking slips into dualistic ways partly because of the structures of language and also due to the way I've been conditioned to see and think about reality, which seems to continuously assert itself. It seems it may be impossible to escape this dilemma and the sense comes that all expression will inevitably fall short. And yet, as you have said, we seem interested or compelled to make the attempt. And it seems like a "good" thing to be aware of this shortcoming of concepts and to wrestle with the interplay of conditioned thinking and self-inquiry or clear seeing; it helps to maintain or access again and again awareness of the nonverbal "space" (again not quite accurate) behind and within the expression.

Hope this is not all too wordy and abstract.

Recently there has arisen at times a profound awareness of the psychological truth of Buddha's supposed teachings concerning attraction and aversion. It seems this may be the whole teaching in a nutshell. Suffering is the result of the mind's strong tendency to be attracted to what gives it security and pleasure and to resist what appears as painful or threatening in any way. This ties in with your words about resistance and the falling away of interest in such. The mind resists not knowing in every way possible and endlessly seeks experience or knowing. Seeing this clearly with the involvement of the whole organism, not just the mind, feels like it has a significant impact and must be transforming, although the actual mechanism and unfoldment of that transformation seems to be often subtle and not easily identified, perhaps because it is functioning largely in the dimension of the "not-knowing," below the level of conscious awareness.

At times there are clearly identifiable results or outcomes like greater peace, love, wholeness, gratitude, and so on. Think I'll stop here for the time being (can time and being go together?) and turn it over to you....

Love

David

20 Mar. 2013
To: David

David,

Want to add a few comments below to your letter and send it in a day or two but right off the bat I have a question regarding your line, "At times there are clearly identifiable results or outcomes like greater peace, love, wholeness, gratitude, and so on."

Our awakening journeys differed in some ways, so I want to get a feel for how it is for you these days. This greater peace, love, etc. you speak of—does it come and go like the sun appearing on a cloudy day only to be obscured again sometime later? Are you ever lost in the trance only to be shocked by a moment of clarity? Then you get lost again in the dream only some time later to have another brief moment of awareness? Or would you say dyad or meditation is more like the opportunity where Beingness blooms? Or is it something else again? Do "you," (by you I mean the story of David) still pretty much inhabit "the cinema of that which aint transpiring?" Is it the case that thoughts still move to the past and present most of the time? Are they equal? A woman I talked to recently said she was rarely in the past. She said she is predominantly worried about the future.

In mundane daily life, when you are not trying to foster mindfulness, does it occur sometimes that you are not in the past or present? If so, has it ever lasted a prolonged period?

If not these days, ever in the past? I am quite curious how the mechanics of this works for you right now.

Also curious how the retreat turned out for you. You just went to one right? Was it illuminating in any way? Why did you go?

Love,
DJ

22 Mar. 2013
To: DJ

Hello DJ,

You've asked some interesting questions which I will attempt to answer in some comprehensible form.

I would say that the peace, love, etc., does come and go and at the same time does not. True nature has a quality of being timeless, and when it is directly known, seems to have always been and always to be present. Over the years it has become more-and-more the case that there is an awareness of that timeless presence which is either in the background as a subtly felt sense or more in the foreground as strong sensations of peace, joy, love, beauty, and so on. When identification with thoughts and feelings is stronger, the sense of my true nature is obscured to some extent, but when identification is less, it appears that true nature was never obscured and has always been here. It seems to be a question of whether or not in any moment it is actually experientially true that there is awareness of true ture. Even as I attempt to conceptualize this in the moment, it is difficult to know exactly what is going on at moments when it would seem that the knowing has faded because it doesn't seem to be the case right now. Many years ago, I sometimes had experiences like coming out of a fog into the clear sunlight, but these days it's not like that. It seems more like a subtle shift sometimes into a greater clarity which by contrast shows me there was some relative lack of clarity before. It's may be like a lens that is slightly out of focus and then becomes more sharply focused and reveals more of the details and carries a sense of heightened clarity with it. It's not as if those details were not accessible all the time, but they were somehow not being paid attention to in the same way.

My experience has also been that strong knowings of love or peace, for example, arise as an expression of the unfolding of consciousness and for a specific purpose such as clearing out or opening the organism so it can contain a greater sense of reality. Once a powerful experience has done its work, it is no longer needed front stage and can retreat into a background sense of being without any particular identifiable qualities. And then there is the question of what happens as perception loses its overriding dualistic tendencies and the subject-object dichotomy dissolves.It seems then that the knowing of true nature becomes more empty, formless, and unidentifiable—and indescribable.There is nothing for the mind to grasp and identify in terms of conventional categories of experience, and this can often result in it appearing that there is nothing of any noteworthiness happening. If I take a moment to tune into the felt sense in the body, almost always there is immediately a sensation of bliss, peace, or joy.

True nature is without qualities and beyond "knowing" or description but as soon as it is invited into the knowing mind, it first shows up as these beautiful flavours or fragrances—including a sense of preciousness. And then often there is just the "not-knowing" where, as I say, it might almost seem that true nature has disappeared when, in fact, it is just so transparent and infinite that it is not being registered by the conceptual mind. So, it seems there are two ways in which I am unaware; one in which identification with thoughts obscures clear seeing and experiencing and the other where awareness is present without an object and, therefore, seems to be nothing

As I write this, I feel there is a subtle effort involved in trying to capture these things in concepts that are as accurate as possible, and when I check into what is otherwise here, there is just the sense of THIS which is beyond all effort. And THIS doesn't really care if the right concepts are found or if the thing (no-thing) can be described or talked about. And yet, here it is, attempting to speak of itself!

You asked if my thoughts are often in the past or the future. Mostly there is the sense of timeless presence within which there may be thoughts of past or future, but there is often no sense of any conflict or duality in that. Presence permeates all thoughts, feings, and experiences and is, therefore, the predominant sense of what is. There is a powerful sense of non-duality. As I think I've said, this knowing of Presence does seem to ebb and flow and change shape in various ways and yet there is an unmoving stillness and silence which is always there within it and permeating everything whenever I check.

So, does that paint any kind of a coherent picture? It doesn't really matter if there are inconsistencies and apparent contradictions, does it? Truth is not in that domain, and there is the sense of something which can't be captured or pinned down. Thank God!

I went to the retreat mainly as part of my involvement with and support for the K centre and didn't have to pay for it. (That would have been a different story). It was somewhat interesting but also kind of boring and not as much to the point as I would have liked. I often feel these days that the potential is just not being met, as I suspect you do yourself, and so there's a level of dissatisfaction as long as I have any kind of agenda concerning what "should" be happening. I wrote a summary of the weekend for Harvey which I think he may post as a blog on the centre's website if you want to take a look. Of course, it doesn't reflect my full experience.

I'm sure there's more that could be done to attempt further clarification but this seems like "enough for today."

Cheers,
David

25 Mar. 2013
To: David

David, you said,

As you suggest regarding the "Faith Mind" poem, the words can be very direct and relatively to the point. But it also seems that the impact is very much dependent on the listener's state of receptivity and just where they are situated in their process of unfolding.

Regarding "state of receptivity," what do you reckon modulates it? Thinking about it for a moment, it seems to me it must be to some degree ego dependent. The degree one opens up to the truth must be dependent on how much less one grasps and clings to the false. Truth is always there to be recognized. It's just delusion that obscures it.

Receptivity to Truth of being seems in some regard to depend on the degree of identification one has with the dream state itself. As one sees through delusion, one becomes more inclined, or more receptive, to regard things as they really are. At least that was the way it was for me. Any thoughts? How receptive are you these days? If not the "Faith Mind" poem,

then what kind of inspiration do you draw upon to help you see what is false? That's a wide open question. It's a wonder to me how ego can orient itself in such a way as to cause its own demise. Using whatever ploys or techniques you currently find at your disposal, would you agree that, ultimately, that is what is unfolding in your case? Crudely, though not wrongly put, is David dying? Would you say that month by month you cling to the David story a little less firmly or is this unquantifiable? Maybe this kind of thing can only be recognized in retrospect. What do you think?

Maybe there are numerous factors which determine the impact of any expression of truth on a particular listener.

Wow, it's interesting to engage in this exercise of considering Truth because I become aware while writing of how easily the thinking slips into dualistic ways...

Wow, indeed! It seems entirely "easy" or very natural to constantly refer to the conditioned mind in order to create a sense of identity, just as you say. In fact it is absolutely how you come to appear to exist in the first place. As you well know, David is entirely a by-product of this paradigm called duality. You define yourself by constantly objectifying things. In fact, basic human experience comes about through the practice of taking even yourself to be an object (not a subject as everyone assumes). You assume yourself to be a discrete individual separate from everything else. I am a human "being" all naturally proclaim, but this is not the case. If one day through meditation or some such practice Beingness is seemingly engendered for a moment (Yet how could reality be anything but this all the time?), then you are simply not. If you "is," you "ain't." When I hear folks tell me they are proud of finding success being in "the now" I know they are not being authentic. No one ever managed to make it to "now." Now certainly is, but no human ever got to write home about it. We both know now = true nature = no-thing = no-body = no-one.

I once heard it said that the biggest trick the Devil ever pulled was "convincing humans he didn't exist." If true that would be one hell of a difficult feat to accomplish. But it pales in comparison to the miracle humanity actually pulls off each and every day. Namely, convincing themselves that they "do exist." That's the real magic. That is where true wonder lies. Or as you simply put it - WOW!

...partly because of the structures of language and also due to the way I've been conditioned to see and think about reality, which seems to continuously assert itself. It seems it may be impossible to escape this dilemma.

Just as you are suggesting and to be clear, "you," the David thing, never escapes duality. David will forever be a dream character until the dream ceases for one reason or another. Awakening is transcending the dream altogether. That, of course, is always available and will certainly be unavoidable when the body-mind contraption passes. But how to dispel your doubt right now? Don't worry about escaping any dilemma. Give up, give in, capitulate, and hoist up the white flag with no conditions. Be surrendered. Dare to see things as they really are. Rise above it all to become the ALL. I keep coming back to the idea of making yourself "grace prone" and being radically honest. By the way, they are the same thing.

Recently there has arisen at times a profound awareness of the psychological truth of Buddha's supposed teachings concerning attraction and aversion. It seems this may be the whole teaching in a nutshell. Suffering is the result of the mind's strong tendency to be attracted to what gives it security and pleasure and to resist what appears as painful or threatening in any way. This ties in with your words about resistance and the falling away of interest in such.

"Attraction and aversion"—that certainly is a great angle to consider deeply. But practically speaking what antidote are you applying to alleviate this tendency. It's one thing to recognize the malady but quite another to employ effectual means to counteract or remedy it. What, if anything, are you actually doing about it? I often find teachers favour being descriptive over prescriptive. Let's look at practicalities once again, shall we? I just asked myself this question and referred to my own past to try to answer it.

Something Adya said was very helpful. It was about not believing any thoughts or seeing how they are all inherently untrustworthy (but just all of them). I guess a large part of it for me was about recognizing non-self. Buddha's sutra on Anatta (non-self) is quite specific on this point. There came a time when first conceptually, then later experientially, self could not be located. From this flowed greater clarity. Thus craving and aversion began to weaken by themselves until finally they were rendered impotent. Or at least that is one way to explain the mechanics of my own awakening. Meditation and growing awareness of awareness (non-objectification) were among some other avenues as well. Practically speaking, how does it work for you these days? What are you doing or not doing?

The mind resists not knowing in every way possible and endlessly seeks experience or knowing.

The mind is the "doer" for sure, endlessly pursuing novel or pleasurable experiences, but you say it also seeks "knowing." I am sitting here wondering if "knowing" was something my mind was ever really interested in. I agree it certainly avoided "not-knowing" in every moment, since that was what allowed it to manifest itself in the first place, but from the viewpoint here, I don't think egoic identification ever knew a single thing in the real sense of the word. If a line was drawn in the sand, and if somehow my mind were to "choose" a side to stand on, like deciding Iraqis were evil and Americans are wonderful liberators, or vice versa, for example. This is most odd as I now know that I could never have chosen anything in my life since my thoughts spontaneously arose by their own accord. So was it actually the case that I "knew" Iraqis were evil? Do I know global warming is an actual phenomenon? Is meat bad? Is Josh an unenlightened ignoramus? I don't know, though my mind may try to inform me otherwise. I just don't take anything it says seriously any longer. This is not a contrived sense of denial. It's clear the little me never actually knew anything ever, so why continue to regard its beliefs as relevant?

My ego perpetually strove to pretend to "know" but when examined carefully, I couldn't help but conclude it was nothing short of a kind of patent medicine salesman. A huckster pushing snake oil. The wonder cure it boldly lauded was fake. But it sure put on a marvelous show pretending otherwise. I know this is a message few enjoy hearing. It doesn't make a great sales pitch either. That is why few teachers mention it this directly. Hard to fill the ranks up with this kind of talk. Nobody cares to hear that they are deluded. That their whole life is premised on a fiction— the fiction of self. How awful to hear this. People have called me crazy or worse for speaking "such rubbish" as they call it.

It seemed that in my awakening journey bitter medicine was invariably the best. I recognize most prefer it sugarcoated. But that kind of adulteration makes the possibility of truth realization weaker by several magnitudes and usually renders the message wholly ineffectual. What I was after was "the Truth, nothing but the Truth—so help me God." You might say I was "dying" to find it. The unexpected part was I never did personally discover it in the end. Like I said before, I simply realized there was nothing but...

DJ

27 Mar. 2013
To: DJ

Hi DJ,

Life seems to be a bit busy and now the Easter holidays are coming, and I won't have access to the library computer from Friday to

Monday except on Saturday. I'll see if there's time for a response to your letter, but it may possibly not come until next Tuesday or so.

Cheers,

David

28 Mar. 2013
To: DJ

Hello DJ,

I think I'll respond to your first comments below today and to the other comments some other day

What modulates "receptivity"? Good question! What does readiness or ripeness look like? How does one bring it about? What at first arises is that ultimately it is totally dependent on grace, as is everything. Within that context it seems that these states are indeed ego dependent as you say. For the moment there is a freedom from the grasping for security through attachment to concepts, ideas, sensations and experiences. The mind is relatively free from positions and beliefs, from its customary "knowing" of how it is. There is space in the mind where attention is not being drawn to thoughts, emotions, and sensations exclusively but is open to something entering from the Emptiness or Unknown. There is space for insight to happen, and insight is not thought. It is a clear seeing in which the ego is not involved, is not present, and which is outside of any thought process. Usually, in the next moment, thought enters and turns the insight into knowledge, as if it has gained something and can then store it away for future use and benefit. It is occurring to me that there are different kinds of insight and maybe we could go into that more fully if it's of interest.

How can we prepare ourselves to be open and receptive? It would seem that meditative practice (i.e., observing the body-mind) and self-inquiry can produce a stillness and spaciousness in the mind and/or a noticing that these are already present as the Beingness. But if the ego is involved in these practices, then it is keeping itself intact while pretending that it is letting go of itself. I'm reminded of your idea of making oneself accident prone. The "accident" of something entering from the unknown (by grace) is maybe more likely to happen when the ego is not controlling the consciousness so strongly. But it's tricky because the ego gets hold of such ideas and subtly maintains control by using them to avoid the unknown. Being aware of all this, seeing through the delusion and the resistance to the real, can weaken the hold of identification with the thinking mind which is creating the dream. This brings about a greater receptivity. Also it must be said that all ideas of somehow manipulating this or strategizing awakening are creating a lesser receptivity.

How receptive am I, you ask? I don't see how it can be measured, but I can answer your question about the sense that David is dying with a definite affirmative. It is just as you suggest in the few sentences on that subject. As for what sources of inspiration I draw upon to support this "dying," I think I must answer that in the next letter. It is indeed quite a mystery how ego could orient itself towards its own demise. Can the ego commit suicide? Is it the ego which is doing this? Is there an ego at all? To be continued...

David

∞ Chapter 6 ∞

April

4 Apr. 2013
To: David

Hi David,
    Thanks for the informative response. Most interesting. I am getting a better appreciation for how this journey of yours is unfolding.
> When identification with thoughts and feelings is stronger, the sense of my true nature...

I think you would agree that by certain convention, or more precisely here I refer to Hindu Vedantic tradition, you or I have learned to say "my true nature." Five years ago, I had never heard this expression. Chancing upon it at that time, it would have been meaningless to me. In a sense I take it now to be a conditioned phrase that I have learned to apply when speaking about aspects of spiritual enlightenment. It is familiar to others, so I sometimes employ it for convenience sake. But I am sure you would agree that there is no such thing as "true self." The conclusion of the spiritual journey reveals that "self" does not exist at all. It's not like finding a "pot of gold" at the end of the rainbow. The end of the path is not like what Dorothy discovered in Oz. The terminus of the yellow brick road does not lead to transformation of self. We don't adopt a new guise. The cowardly lion never discovers that he was actually brave all along. The scarecrow never finds his "true self" was wise beyond compare from the get go.

When the searching ceases, so does self. Bernadette Roberts calls it "no-self," as in "the no-self experience." I think the Buddhist concept of Anatta, or "not-self," or "non-self," is a bit more useful. Why? Well, to be clear there is neither self nor its corollary "non-self" waiting to be discovered at journey's end. Waking up reveals neither a negation nor an affirmation of self. But if I have to use dualistic terms, then I prefer to speak of truth realization like awakening from a dream and leaving the dream character entirely behind. So where is the self in that? It seems that I rarely describe waking up to reality as like discovering my "true self." I guess the profound sense of emptiness tends to preclude that inclination. You speak about this emptiness in a similar manner below. There is no great distinction to be made here as all distinctions are irrelevant. More of an observation I guess.

...like coming out of a fog into the clear sunlight, but these days it's not like that. It seems more like a subtle shift sometimes into a greater clarity which by contrast shows me there was some relative lack of clarity before. It's maybe like a lens that is slightly out of focus and then becomes more sharply focused and reveals more of the details...

"Details"...can you describe what you mean here? For example, what are some of the discrete qualities or characteristics that come better into focus?

So, it seems there are two ways in which I am unaware; one in which identification with thoughts obscures clear seeing and experiencing and the other where awareness is present without an object, and, therefore, seems to be nothing.

So you said that there are "two ways that I am unaware." If you think about it again, would you be willing to entertain the possibility that it was really only one? Perhaps Maya or duality has clouded clear seeing here. I would propose that there is indeed only one way that you are unaware. I would say that David is no more than a premise and the nature of this premise is ignorance. So, yes, it is quite true that David is utterly unaware. He counts on this to manifest himself. But what about this other way you think you are unaware. You said, "I am unaware when awareness is present without an object..."

Is this so, really? I think not.

This awareness in fact has nothing to do with David nor with anything else. Or it has to do with everything, but not anything in particular. Awareness is simply aware of itself. David does not exist. David was never born. So pure Beingness is not really a case of you being unaware. It is a case of you being "not." But this is never conceptualized. It's just awareness awaring itself. What does this have to do with you? The most fundamental way that David is unaware or ignorant is through the very fact that he takes himself to be real. In truth you are no more than a thought believed in. Where in abiding non-dual awareness is David found? So could we say that your "true nature" is more akin to pure awareness itself stripped of any semblance of self? Not David no longer being aware of objects in his field of awareness. For a guy like me who claims that distinctions are irrelevant, I would say this is an important one.

You asked if my thoughts are often in the past or the future. Mostly there is the sense of timeless presence within which there may be thoughts of past or future, but there is often no sense of any conflict or duality in that.

So would you say that your mind still spontaneously calls up the so-called past or projects to a fantasy future pretty much like it always has? Just a constant stream of uncontrollable gibberish. Monkey mind stuff. Do you ever have a respite from the noise? I am sure you do when meditating. How about during normal routine? I asked you before, though you never responded, whether you ever had a prolonged period of utter silence such that you found it quite impossible to dredge up past or project to future. Have hours or maybe even day(s) gone by for you when the chattering monkey mind ceased entirely, or pretty much so? It is of no importance, I am just curious. Do you remember Roberts spoke of this occurrence, and it took her aback? In my case it occurred several times for brief periods before the paradigm entirely shifted. It felt very weird to say the least.

It doesn't really matter if there are inconsistencies and apparent contradictions, does it?

It may not matter in the least, but we must be careful here. The ego has a propensity to justify its enduring ignorance through such talk. It's not truth that must be wary of ignorance, but certainly ignorance is always wary of the truth. If identification is entirely outside of the dream then as you say inconsistencies here, as in everything else, are of no import. Otherwise, we still must be vigilant. I find it best to assume that ignorance could pop up at any moment and live life accordingly. Letting one's guard down may not be prudent. However, if it is entirely clear to you that you never had a guard to begin with, then, of course, all is well. Only you can determine how it is for you. Once again, radical honesty is your ally here.

DJ

6 Apr. 2013
To: DJ

Hi,

Many very astute points were in your letter—quite revealing. I see the "my" did slip in once I think, whereas otherwise I referred to "true nature" without the possessive pronoun, which seems more to the point. I do agree that the idea of a "true self" can be misleading. Many teachers seem nevertheless to use such terms as "true self," or Self, and even to speak of it as if there is an owner ("your very own Self," etc.). I must say that such talk usually strikes "me" as inaccurate and still within the duality of a subject and an object. "True Nature" is one way of attempting to speak of Truth in a way that avoids the word "self" and makes it less personal, but of course as soon as I say "my" true nature, it is already personal. As to the question of whether there is a self or not, it seems that Gautama's words were (if we can know what he actually said), as you say, that there is neither self nor non-self.

And that accords with "experience" when I look for a self and find the indescribable. As you point out, it is not David that finds anything. What is found is that David is just a thought. As you say, it is not like the scarecrow finding that "he" was always wise but more like finding that he never existed. And yet does not wisdom arise when needed from or in or as that indescribable Is-ness that you are calling Emptiness? We can't say that nothing is there (here), can we? Neither can we correctly say that "something" is here. THIS (or THAT) is non-dual, neither this nor that.

This brings me in present experience as well as in the narrative to your question about the "details" which become clearer. What I was feeling into there, was the sense that the subtle (or not so subtle) ways ignorance manifests are seen at times more clearly than at others and also words can be spoken which carry a stronger sense of truth and authenticity in describing aspects or qualities of Consciousness and how Consciousness (to use this word for the moment) unfolds into itself and becomes aware of itself while at the same time never having been other than itself.

Maybe it could be described as the light of awareness shining more purely, less obscured by veils of ignorance or duality.

You speak of awareness becoming aware of itself and "true nature," if we are to use this expression, being akin to pure awareness stripped of any semblance of self. This seems accurate in my experience, and at the same time, I have a question about it because it seems that pure awareness is not aware of itself in any conventional sense (objectively) but that there is a different kind of "knowing" or awareness which is a "not-knowing" and about which nothing can accurately be said. I suspect this is close to what you are pointing to...

Library is closing and I have to end this communication.

    Bye for now...
    David

10 Apr. 2013
To: DJ

Hello DJ,

I'd like to respond to two paragraphs you wrote. On the topic of having a respite from thoughts, I've been contemplating how to describe my experience. I think I could say that there's a spectrum of thought activity. At one end is such a complete absence of thought that there is no knowing of any experience at all, no sense of time, place, location, or any "me" to know anything. There is no knowing of being alive or dead, awake or asleep, aware or not aware–complete nothingness, and not even a knowing of nothingness or anything else. If there is any knowing, it is so subtle that it can barely be perceived by the mind and it seems more like a total gap where there is no recording of anything going on. I'm thinking that this may be at least an aspect of what you refer to when speaking of awareness stripped of any semblance of self.

It is only when for whatever reason consciousness starts to reform a sense of a reality—location, time, presence of some knowing or experiencing—that it can then be said that there was a gap. It's more a conceptualizing of an emptiness in relation to the somethingness that appears as reality is constructed out of apparently nothing describable. This type of non-experience happens for "me" sometimes while in a floatation tank (very relaxed) or when meditating, and of course, in deep sleep. But in the ordinary waking state I think (but can't be sure) it is fairly unusual and not long lasting in terms of clock time.

Then there are states where thought is very quiet and may be hardly functioning at all. There is more and more a sense of deep stillness as the foundation of being even though thought activity is going on. At those times there is no pull or almost no pull from thoughts to engage with them and no real interest in what the thought process is projecting. This silence is not the opposite of noise, and it is not bothered by some noise being present as thoughts. In fact, the noise is no longer really noise because it has no real legitimacy in the face of the deeper stillness. There is a sense of power and significance in this type or expression of awareness, even though nothing is being known in terms of information.

The other night in a dyad there was a strong experience of this state, which then turned into a realization that the awareness that is the essence of what "I" am (as emptiness) is the essence of everyone and everything else. The experience was one of unity with all, being "inside" everyone and everything, although not really inside because there are no boundaries or borders for awareness. It was more of a subtle sense of intimacy with all as a unity or non-separateness and is hard to describe in words, but I suspect you can relate to this. You may say there is no such thing as "essence," but that was how the mind ("my" "mind") was conceiving it.

At the other end of the spectrum is thought activity that has a great charge, full of emotion, and which pulls the attention to engage with it and believe in the reality that it is projecting. There is at that point very little conscious witnessing of the thought process and an almost complete identification with it. Overall, there is every state along the spectrum manifesting, in whatever ways it does, at any given moment. To touch into your earlier question about what kinds of practices I use to deal with the persistence of thoughts (and ignorance), the "practice" of mindfulness or witnessing whatever arises is an important one for me. Witnessing takes the energy out of the "mind" and supports a falling back into Being or Silence. Then, there is the "practice" of keeping the attention on the sense of being or stillness. This supports a dropping out of the mind and thoughts and a resting in what is more essential or "real."

Then, also, I find great value in self-inquiry or exploring the nature of what is here. This includes the questions, "Who am I?" and "What am I?" and also such questions as "What is This?", "What is love/life/another," and so on. As you know, I like to explore these questions in the dyad format used in "Enlightenment Intensives" as the kind of attention that emerges while sitting in presence with another being has seemed very useful and significant. In the past I have also felt meaningful benefit from the experiments of Douglas Harding on seeing who or what we really are (I took some workshops with him) and make use of those from time to time. Then, there is listening to teachers like Mooji, Rupert Spira, Adyashanti, and many others—and occasionally going to retreats or satsangs with such teachers.

There seems to be a lessening of focus on teachers and strengthening of the trust and focus on "doing the work" myself, so to speak. It seems to be mostly a spontaneous flow from one "approach" to the other and they all seem to be inherently one process without any significant differences. Maybe the essence of my practice is the looking into and questioning the truth of whatever arises as thought or experience in each moment. Who or what am I taking myself to be in this moment, and is it true? Who is experiencing this, suffering this, and so on? What is the entity called "me"? The various "techniques" are just slightly different ways of exploring and being "vigilant" as you put it, and are used as seems appropriate at any given moment. And the question must regularly be asked, "Who is making use of any practices, and who is expecting to benefit from them—if there is such an expectation?" I don't know if I'm rambling here or how interesting such information is to you, but I think you did ask. I suspect you may come up with some pointed questions as to the relevance and effectiveness of such practices in relation to awakening or may have some interesting comments on such. It could be a topic for further exploration.

In terms of the uncontrollable gibberish or monkey mind, I would say my experience is much more often of a core peace within which thoughts and feelings arise and float away. And there is often a sense that the mind just does not move towards objects of perception and has little interest in them. When this is felt strongly it can, as you say, seem a little, or more than a little, weird. Then, as I say, at other times consciousness is more interested in and engaged with "the world" or the projections of itself. And ultimately, as you also suggest, what the mind is doing may have little import in terms of "waking up." Okay, enough for today...

Cheers,
David

16 Apr. 2013
To: David

Hi David,

Thanks for that. I really look forward to all of your replies. I have a better idea now of what it is like for you these days vis-a'-vis truth realization and your state of mind/no-mind. It's not often you see this kind of thing described in print or else-wise talked about in detail during satsang. It's investigations like this that tend to keep us honest, I think. In a very pragmatic way it helps us see just what the heck is really going on. I still find it interesting to compare and contrast others' journeys to my own. Thanks for the opportunity to learn a bit more about how this kind of thing is unfolding for others...or "apparent" others as Josh would have it.

While reading through your answer I was struck by how similar your awakening journey is to the one that unfolded here. I seem inclined to say that fundamentally our experiences differ only in degrees of ego loss but not kind. What you have written is very familiar to me. We both know each journey is unique in specific detail but there appear to be some common attributes or threads of direct experience running through many of the famous awakening stories—and yours and mine as well. These states of mind and realizations seem to naturally manifest over time as the self is dropped and the pattern seems to unfold in a somewhat prescribed manner. At least, there are some general common milestones that I see mentioned often, found reflected in my own journey, and now see here relayed in your account as well.

I am not a fan of the school that says "fake it until you make it." This stuff arises only through genuine spiritual maturation/ego degradation. It can't be faked. This maturation may occur relatively quickly or over the course of decades as in your case. Ultimately, self may seem to disappear entirely through an earth shaking, unfathomable act of grace (as occurred here), or it may alternatively, so I am led to believe, and you seem to be a case in point, almost imperceptibly fade away bit by bit as though a camp fire starved of new logs might slowly die out over the course of an evening. As well, it could be a bit of both I imagine. I'll comment further on several topics below.

At one end is such a complete absence of thought that there is no knowing of any experience at all, no sense of time, place, location, or any "me" to know anything. There is no knowing of being alive or dead, awake or asleep, aware or not aware. Complete nothingness, and not even a knowing of nothingness or anything else.

Yes, this is one way or aspect of describing what the actual "sense" of non-self is like. You did a great job of describing some of the salient qualities of emptiness—if we can say it has any qualities at all—again that damned paradox.

Did you or do you have any perceptual side effects just prior to or after exiting this state like seeing a bright light, hearing something or feeling bliss or fear, for example? How about that tight knot in your gut? Do you ever get that these days? If so, when or why?

This type of non-experience happens for "me" sometimes while in a floatation tank (very relaxed) or when meditating, and of course, in deep sleep...

When you say that this nothingness arises during meditation for you, this was precisely my own experience as well once I became adept at letting go. It was ridiculously easy to conjure up this state. It arose almost instantaneously. Not more than two or three seconds would elapse from so-called normal waking consciousness to...well who can say. In retrospect I can understand why it was so easy to elicit. This is how things really are, so what could be more natural? It's the contrived head space that passes for normal waking reality that is actually the difficult bit to pull off.

In the terminal stages that is how every meditation went, and at that point I was doing about seven to eight hours a day. Then, one day, what had up until then been only a state-induced experience, suddenly became the norm. What had been my "meditative state" somehow suddenly became the way things were whether I closed my eyes or not. Emptiness blossomed but not in a freaky disassociated way as the ego might suppose, but rather appeared entirely "normal" and imbued with an overwhelming sense of love and preciousness or dearness. It's impossible to relay this feeling. To say my heart exploded with peace and joy is putting it mildly.

And I was not separate from this. It was like MIND suddenly came to see that "meditation" and life itself were not different. In fact, nothing was separate or differentiated from anything else. Wholeness recognized itself. It was absolutely apparent that things had always been this way. What a leap of faith to believe otherwise, but that is Maya for you. So simple and unbelievably familiar. This emptiness you speak of above is IT, and you are THAT. Fear not. Dare not to avert your gaze as you look into the mirror and in a moment out of time come to discover that you are none other than the mirror itself. Stop resisting. Of course, that is impossible. You cannot through your own will and efforts stop being, David, for that in itself would require yet more resistance. I am aware that you already know this. So what do I mean then? Maybe it's more like seeing that efforting is futile. But just ALL efforting.

LIFE, and here I am not speaking of your life but all existence, turns out to be much like a deliciously accommodating and comfortable plush overstuffed recliner just waiting for you to flop into it and take a load off. Watts puts it well in the link below.

http://www.youtube.com/watch?v=Hu5oaty0uJM&feature=player_embedded

You won't regret it. Though your mind may be dubious, I tell you flat out that David is not the one having awakening experiences but rather awakened mind is having the David experience. Well sort of.
This silence is not the opposite of noise and is not bothered by some noise being present as thoughts.

This "silence" that you speak of that is neither the presence nor absence of sound is most illuminating and certainly familiar to me. Remember the time those kids were annoying you with their rowdy behavior as they floated in the middle of the pond you were meditating at? Remember how I said that they were your best teachers despite your inclination to grab (I know you were being metaphorical when you said this) a knife and slit their raft to shreds? Would they bother you in such a visceral manner now? Have things changed over the last few years for you or does this kind of behavior still piss you off from time to time? When you bump into life in this regard, is it a little more difficult to get the old juices flowing to such a degree compared to when we first met? Do you ever get embroiled in this kind of interplay and then have a moment of clarity and sort of laugh at yourself for engaging in such tomfoolery? It really is all just a big put on. Spirit playing tag with itself, as it were.

I remember Rob telling me how he was irked by noisy environments while meditating. I told him it was not the noise that was the problem. I encouraged him to seek out the most "disruptive" places he could find. I used to look for the noisiest spots to meditate in as a kind of a challenge like a pool full of fifty or so screaming kids being yelled at by several highly animated coaches or auditoriums full of hundreds of attendees awaiting the guest speaker's arrival. Things couldn't have been any more peaceful for me than if I was floating in that isolation tank you spoke of. The truth of the matter is that if your serenity is dependent upon your external environment, peace will never be afforded you. Ultimately, your very nature is peace itself which, of course, is not dependent upon anything. If your mind says differently, then very well. And YOU will certainly have a lousy time of it. By the way Rob didn't appreciate any of this at the time. How's the old chap doing these days?

> The experience was one of unity with all, being "inside" everyone and everything although not really inside because there are no boundaries or borders for awareness. A subtle sense of intimacy with all as a unity or non-separateness. Hard to describe in words but I suspect you can relate to this. You may say there is no such thing as "essence," but that was how the mind ("my" "mind") was conceiving it.

Yes, I had that exact same realization (awareness as SELF) at one point, pretty much to the letter as you have described. There was, of course, still further to go, or a gap still to be closed, but this is a highly relevant awakening experience. Your recent letters suggest to me that you are further down the pathless path than I might have suspected. Of course, this is just a relative judgment, so don't make too much of it. Back in the day when I was new to all this spiritual stuff, I recall how my ego was keen to compare and contrast its accomplishments with those of others. This was not useful for, as we both know, it is a case of making yet further distinctions. Eventually, this inclination was dropped. You spoke above of recognizing unity. That's IT. In a sense, we both recognize that Truth gets a kick when it catches a glimpse of itself. If we forget the neo-advaita thought police for a moment, what's the harm in saying *well done*?

Layman P'ang, that renowned Zen sage whom I admire greatly for his inclination not to join any organized monastery (come to think of it, I guess we share said inclination), comes to mind:

> When the mind is at peace,
> the world too is at peace.
> Nothing real, nothing absent.
> Not holding on to reality,
> not getting stuck in the void,
> you are neither holy nor wise,
> just an ordinary fellow,
> who has completed his work

Waking up for him, I gather, engendered a feeling much like an ordinary bloke might have when he comes home after a particularly hard day's labour and thinks to himself as he flops into that easy chair I spoke of previously—"Well done"…Nothing more than that just, "That was a good day's work." I might be inclined to say an eternal sigh of relief might also describe the moment in a similar way.

So, well done it is then! Fuck those party pooping nondualists. Or God love them, so go give them a mighty big hug. But then they will be moved to immediately ask, "Who is it that you think you are hugging?" "Who is the one you think is doing the hugging?" And at that point I would admit that they had me stumped. So I might as well stick to my first inclination. Simpler. LOL

If you tweak your identification, and by this I mean keep backing away from what is false just a wee bit more, by Jove I think you'll get it. By the way, I couldn't have articulated the realization you wrote above any better. Ever notice how it is much easier to express the truth of things rather than how it goes when writing about the spurious stuff the ego wants to bring forth? I encourage you to stick with what you know. That stuff is beautiful.

> ...the "practice" of mindfulness or witnessing whatever arises is an important one for me. Witnessing takes the energy out of the "mind" and supports a falling back into Being or Silence.

This "witnessing" and "awareness" business is a tricky matter. I find it challenging to articulate all the nuances the subject encompasses. Who, if anybody, is doing the witnessing? If SPIRIT is no-thing, then can we take this idea of witnessing seriously? Does it truly exist? Still, during my journey I could have sworn such a thing as "witnessing" did indeed occur.

In my case it was kind of neutral and detached but, in great regards, still "egoic" character that first engaged in this witnessing business. Later "I" took a step back, and it became difficult to discern who was doing this witnessing. Later, still no one was doing anything, so perhaps witnessing morphed to pure awareness itself. I say "awareness" since witnessing suggests a "witnesser." This progression was very natural and uncontrived and seemingly progressed over the course of many months by its own accord.

The guy whose video I watched that somehow seemed to trigger my final awakening wrote his one and only book (now, sadly, no longer available) entitled precisely what you are pointing at here: *The Awareness Method.* Adya once said something to the effect that if one were to be aware 24/7, he would guarantee their awakening. This week I heard a Thích Nhất Hạnh devotee say that their master prescribed constant mindfulness as the vehicle to final liberation. I told her that was true, but in one sense not quite possible if it was the case that "someone" was being constantly aware. Oh no, she said, "It's all about 24-hour awareness. "Really," I said, "ever done it?" "Well, no," she defensively replied. "Know anyone who has?" I asked. "Not really," she replied. "Well, I do" I stated.

I then proceeded to inform her that it was not feasible to be aware all the time as it made restive sleep impossible. Sure it could be done, but if it was the case that there was a self attached to the awareness, it could simply not be maintained forever. At least not with a self doing it.

During my stay at the hermitage I found my single-pointed awareness becoming so pronounced that it actually was carrying on into the sleep cycle. I was aware of all stages of the dream cycle, which included hypnogogic sound and vivid visual imagery. This I found disturbing in the way a psychedelic trip might be. Awareness jolted me back to wakefulness again and again. This went on all night. Also lucid dreaming occurred, which furthermore disturbed my restful sleep. These days, while I am able to lucid dream whenever I choose, I generally don't as the body-mind complex prefers to entirely shut down for a bit. So am "I" aware all the time? Nope. Here I am referring to relative reality where an "I" has to be present in order to be aware of objects in the perceptual field.

The other "AWARENESS" we speak of is quite different. You and others say that this awareness is present all the time, even during deep sleep. My inclination is to say this is probably so, but I really don't know. At times we label the great mystery "AWARENESS" and say it is everything and nothing and neither, the ground of being. So, it is common to hear that it is present during deep sleep. But here a distinction is being made. Who is the one who is deep sleeping? Does David know for a fact that awareness is present during deep sleep and that he is separate from this? For me this proposition simply does not compute one way or the other.

I suspect you may come up with some pointed questions as to the relevance and effectiveness of such practices in relation to awakening or may have some interesting comments on such. It could be a topic for further exploration.

The relevancy of spiritual practice? That's a hot button topic for sure. We've broached it before. It's a difficult one. The bottom line is, if it helps promote awareness, then why not? If it aids an aspirant in shedding (the apparent) self then why not? Couldn't hurt. In the realm of "doing," whatever practice one does that reveals the illusory nature of self is probably better than one that doesn't. I doubt Joe six-pack gives much attention to the kinds of things we are exploring here. Is he already THAT? Undoubtedly, but he sure is not aware of this fact. Is he worse off? I suppose if awakening is of no interest then not really. Ultimately, spiritual "practices" or "tools" are still a part of Maya: They are all illusory in nature, still relics of the dream state. And we both know dream tools can only tweak dream nuts and bolts. You can never utilize them to escape the dream. Yet, like a wrench which can be used to tighten bolts, such tools can also be used to loosen them as well. It is this loosening, this disassembly of self, that we are after. Loosen enough bolts on a bicycle and an accident is quite likely to ensue.

Once again I get back to making yourself accident prone. I heard my favourite STARS (Canadian pop group) song the other day. Opening line caught my attention. "When there is nothing left to burn you have to set yourself on fire." I think spiritual practice aids in the self-immolation process. Whether there is actually anyone there to be set ablaze (as certain neo-advaitists are fond of pointing out) seems to be a point rendered moot by the scars I bear. When I suffered third degree burns to a quarter of my body the intolerable pain seemed very real at the time let me assure you! Likewise, it seems very real that ego can be seen through and its pull weakened through deliberate spiritual investigation. Whether this is ultimately the case or not, I leave for you to discern.

Love, DJ

Chapter 6 | April

PS. A question. A while back you spoke about being sceptical or dubious of awakening in order to discover abiding nondual awareness. I would like to speak of this inclination towards scepticism but would ask that you describe your thought more fully. What exactly were you noting or pointing at a few letters back?

DJ

17 Apr. 2013
To: DJ

Hello DJ,

I very much enjoyed the Alan Watts video, so thanks for that. Also enjoyed your letter and will respond in black to your questions or comments highlighted in **BOLD**.

Did you or do you have any perceptual side effects just prior to or after exiting this state like seeing a bright light, hearing something or feeling bliss or fear, for example? How about that tight knot in your gut? Do you ever get that these days? If so, when or why?

I don't remember seeing any lights or hearing anything, although I'm reminded that sometimes out of this emptiness I have heard a voice, usually female, calling my name. This has also happened in sleep, and I don't know what to make of it. I haven't given any real importance to extracting meaning from it. It seems like Consciousness itself in a personalized form speaking to "me." It has never given any further message that I remember. Have you had such experiences yourself? One time there was an image and sensing of something like a whirlpool of consciousness out of which the voice was speaking. Anyway, I don't think we are going to place much emphasis on such phenomena, but of course, it can be interesting at times to play in that field and compare experiences for fun and possible edification.

Bliss and fear I relate to for sure. After exiting the "gap" there has often been a sense of blissful well-being as if the body-mind had bathed in a nurturing energy like having a deep sleep but somehow different.

But also immediately while returning from the "void" to consciousness of a reality, there has sometimes been a reaction of the

149

mind as it attempts to gain some reference points to establish a sense of location and orientation in space. A kind of panic. This has, as I remember, passed quickly as a sense of knowing of location is established. But it seems there were moments where it was okay and even interesting to be un-located in time and space.

About the tight knot, I remember speaking of it more as an empty hole in my gut or solar plexus with a sense like fear in it, a fear that seemed to have no reason and no connection with anything in particular. I think I did say that it did seem like pockets of mental identification or thought "entities" or fragments of self concepts that were appearing with a knowing that they were unstable and having no essential reality to hold on to. In other words, they were bits of "self" that were in process of dying or dissolving. I remember your seeming to agree with that analysis in your own experience. I may have said that it could feel like a tight knot, but I think the sense of it was that there wasn't really a holding or contraction at that point but more just a phenomenon. This seems to happen less lately but has definitely been felt at times. I don't know if I can say that it comes at any particular time or for any reason other than what we discussed about it. As I say, it seems to be a precursor to a letting go of some piece of (conceptual) self.

Any further comments?

Your description of entering into the natural state of emptiness is most interesting. I feel drawn to add my own comment on the idea of non-effort based on my experience and concepts arising from such. When it is seen that every creation of thought is essentially and ultimately untrue in the sense that it has no substantial reality and never can or will, then it is also at the same time seen that all effort can only be towards a concept of something that could be realized and sustained in some way. Nothing in the domain of thought can be sustained as it is always flowing towards dissolution or change. There is only a river of consciousness flowing onward and rising as waves of experience which then subside into the body of the river itself, to be followed by new waves of manifestation. Everything is naturally dissolving into emptiness or formlessness. What is aware of this? Is that which is aware something beyond the changing phenomena, something unchanging? Or does it not even conceive of itself in such terms? Any conception of itself is immediately back in the realm of thought and concept, which is just a wave in the river.

I'd like to stop at this point and answer your further questions in my next letter, so perhaps you could wait until my second installment arrives before replying.

Love, David

18 Apr. 2013
To: DJ

Hello DJ,

To continue my response to your last letter (excerpt in bold)...

This "silence" that you speak of that is neither the presence nor absence of sound is most illuminating and certainly familiar to me. Remember the time those kids were annoying you with their rowdy behavior as they floated in the middle of the pond you were meditating at? Remember how I said that they were your best teachers despite your inclination to grab (I know you were being metaphorical when you said this) a knife and slit their raft to shreds? Would they bother you in such a visceral manner now?

I remember well the incident at the lake and our heated discussion of it, and I assure you that my desire to slit the raft with a knife was more than metaphorical. On that score I've noticed lately a number of occasions when there was a lot of noise going on which was being experienced as greatly distracting by others, but I was experiencing complete peace without any sense of being assaulted by the noise in any way. It certainly, in these cases, has been very different from the lake experience. I wouldn't take that as meaning anything has been permanently attained or that another disturbance to Being might not happen at any time.

I remember being in India four years ago in a town (Tiruvannamalai) where others were reporting they felt overwhelmingly disturbed and distracted by the sounds, the pollution, and the people in the streets. For three months I hardly ever felt disturbed: It all seemed to flow through me like nothing. The lake incident came after that in time, so the previous peacefulness was obviously not beyond being upset. Nevertheless, it seems that the movement or unfoldment is definitely in the direction of deeper peace and less disturbance, without any effort to make it so. Also, it seems the laughing at myself, when embroiled in some drama, happens ever more quickly and often. Hard to take things so seriously most of the time.

I came across some talking by Darryl Bailey in answer to a question from a seeker who found himself becoming disturbed and annoyed by some people in his life and asking Darryl for advice on dealing with it. Darryl said he could only comment from his own experience which is that he also finds certain situations annoying and some people "bug the hell" out of him. He even, so he said, avoids such people as much as possible.

However, no matter how much Darryl feels annoyed, he recognizes that each "person" is a legitimate expression of Life or Consciousness and as such has every right to be just as they are. I find that interesting. The difference there seems to be that in my case there was at that moment no real acceptance of the legitimacy of those guys to be as they were, a legitimacy that I remember your bringing to my attention at the time. I remember begrudgingly admitting (perhaps only to myself) that it was true, but certainly on an emotional level, it wasn't true in my experience and part of my mind was strongly resisting the idea.

As I write I am also moved to mention that it seems not to be of any value to say I shouldn't have been feeling what I was feeling, nor to have made an effort to change it. Being fully present with things as they are, without judgment or rejection, seems to me to offer the best possibility of being in a state of mind (or no-mind) that is least dualistic and allows for a natural transmutation of the energy of the situation and the position being taken by the reactive mind. I'm aware that at the time I was in fact not taking such a position of non-judgment. Or was I? Even while my body-mind was reacting there was an observing present which just took note of the whole drama and all the reactions arising, including those during our conversation about it.

The more of this the better one could say, and at the same time from the non-dual view (or non-view) everything is just happening as it is without any better or worse. Even the justification of ignorance is just a happening, which from the absolute perspective is of no consequence. From that perspective there is actually no such thing as ignorance and all that manifests is only Consciousness in the absolute sense arising as that expression, with no loss if it's absolute reality. This has been a powerful direct experience at times which completely turns everything upside down, so to speak, but is certainly not in my case an ongoing direct knowing, but more usually a memory and, therefore, a concept.

You asked about Rob. He's pretty much as before, but I must say I've noticed recently that sometimes when he speaks there seems to be a deeper clarity and "truthiness" to his expressions. The other day we were speaking of journeying with a little help from our friends and he admitted, in a moment of candor that I appreciated, that he's a "coward." He said he likes someone he trusts to go ahead on the trail and report that all is safe before he will venture forth himself. He says he now feels ready to do some experimenting when an appropriate opportunity arises, so we'll see what happens. I have no expectations one way or the other at this point. I don't think I mentioned that Meghan and I did another Aya night recently, which could be a whole other story I guess. There is so much I can respond to in your last letter that I feel I can write several more replies before exhausting the material and, in fact, could probably go on endlessly.

I liked the Zen poem very much. I would even say that to call himself an "ordinary fellow" is too much identification, but as you say, let's not be advaita party-poopers!

Until the next time...
David

22 April 2012
To: David

You said,

I don't remember seeing any lights or hearing anything, although I'm reminded that sometimes out of this emptiness I have heard a voice, usually female, calling my name. This has also happened in sleep, and I don't know what to make of it. I haven't given any real importance to extracting meaning from it.

"No importance extracting meaning." **Same here.**

It seems like Consciousness itself in a personalized form speaking to "me." It has never given any further message that I remember. Have you had such experiences yourself?

Nope, I've never had a voice or anything else beckon me. During meditation in the mid-stages of my journey, a very bright golden light would appear in "my" visual field. Its intensity would increase as though controlled by a dimmer switch. The more I let go, the brighter it got until eventually it became overwhelmingly luminous. Quite disconcerting at first. Research showed me it was not that uncommon a phenomenon. Some traditions have labeled it. It goes away as the I drops. Rarer is a second phenomenon I first encountered as a momentary experience then later found it to be occurring all

the time. It is here now as I write if I care to note it. I struggled during my search to find it mentioned in the literature, though finally I heard Adya speak of it in a cursory manner. Recently, Josh mentioned it by name, so now I can put a label to it. If I ever meet him, I will be sure to thank him for that. What I am speaking of here is called Anahata Nada. Here is a brief overview I pulled from the web:

One of the koans of Zen asks, "What is the sound of one hand clapping? This sound is known in the Sanskrit tradition as "Anahata Nada," the "Unmade Sound." This means a sound not made in the way we know of – it is the "sound" of the universe, the primal sound of energy itself.

Ancient tradition says that the audible sound which most resembles this unmade sound is the sound of "AUM" (OM). (Brahma Randhra: Brahma-aperture; opening in the crown of the head; "the tiniest of apertures, in which is the silent, primordial sound, which gives you the impression that you are, but you really are not" [Nisargadatta]). According to the Vedas, AUM is the most sacred of all words, out of which emanated the universe, the symbol of both the personal God and the Brahman or Absolute. AUM is regarded by Hindus as the greatest mantra, being of incalculable spiritual potency.

Experientially, the best way to describe it is like hearing a constant white noise generator or listening to the static on an un-tuned TV or radio channel. It is definitely a by-product of the dropping of the self and not tinnitus, for it showed up briefly one day during my first two-week meditation retreat when the self dropped for a moment or two. Really took me aback. Much later it showed up again and never left. Curiously, this was before the entire self dropped. I heard a guy at an Adya satsang describe it, and he was not pleased. Actually pissed him off quite a lot. As I recall, Adya said his father got it though he himself didn't. Never bugged me, as who would be the one disturbed by it? In a similar way, I can now see eye floaters if I turn my attention in that direction. I assume that they were always present but my mind (and everyone else's, I presume) filtered their presence out. Waking up seems to relax this kind of perceptual filtering. As you know, senses generally become sharper as the I falls away. This kind of effect can also be temporarily noted during psychedelic use and lucid dreaming when everything appears better defined, crisper and cleaner.

About the tight knot, I remember speaking of it more as an empty hole in my gut or solar plexus with a sense like fear in it. A fear that seemed to have no reason and no connection with anything in particular.

Yes, if you recall, I said I thought of it as a kind of existential angst or fear, and the last refuge of the disintegrating ego. After my great epiphany, I carried that feeling in my gut for at least a year. But by and by it decreased as the last vestiges of the gap between self and other closed. Speaking of this makes me recall Adya's observation of awakening in head, heart and gut.

There is only a river of consciousness flowing onward and rising as waves of experience which then subside into the body of the river itself, to be followed by new waves of manifestation.

Just a wave in the river...And what is the river...???

Cheers,

DJ

23 Apr. 2013
To: DJ

Your last question, "What is the river?", brings me to the realization again of the limited nature of words and concepts. Is Life like a river? Here's what emerges...Experiencing emerges from the Unborn, the Invisible, the "Implicate Order" (Bohm). The source of thought, conceiving, and experiencing is invisible and unknowable to the rational mind. It's not a river or anything else conceivable. Somehow out of and as an expression of this Unknown, arises conceiving and experiencing as if a wave or a bubble of consciousness and knowing.

The knowing then dissolves into not-knowing. The creations that arise as experience seem to be partly comprised of material that is stored as memory, as conditioning. One of these creations that arises regularly is the I concept. It has some strength of belief associated with it; it is more or less believed to be real and, therefore, has more or less potency and effect in shaping the behaviour of the body-mind organism.

I was listening to some Rupert Spira material the other day wherein a question was asked about where the sense of I dwells. The questioner pointed out that Rupert has said that there is really no such thing as mind other than the thought arising in the present moment. He also says that there is a thought-created sense of a separate self. The questioner said that he is not consciously inviting the idea of a separate self, but it just spontaneously arises within the content of most thoughts and feelings. So, he asked, Where is this idea of a self abiding or dwelling that it can insinuate itself into almost every thought and feeling that arises? One would normally assume that it is residing in memory, but Rupert seemed to be saying that there is no such thing as mind in itself, which would be the same as memory. I hope I'm getting the issue clear. Rupert went on to speak of conditioning and repetition of the self-concept, which it would seem, would involve memory. Anyway, I didn't feel that Rupert actually answered the question.

What is relevant in my own experience is that this "I" sense does arise regularly and is still felt to have some potency and some affect in terms of how I feel and act. There seems to be no way to stop it, get rid of it, or control it. It does seem that the awareness of it, the silent witnessing, and the action of self-inquiry, is (or are) a force of dissolution or disempowering of the sense of the separate I and that there is a natural, effortless surrendering or letting go of self, a kind of letting go of the steering wheel or the rudder. Perhaps what the river is can never be spoken, but there can be a surrendering into it and thus a knowing of it beyond concept and an enjoyment of its qualities as "It" manifests itself in the realm of knowing and experiencing. In this way the Absolute can know itself through the lens of consciousness which must be comprised of at least some subtle duality - or apparent duality. And it can have the experience of knowing itself more and more deeply, a never ending unfolding of itself into itself, a most amazing experience!

It's interesting and perhaps useful to investigate the nature of reality in terms of conceptual understanding, but it seems to be most useful to look at what you have called prescriptive rather than descriptive understanding. What can be said about the "how" of releasing the grip of the separate "I" which seems to be the root of suffering? I've noticed lately that so much of what passes for serious spiritual discussion is actually speculation and conjecture which has no real power to transform anything but merely keeps the mind busy thinking it's doing something noble and useful. Where does the power lie to actually respond to our condition in an effective way and really get to the bottom of it? Hopefully, our discussions are on target and pointing to the actual "practice," "implementation," or whatever we would call it. And then we can also enjoy the far-ranging examination of details. I'm thinking just now that all inquiry with an attitude or energy of really seeking to know what is true in terms of actual experience is effective, and inquiry that remains at a mental level only has relatively little power. These ideas are just emerging in the moment.

I think there is still much to consider in your letter before this last one, and I hope to address some of the issues more completely. The question of witnessing and awareness seems to be definitely of potential in grokking what can be effective inquiry and self-examination.

Enough for today,
David

24 Apr. 2013
To: David

Thanks for sharing. I did find that JK piece interesting. Hope the following reply entertains as well...You said:

I'm aware that at the time I was in fact not taking such a position of non-judgment. Or was I? Even while my body-mind was reacting there was an observing present which just took note of the whole drama and all the reactions arising, including those during our conversation about it.

For me, or more pointedly how life unfolds for non-me, things are not quite as you describe them. The capacity to take things personally just isn't possible. I am not implying that I am special. As I say, more like I am not. Getting enmeshed in drama doesn't occur, and it is not a matter of conscious momentary transcendence. It is as Huang Po says, "Mind is not of several kinds." There is not one mind that is above all this and another that struggles not to be sucked into the drama and yet another that is asleep at the wheel.

But this does not mean that people never irk me. In fact, there is an assistant cook who works from time to time at the kitchen where I volunteer who strikes me as a most annoying individual. I try not to show up on the days he is scheduled to work. But this is not a personal thing. He annoys me as a mosquito might do, and I sure try to stay away from those suckers as well. But it would be ridiculous to say I hate this cook, just as it would be the same to say so of mosquitoes. I hold them to be expressions of life just as Bailey puts it. They are just as dear to me as anything else is. But again I choose to avoid them as I would a foul odour. It's not personal. So there is no dual movement of mind as you describe it. There quite simply is not two of anything. True mind is not unified mind for this suggests more than one to begin with. When the true state of affairs is realized viewpoints, distinctions and complexity ceases. Peace. Of course, I am not implying that things are "wrong" for you at this time. They are as they are. Like you say "no better or worse." But perhaps "different" from how it is here.

...that he's a "coward." He said he likes someone he trusts to go ahead on the trail and report that all is safe before he will venture forth himself.

It's quite natural to be fearful while engaging in authentic spiritual investigation. I was perpetually leery of the unknown but ventured forth nevertheless. Avoiding uncharted waters is just good common sense. Yet striking off into the unfathomable is what is demanded of us if we are to proceed. Eventually, there is no one who can blaze the way for us. Everyone who has ever awakened did it entirely by him- or herself. But this fact runs counter to the ego's desire. On the level of safety and security it always wants to know ahead of time if there are natives and whether they are friendly or not. This is natural. But as one proceeds down the pathless path, one day you come to recognize that there is no one left out there with you. You have to leave the sangha and teacher behind because they don't have a clue or can't offer aid. You are utterly alone. None can discern the way ahead for you. There are no maps. At this point the territory is unknown for it is unknowable.

Like Neil Armstrong stepping off the ladder onto the dusty moonscape for the first time, you're it. You're that guy who has to find out for yourself. But unlike Armstrong whatever you learn cannot be passed on to others. There is nothing to learn. True spiritual pursuit is the most solitary of endeavours. So, of course Rob is frightened. Isn't that the great fear, the fear of death? Aren't we all burying our heads in the sand so that we might put off for just a little longer the necessity to come face to face with reality and see clearly that there is not two? The book *The Haunted Universe* makes the case that this is a horrible thing to realize. There is nothing more terrible than being alone in the universe. But only if you believe this. From Twain's "Mysterious Stranger":

It is true, that which I have revealed to you; there is no God, no universe, no human race, no earthly life, no heaven, no hell. It is all a dream—a grotesque and foolish dream. Nothing exists but you. And you are but a thought—a vagrant thought, a useless thought, a homeless thought, wandering forlorn among the empty eternities!

No thought = No haunted universe

Cheers,

DJ

The Clothes Have No Emperor

∞ Chapter 7 ∞

May

1 May 2013
To: David

Hi David,

May already. Hope you are still enjoying our investigation. I sure am. Your insights refresh me like the flowering cherries do here in town.

Your last question, "What is the river?" brings me to the realization again of the limited nature of words and concepts. Is Life like a river?

"Is life like a river?"... Well, let me see. How long is the river? Hmmm...What colour is it? Hmmm... Some may think this kind of contemplation is, or deconstruction is, too simple, but it works every time. For example, I might hear someone say, "God/Krishna is a separate entity from me. He exists." Then I might well ask that person how big is this "God" (as I did of the owner of the local Hari Krishna restaurant but a few days ago—apparently one of their beloved texts provides a readymade answer with an empirical measurement purporting God's exact dimensions. What to say but note once again how pernicious Maya truly is?)

To be as forthright as possible, I have come to envisage the great mystery as "Snoopy." Every question regarding qualities or attributes of the ineffable elicits "Snoopy" in reply. Someone asks me, "What is it all about? Tell me the great secret," and I reply, "Oh, it's Snoopy." "What does Snoopy look like?" they want to know. And again I give my best estimate, which is "Snoopy." "So, where does Snoopy dwell?" they ask. "Snoopy," I say. "Ok, so when I find Snoopy what will be revealed?" "Don't you get it?" I admonish them in exasperation, "It's Snoopy. It's always been Snoopy. Just Snoopy!"

Here's what emerges.... Experiencing emerges from the Unborn, the Invisible, the "Implicate Order" (Bohm).

The source of thought, conceiving, and experiencing is invisible and unknowable to the rational mind.

I say that there is no source, FULL STOP, PERIOD, but then I let this concept slip away as well…. This is exceptionally clear from the non-viewpoint here. After all, when the ineffable turns in on itself and recognizes the ALL to be the ALL, from what point of view can source be discerned?

As you know, our friend G. told me he "discovered" the source. I can't imagine, and I sure tried, what the heck he was talking about. Source as opposed to what? If one has embraced non-duality purely as a conceptual philosophy this is an easy one to see through, but that is not what I am pointing at. When things appear as they really are there is no more "other" because there is no more self. There never was other, nor source nor non-source. It was all a charade, simply smoke and mirrors, mere appearance.

Like that wonderful Huang Po quote states, "There is not a multiplicity of minds" (or anything else for that matter). There is no source of anything. And, furthermore, consider this "anything" which I say is "sourceless." Is there "anything" to begin with? Does "something" discretely exist of and by itself? Outside of thought, point to something and confirm its existence.

Such distinctions can't arise for as I said, within what viewpoint do you ground such distinctions? This is not Philosophy 101; this is how things really appear when the apparent self drops away. This is how it is when dreaming ceases. I remember Jeff Foster at one time used to say, "Everything is just happening," as in there was no one present to claim any experience. Hearing that, I was more inclined to say "NOTHING is just NOT happening all the NON-time." But it is not really that way either. It takes as much of a somebody to judge that something is happening as it does to say something is not happening. It is always at this juncture that words fail me.

Looking again at what you said, "The source of thought, conceiving, and experiencing is invisible and unknowable to the rational mind," I ask you to define the source (since you stated that there is one). Is "it" unknowable to rational mind or simply unknowable period-- end of story? I bet you come up with questions on both counts. So ? + ? = ? You see what I mean? As well, is "rational mind" truly separate from the ALL? How do you arrive at this distinction?

How can you say that there is a source and yet not be able to ascribe any qualities to it? You are still attracted to seeing things in a subject/object (dualistic) relationship. There is an "I" (subject) that perceives things (objects), ergo there must be a source of these things. Reality shows that this is a fiction. There truly is no subject and object. Never was, but appearance certainly may convince otherwise.

"Experience emerges from the unborn." Really? Look again and tell me if this is actually the case. So is this unborn the source then? Does it follow that there is in fact "the born"? Would you say that David was born? If you are being honest you probably will have to say yes. Yet the strange thing is, you can't locate the self anywhere. So this "David," who was very evidently born (his mom made sure he had the pictures to prove it) goes looking for David but comes up empty handed. There is obviously a disconnect here. Something is not adding up. What could this mean? Maybe things are not adding up since there is nothing to be possibly added to. I say the Absolute (which is not an object) is more akin to "zero before a one" than any other way of looking at it. What labels can be affixed to nothing? That is, how it really is. David was never born, so of course he is "unfindable." There is no source and there is no not source. If it seems that experience emerges from the unborn, then I cannot argue that that is apparently the case for you, but would it actually be the case if "you" realized you were not present? If you were "not," what could you hold to be true or not true? This subjective experience is Maya's trickery. Bohm was a great thinker but therein lies the problem. His implicate/explicate order is just more dualistic philosophising. As far as Reality goes, the man was clueless. Bohm is a character in a dream as is David. What the hell could a fictional character know about the true state of affairs? I can't say it clearer… Bohm came to his senses on the day he died.

I was listening to some Rupert Spira material the other day wherein a question was asked about where the sense of I dwells.

"Question about where the sense of I dwells"…well…that seems to me to be a Rubes game. Who cares where it dwells? If "I" is only a phantom, then why place importance on where it hangs out? Unmasking "The Batman" is the important thing here, not finding the location of the bat-cave. When the mask drops so does everything else.

…this "I" sense does arise regularly and is still felt to have some potency and some affect in terms of how I feel and act. There seems to be no way to stop it, get rid of it, or control it.

Like I alluded to above, The Dark Knight is a furious force to be reckoned with, "unstoppable" as you rightly say until…until he is unmasked. That was Batman's weakness, and he was in constant fear of exposure. Once his true identity was revealed, he would be rendered impotent, and he knew it. Rip off Batman's mask, and he ceases to exist. That is what is always being pointed at here. Where does identity lie? In the relative or the absolute? Can we truly speak of identity at all and keep a straight face? If not, can it be "located" then? What is identity but an adopted persona?

Does David truly want to be unmasked, rendered impotent? Or, rather, does he continue to aspire, as the Caped Crusader did, to be a force to be reckoned with, a righter of wrongs, and a perpetual good DOER (human doing versus human being)? You can't play it both ways and be authentic (that seems like a pretty big position to take, but it seems to be the case, so I'll let it stand).

Batman was a rather neurotic, unstable character. Eventually, he gave up trying to straddle both sides of the fence. As I recall, years ago one graphic novel I saw had Batman committed to Arkham Asylum, an institution for the criminally insane, where he got to hang out with his old nemeses like the Joker, the Penguin, etc.

The current movie franchise has him simply "retiring" (blowing up) in a grand selfless act of valour. David, sometimes I wonder why you want to ruin a perfectly good cartoon character? Look below to something I grabbed from the web, and you might see what I mean. Seems like you have a pretty good "story" going on there.

The web page exclaims, behold a "Smartest People," a "Big Ideas" guy, named David Bruneau. And we have the picture to prove it. Once again, this is confirmation that David was born and is certainly alive and well in the world - and apparently is a pretty smart guy.

THE SMARTEST PEOPLE · THE BIGGEST IDEAS

D-A-V-I-D

How does one ever awaken when we are subjected to a constant barrage of conditioning that reinforces the idea of a self? This conditioning comes from within and without, but it is the self-generated reminders that are the most insidious and hardest to deal with. I guess in the final estimation it is all self-generated, isn't it? One thought believed in: The thought of "I."

David, when you look at that picture, I wonder who/what you see?

I note your words immediately below that speak of "surrendering" and "disempowering." Do you think that that could be a part of the "unmasking" that I referred to in my analogy above? I would tend to think so. In fact, they might be synonymous and could well lead to the dissolution of the self as you suggest.

I'm thinking just now that all inquiry with an attitude or energy of really seeking to know what is true in terms of actual experience is effective, and inquiry that remains at a mental level only has relatively little power.

I liked that last bit. As Adya always says the truth game should be results-oriented. Considering Buddhists, for example, how many of them actually awaken? Buddha we know literally means "awakened one." How many take after their namesake? How many are truly "awakenists"? I recently spoke to a self-professed Buddhist who flat out told me she had no interest in awakening - ever. WTF?

More than enough for today, eh?

Cheers, DJ

8 May 2013
To: David

What follows is mostly descriptive rather than prescriptive. Though if considered as a whole, perhaps what is ultimately being pointed at here is the requirement to place little importance in conceptualization vis-a'-vis the larger picture. Abiding non-dual awareness has nothing to do with what you think and everything to do with what remains when conceptualization ceases. I think it is helpful to remind ourselves of that fairly frequently. Maybe that reminder then falls into the "prescriptive" category. Note to self: "Let's be honest here; you really don't have a clue do you?"

Your Snoopy answer to the Great Question is funny (maybe) but I must say I'm in the category of those who don't get it. I also don't get how God can have specific dimensions: that's a good one!

My Snoopy "shtick" is actually born out of quite a profound realization and not meant to be funny per se. At the Jac O'Keeffe, and a few weeks later the Unmani retreat in Costa Rica, I was impressed deeply by the way those couple of truth tellers refuted any label, quality or attribute anyone tried to ascribe to the "Absolute." They took great pains to point out that whatever concept the mind wanted to apply to the ineffable, ultimately proved to be "Teflon coated," that is, nothing stuck.

I offered to Jac my feeling that the so-called awakened state had a sense of "knowing" or knowingness about it but then added, "and then take that away." Jac would have none of this. She negated whatever I and anybody else said about it. *Neti neti*. All concepts were nonsense. The true state of affairs was best summed up as a "nothingness or emptiness" she asserted time and time again. Not even a "mystery" could be applied to it, she said.

Did I immediately accept this? Hell no, but soon I began to see that this was indeed actually the case without question. It could not be denied that the ineffable was quite simply that. One was brought back again and again to the silence. Any labels or features that I may have tried to ascribe to the Absolute were seen to be false. To believe in any of them was pandering to the absurd. So in a kind of *reductio ad absurdum* I pondered what absurd label I might henceforth apply to something that "didn't exist," and yet which the conceptual mind seemed hell bent to conceptualize into symbolic reality, and voila, Snoopy popped into my mind during a lull at the Unmani retreat. For me, Snoopy and Source are equally ridiculous concepts. For others apparently it's "turtles."

I stumbled upon this little gem just last week which illustrates my use of SNOOPY but here substituted with "turtles," in a similar fashion. Apparently, it is quite famous and oft quoted in one form or another. Perhaps you know it already:

There's an old story of an Eastern guru who was asked by a seeker to explain the nature of the world. The guru replied that the world was a flat disc resting on the back of a giant turtle. When asked by the clever seeker, "Ah, but what does the giant turtle stand on, the master replied, "Another giant turtle." When asked what that giant turtle stood on, the guru paused, then answered, "Don't you get it, it's turtles all the way down."

Is there a source? Many teachers speak as if there is indeed one and even as subtle and profound a book as one of the Dzogchen classics is called *The Supreme Source*.

Instead of quoting others who are not here to defend themselves, why don't you tell me directly about this source of yours and whether it is "supreme," all the better. Citing others in hopes of propping up a belief system doesn't cut it. What do you know yourself? It was you who used the term, so flesh it out a bit for me. You may or may not have noticed that I speak from direct experience and only cite others as an addition or adjunct to complement my own experience and not as a replacement for it.

Though to be sure you are correct to say many teachers bandy the term "source" about quite frequently. The question I like to ask is, "Do they believe their own bullshit?" I felt G. actually seemed convinced a source had been found. By whom, I wondered? Let me quote Huang Po, to give you an example of what I mean. Yes Huang Po does mention source from time to time, or at least that is what the translator thought, but to be clear, source was just a manner of pointing to the ineffable. Clearly what he says below refutes the possibility of an actual source existing or not existing:

> If you students of the Way desire knowledge
> of this great mystery, only avoid attachment to any single thing
> To say that the real Dharmakiiya of the
> Buddha resembles the Void is another way of saying that
> the Dharmakiiya is the Void and that the Void is the
> Dharma kaya. People often claim that the Dharmakiiya is
> IN the Void and that the Void CONTAINS the Dharmakiiya,...

(similarly we are not in the universe, the universe is in "I" or more pointedly the universe is "I" or just is. IS and I being the same thing. You could just as easily say there is no universe too.)

> ...not realizing that they are one and the same. But if you
> define the Void as something existing, then it is not the
> Dharmakaya; and if you define the Dharmakiiya as something
> existing, then it is not the Void. ..
> ...Well, so much for the City of Illusion,
> but where is the 'Place of Precious Things'? It is a place to
> which no directions can be given. For, if it could be pointed
> out...

(saying "I found the source" is certainly pointing it out isn't it…?),

> …it would be a place existing in space; hence, it could not be the real Place of Precious Things. All we can say is that it is close by. It cannot be exactly described, but when you have a tacit understanding of its substance, it is there.
> Huang Po

"Tacit understanding…" I like the way Huang Po puts that sentiment across. I also appreciate his use of the term "void" which is less tangible and more nebulous compared to found in space and time "source." Tacit understanding is kind of what I was trying to put forth to Jac when I said it's like "knowing" but then take that away. Kind of like knowingness itself without any object of knowing, or as Huang Po says an understanding that is implied but can't be stated: silent knowing. Though, these days I no longer feel this way. For what reason, I know not. Lack of a "gap" perhaps. Not-knowing and not not-knowing and neither and both. In the final estimation Jac proved correct.

Anyhow, what H.P. is so eloquently stating above is how it is seen here as well. Here is my attempt at pointing out the same thing. Be assured these were not gleaned from some other guy's book.

If it all springs from the source, if indeed ALL is SOURCE (and I assure you it is) then what's the difference? How/where is distinction arising? ALL = SOURCE = NO OTHER

It all depends on which side of the fence you are on. Here I might say I see a tree or rock or, perhaps peering more deeply, SNOOPY. There I don't. I mean there I don't "see," nor do I "I." And come to think of it, how did I ever imagine there was a fence to begin with? That there was a "there." The "suchness" of existence. Vibrant aware silence.

If Spirit is everything, but just everything, then tell me where should I look to find Spirit? If there is source then what is not source? If everything is ONE, how then are you getting two?

If Reality is Unity, if the ALL is the ALL, how is it that you perceive disunity? Is source a belief stemming from duality or the way things actually are?

If ONE realizes true nature, ONE has realized ONE. How then does a distinction between source/non-source arise? How is source/non-source ONE? How is source/non-source not ONE?

Source, by definition, means point of origin. So "something" has gone somewhere. How ridiculous this notion seems to me. If there was a world comprised solely of an ocean could the water go anywhere? Well, you might try to be clever and say, "I would blast some of it off into space." I would then remind you that the rocket would have to be made of water and also then inform you that everything else in that particular universe was also water. It was all water. That's it. From what point of view do you judge the ocean to start? Where does it begin? Where could it go? And is there even an "ocean" to begin with, when there is naught but ocean everywhere? You might say, "Very well then, but this ocean has originated elsewhere." And I would ask where might that be, 'cause from the view here it's "ocean" "all the way down"...or up or left or right or anywhere or everywhere or nowhere. So once more, please tell me where this source of yours lays?

There is no alpha and omega. Only your mind suggests otherwise.

Very well, call it the source if you like. But that is duality objectifying itself. Realize the ALL, Be the ALL, and then dare to open your mouth.

From the position of "THAT" there is no that and no position as well. That's ALL folks.

And, finally, it would be as equally preposterous of me to say that there is no source as to say that there is. Let's make sure we are clear on that point. We can apply or refute the use of "source" over any other term we choose to denote the ineffable, but let's not take ourselves too seriously here. After all, language is symbolic. Not the thing/no-thing in itself.

And now to quote a couple of your favourites. Not because I need to but it is fun to see the same thing articulated once again from an apparent "others" mouth. Kinda like at times what has transpired here in this forum. From J Krishnamurti:

> The unknown is not measurable by the known. Time cannot measure the timeless, the eternal, that immensity which has no beginning and no end. But our minds are bound to the yardstick of yesterday, today, and tomorrow, and with that yardstick we try to inquire into the unknown, to measure that which is not measurable. And when we try to measure something which is not measurable, we only get caught in words.

Here is a snippet I spied today on the net from Mooji. He mentions the "mask" thing I spoke of last time as well as uses "source" in his pointer:

> Truth transcends language and mind; truth has to ring through the mind as mind is not different from source; the person is only the mask over the Beingness.

Here Mooji reminds us mind is not different from source. And I am sure he would say nor is anything else different from source as well. Just as I have done above. If it's all the same, then what is this source exactly?

You are probably very bored of the next one but seen with fresh eyes it is quite wonderful...

> The world is illusion.
> Brahman alone is real.
> Brahman is the world

as is this one:

The authorities say that God is a being, an intelligent being who knows everything. But I say that God is neither a being nor intelligent, and He doesn't 'know' either this or that. God is free of everything, and therefore He is everything." "If I had a God I could understand, I would no longer consider him God." Meister Eckhart

Meister Eckhart has a lovely way of pointing directly to the heart of the matter. Spirit is ALL and ineffable. And as an aside, here again we see someone stating the great mystery is not an "intelligent being." My feeling as well, if you recall from our previous discussion.

When you raise the questions you have it invites an inquiry which at the moment I feel too tired to grapple with, although on an initial reading it does strike me as being worthwhile to deconstruct the concept of a source in the way you are suggesting. For now I say the answer is Snoopy and will explicate further at some more opportune time.

You ask what I see when looking at the picture of "me" at the Ideas Conference... you may say I'm avoiding the question but really I don't get the point of the question or the point of any answer. He looks like Snoopy.

Well then, Snoopy it is. You are right. It was a ridiculous question. Maybe the answer could serve though as a reminder the next time you become embroiled in the drama and vicissitudes of life. That would include what I write here. Getting PO'd would seem to be ridiculous in light of what you have said above, wouldn't it?

Cheers, DJ

PS Any interest in addressing that question I asked you a couple letters ago or so about "doubt" arising over the reality of "liberation"? Does liberation differ from no longer "dreaming?" Maybe you could define what enlightenment, etc., means as an aid in clarifying your statement. Here is what you said some three months back:

No final liberation has taken place. Does it ever? There is the concept of final enlightenment or transcendence of ego and separateness, but I'm a little suspicious as to its veracity.

8 May 2013
To: DJ

Hi DJ,

I seem to be a little short on time and energy to get into this exchange fully as I'm involved in last minute preparations to go to an Enlightenment Intensive (EI) tomorrow. I'll be out of communication for a week and then will likely be able to reply after that.

I found it a little strange that you interpreted my quoting the name of the book *The Supreme Source* as an attempt to prop up a belief system and that I have some kind of ownership of a concept called "source" to which I am attached. There may have been an unconscious acceptance of the concept as containing some reality, but I don't think I had any (or much) investment in it, and I had also said that I could appreciate the value of deconstructing it as you suggested. At the same time I do appreciate your statement below that you are NOT saying that there is NOT a source. So long for now
David

**8 May 2013
To: David**

Have fun!
DJ

23 May 2013
To: DJ

Hello DJ,

Well, it was an interesting retreat and very "fun" in a way that may not be the usual type of enjoyment engaged in by most people, but which I think you share, with many insights and openings to less mind-y states of consciousness. It's now been almost a week since returning home, and how quickly the time has flown! The retreat seems like old news now, so it will no doubt be expressed in whatever communication we enjoy, but I'm not sure I'll be relating any specifics in any kind of logical, linear fashion. One thing I do remember at the moment is the experiencing of a consciousness beyond the human, if you know what I mean. Very "trippy" and awesome... Probably just what IS when not being conceptualized in the usual way.

I just reread your letter of May 8 and feel coaxed into silence and not knowing. I don't think I really had any attachment to the concept of a Source, and when I follow your meditation on the subject the whole idea loses any ultimate validity. Your last questions similarly leave me without any real answer. What is enlightenment? I have no idea! I've heard many definitions which vary significantly. And how would I know which is true as I'm not claiming to be enlightened myself? Can any of them be true? It would seem, as you suggest, having something to do with seeing through the dream being "created" by the mind with its illusion of a separate self. I was expressing a doubt that "people" go beyond all conditioning and are no longer subject to human frailties or tendencies of conditioned behaviour. It just seems that to claim some kind of perfection or infallibility leads to all kinds of trouble. But I sense that I really don't know and moreover really don't care. In fact, there seem to be many aspects of the self-realization game that I'm just not that interested in. For example, the sound the universe makes. Perhaps if I hear it and it means something, then it will seem significant.

I'm getting the sense that maybe I shouldn't be writing at present because there seems to be a kind of disinterest in conceptualizing anything. Or maybe that's a good time to be writing. I'm experiencing a sense of being slightly disassociated, kind of spacey, and yet there's a sense of aliveness and clarity of being. A bit strange, and curious.

You said you sometimes wonder why I would even be interested in questioning my existence as by conventional standards I might seem to have a pretty together life. People used to say the same thing when I retired from ski racing and then coaching in my twenties. They had no idea of what was going on "inside" me, of the quiet suffering, the fear and self-consciousness that was never far from my awareness. So that was no doubt part of it. But also I don't think the motivation to search is just about suffering, as many who suffer never take up self-inquiry. I started contemplating death at about six years old, trying to understand it and see beyond it, to no avail. It seems that some force beyond my control was at work, and when a friend gave me a Krishnamurti book in my adult years there was an immediate affinity, and a deep interest in what was being pointed to soon developed and went on from there.

The Clothes Have No Emperor

I'm off to Mexico tomorrow for some dental work and a free holiday from the dental savings and air miles. Meghan also needs a root canal and crown, so we'll be saving big time between the two of us. Probably won't be at a computer until after we return on June 2.

Hope all's well with you, my friend,

David

∞ Chapter 8 ∞

June

5 June 2013
To: DJ

Hi DJ,

    Mexico worked out well. I've been super busy since getting back to Victoria. How are things with you? You may say there are no "things" and no "you" but we'll see what will be shared...

    On the spiritual front there is a sense of silence and lack of a need to conceptualize anything. It has become ever clearer that any movement of mind towards anything is a movement away from what is already here behind or prior to any seeking of anything. What is already here is silence, love, peace and even more truly cannot be objectified or identified without in a sense losing the truth or reality of what is. Truth or Love or whatever is not accessible to the mind (thought). Accessing it is a kind of surrendering or collapsing into what already is or, perhaps more accurately, is a complete non-doing in all ways conceivable. Seeing this clearly in a dyad the other night was quite a wondrous happening, a simplicity and clarity, joyful and empty at once. It's already here! And what "it" is, is what I am, which again can't be objectified and remain purely true. Awareness is effortlessly present and notices all that arises in the field of itself without needing to "do" anything about it. Again, even to say this requires some degree of objectification. Hence the primacy of silence. But the silence is not disturbed by any words. The above just emerged in response to a wondering what there was to communicate...

    Love, David

7 June 2013
To: David

Hi David,

Nice to hear from you. Very nice indeed! I was wondering if you had given up on this forum so was a bit surprised to receive your letter. Even more so given the subject line of "Already Here"!

I paused quite a while, wondering what it could mean. Of course, I was really wondering if it could apply to anything else but The Truth. So, I was really delighted to discover that indeed it did regard Truth-realization and was further thrilled by your description of your recent awakening experience.

What to say? From the experience and perspective here your description seems totally apt. I concur with it wholeheartedly in that you have described what non-self or emptiness feels like when objectified. It's not what you think it is, is it? I mean this in two ways.

First, when grace occurred for me such that everything finally ceased, I was truly gobsmacked. Not what I expected at all. I could never have imagined this into existence in a thousand lifetimes. Indeed no one can, as it has nothing to do with thought at all. So, again, it is not what you think. Not as in you are "thinking wrong" so you must adjust your thinking but, quite simply, your true nature or no-mind has nothing to do with thinking at all. And this is what you have seen directly. A few more comments follow below.

Mexico worked out well. I've been super busy since getting back to town. How are things with you? You may say there are no "things" and no "you," but we'll see what will be shared...

"Things" with "me"??? That truly is a paradoxical question. I can say that I have just spent a full three weeks sussing out a computer problem. Could have been terribly frustrating but was simply taken in stride. No drama I am afraid. All is well.

On the spiritual front there is a sense of silence and lack of a need to conceptualize anything. It has become ever clearer that any movement of mind towards anything is a movement away from what is already here behind or prior to any seeking of anything.

Yep. A little more broadly than "any movement of mind towards anything," we might as well call it as it is: Any egoic identification in any form quite simply is ignorance personified, untruth, or resistance to what is. In one sense the quest to awaken is one of turning away from such self-deception and realizing what has always been.

What is already here is silence, love, peace and even more truly cannot be objectified or identified without in a sense losing the truth or reality of what is.

Bingo! It's the difference between talking about "Being" and actually abiding as non-dual awareness itself.

Truth or Love or whatever is not accessible to the mind (thought). Accessing it is a kind of surrendering or collapsing into what already is or, perhaps more accurately, is a complete non-doing in all ways conceivable.

Radical relaxation is another way of looking at it. Flow. The "don't care" attitude which is most disturbing to egoic identification. The ego certainly abhors an attitude of laissez faire and "let it be." Beingness itself. The ego doesn't know what to do with this. Skepticism may result. Pay this no heed. Restrict the fuel and it will snuff out on its own accord.

Seeing this clearly in a dyad the other night was quite a wondrous happening, a simplicity and clarity, joyful and empty at once. It's already here!

You say, "already here." That's it, indeed. Astonishing isn't it? The end of seeking. What's to be found that is not already presently here? Oneness was here all along but through simple misperception it was overlooked. And when the seeking ends, so does the seeker. The story of ME comes to fruition. The little game of tag is wrapped up. But nothing really ceases for in truth nothing ever began.

"It's already here!" To the uninitiated it sounds like drivel. From the viewpoint of direct experience it is one of the most profound and, as you say, "wondrous" experiences you can get. Who could have thunk it? There all along. Never saw that one coming.

And what "it" is, is what I am, which again can't be objectified and remain purely true. Awareness is effortlessly present and notices all that arises in the field of itself without needing to "do" anything about it. Again, even to say this requires some degree of objectification. Hence the primacy of silence. But the silence is not disturbed by any words.

So it seems that you are settling ever more into the ground of being. Self-ignorance falling away. But of course there is a huge difference between recognizing true nature and abiding as it. In my case, much as in Scott Kiloby's I gather, I had a short period where I could turn on/off enlightenment at will. This was nothing but a simple parlour trick. At this time the ego still sufficiently held sway. This was not true awakening, though I did not recognize this at the time. Though being warned that the ego often re-exerted itself after one ceased to dream for a period, I was at that time still in delusion. There was still a bit further to go. Then I snapped out of it again; or, more precisely, the story teller ceased to orate entirely. Full stop.

When all was just "IS-ing" itself merrily along, when the past and future ceased to come to mind, when I was essentially "not" and "The ALL" or "oneness" was simply always at hand, then I might say abiding non-dual awareness truly realized itself. Later still, not even this much could be recognized. Just peace and not-knowing.

      Love, DJ

17 June 2013
To: DJ

Hello DJ,

Just a short response today. I very much appreciated your letter. Near the end, you comment on the difference between recognizing true nature and abiding as it. Yes, in my case the so-called ego still seems to hold sway, as you described in your own case at a certain point. Identification with a "me" still happens to a degree that creates emotions such as depression, anxiety, insecurity, and so on. I can be and am affected by potential loss of money or attention from loved ones. There is a witnessing of reactions of the body-mind organism and at the same time it seems there is still an identification with the "I," more or less. Or is the more or less only in the realm of phenomena and the identification actually a more subtle but stable, entrenched psychological belief that has not yet been rooted out? What does it mean? It is what it is and means nothing sometimes and something at other times.

Hope all's well, David

21 June 2013
To: David

I take your appraisal of "where you are" spiritually speaking to be refreshingly frank. You are just calling it as it is. Bits of the old "truthiness," as it were. I appreciate such candor. You proffer the question, "What does it mean?" (exhibiting egoic identification at times...others not...). Then wisely answer it with, "It is what it is." No more than that. Just a statement of fact.

Contained in this admission I see an important facet of the Truth realization process. I would suggest that only your ego would be moved to seek out significance here, try to adjust its perceived shortcomings, etc., and you are clearly aware of this fact. Yes, so "sometimes my mind moves towards egoic identification and sometimes moments of lucidity are the case —so what?" So what indeed. That's just the way it is. Sometimes there is clarity, sometimes not. Yet always the inclination to awaken remains.

I used to be thrilled by temporary breaks in the dream state when a moment of clarity erupted during life's normal routine. I gather some have the propensity to beat themselves up upon realizing that they were once again fully ensconced in the dream state, instead of considering how precious such a moment of lucidity really is. Who cares if one is lost in delusion? How marvelous when one isn't! As I say, these short respites always gave me such a thrill. Don't you find even a second of clear seeing to be sublime? How wonderful it is not to be entranced if only for a second. In the early days it was always such a shock to find the craziness of "ordinary reality" momentarily replaced by sanity. In fact, one could call the enlightenment process the drive to re-establish "normalcy." Waking up is simply becoming sane.

Over time these brilliant still moments became ever more frequent with longer duration. The "awareness" engendered through long hours of meditation, plus a new found disposition to be inclined to stay "awake" even while not atop the cushion, seemed to orient the self ever more away from delusion. It is like the old programming naturally subsides to be replaced by lucidity of BEING. Truth realization becomes one's new-found raison d'etre. And, as this "clear-minded no-mindedness" is your natural state of being, it is actually a pretty simple state of affairs to realize. Seemingly all it required was a certain earnestness to awaken in this lifetime and an honesty to confront things as they actually were (not as I hoped or wished they were). This last sentiment I find reflected in the following passage:

…as there was presence, being fully there, there seemed to be no possibility of moving into "problems." In fact, there was no such thing as problems. The sense of empty fullness permeated everything.

Yes, indeed, that is one of yours, David. Certainly penned as a result of a moment of clear seeing. Now to discover that there really aren't moments of clarity. Rather, you are currently dabbling in a game of deception that requires "endarkenment" or non-clarity of seeing to be ever present in order for the charade to be artfully pulled off. The view (not mine or yours) has always been crystal clear. You are just momentarily pretending otherwise. You don't really ever discover your true nature. After all, it is called your true nature for a reason: It is what you already are. (How could you really be anything but what you truly are?) Rather, you just shed your play-acting false persona. A little tweak in perception is ALL. Your recent awakening experience suggests that you are currently engaged in putting your costume back into the tickle trunk from whence it came.

At one time or another we all mistakenly entertain the possibility that this garb is ours to keep forever (I'm eternal since my soul will persist...gonna go to heaven, etc. Some may believe the old suit is replaced with a fresh one from time to time, a la reincarnation. Most incredible of all is the fact that we mistakenly perceive simple actor's vestments to somehow be who/what we actually are. Objectification is where our identification lies.

You have directly realized this is not the case at all, haven't you? About time to shuffle off the stage, isn't it? Or perhaps "grow-up" in the manner of the quote which follows below. Or does this kind of talk disturb you? Or is it of no interest whatsoever? Is it counterproductive? I certainly would be the first to suggest that "silence is golden," yet I do recognize that dyad inquiry is helpful to you and wonder if this forum has been of use as well (and thanks again for providing me with a venue to try to articulate that which is ineffable and at the same time providing your own wonderful descriptions of how it is to awaken in one's own lifetime). If not, we could cut our proposed yearlong investigation short but, seeing as we are half way there, why not continue? What's another six months out of an eternity?

Love, DJ

When I was a child, I talked like a child; I thought like a child; I reasoned like a child. When I became a man, I put the ways of childhood behind me. Corinthians 13:11

The Clothes Have No Emperor

25 June 2013
To: DJ

Good day, DJ,

Your letter was right on the mark and very much attuned to how things have been unfolding for me. It brings joy to share these subtleties of the journey, and it is not such a common thing that such sharing can happen. Therefore, it is all the more precious and at the same time totally "ordinary" or just "what it is."

I agree that there is a thrill in the moments of clarity. And also what you say about the view being crystal clear at all times is worthy of contemplation. As you say, our "true nature" is always present and that is what sees and experiences the apparent confusion, limitation, or ignorance with a crystal clear view. The capacity of what we are to objectify itself is what "creates" the sense of lack or limitation. At least that's what I think you said.

As far as finding your words about shuffling off the stage or growing up to be disturbing, of no interest, or ???, it seems that the idea of a doer who could shuffle off the stage or grow up doesn't seem to hold any real relevance, but that these apparent events could happen within this unfoldment holds some kind of reality. Or does it? Who would have been on the stage or have shuffled off it other than a concept?

Our sharings have I think been of "benefit" in inspiring a more thorough looking into the way things are and have been a significant part of my unfoldment into a deeper "knowing" of how it is. This sounds a bit relative, and yet that seems okay as it can be present within the awareness that all is just as it is and there's no unfoldment in the Now—only THIS. Unfoldment requires thinking and the concept of time and movement. Perhaps it could be called an unfoldment without thought or time. Another (apparent) divine paradox!

I'm happy to continue our dialogue. It's good to look ever more carefully, to exercise the expressive capacities and reflect on what is being said and heard, and to engage with your subtle perceptions and "truthiness." If summer ever arrives, I will likely be spending more time at the lake and such outdoor places so may be less at the computer. Enough for today, David

28 June 2013
To: David

Hi David,

You said, "Our true nature sees and experiences..."

This may be "felt" to be the case by you, David, or perhaps common sense would dictate that this is so, but I suggest you consider again if this is truly the case. Most of the awakening journey defies common sense, and this is another case in point. So what I am now about to point to will be decidedly counter-intuitive, but it is actually the case nonetheless. Of course, I can point this out only through the benefit of hindsight. Prior to the dream state ceasing I can well imagine things would seem to be as you say. Awareness (my true state), I could have well gathered, was the one that experienced Maya (the illusion which was not really me). This is not the case at all, but I can't adequately explain why, though I will try now (and freely admit expect to miserably fail).

It was misleading of me to say that the VIEW is crystal clear yet at the same time it is quite so. It is as Corinthians 13:12 says,"For now we see through a glass, darkly." Upon awakening there is found to no longer be any Vaseline smudged mirror distorting reality (also in a sense no reality at all), nor a "we" from whence to view it. That is, distortion disappears and so do you. That is, object disappears and so does subject.

Thus, I ask you who or what is there to "see" or "experience" anything? Therefore, I refute my previous assertion about there being a "view." There is no view whatsoever. What nonsense!

Yet true nature is indeed crystal clear. In fact, it is clarity beyond compare. It's just that nothing is seen or experienced. This is the actual state of affairs. But again I refute what I have just said and state for the record that there is nothing happening at all, so what misleading rubbish to intimate to you that there is a "state of affairs" to be found upon awakening. And if nothing is happening, who would be daft enough to state that there could be any kind of view, clear or otherwise, to be found anywhere, since a view must include something objectified, and furthermore, it infers a "viewpoint" taken as well as a "viewer" to be present. None of that is actually the case.

Presently, as life unfolds here, I might say that there is some kind of loosely held viewpoint (i.e., two eyes seemingly looking out upon creation) but no viewer present to "own" this point of view.

Our true nature does not see or experience anything. Yes, my peepers regard objects seemingly held in space, but at the same time I stress that there is nothing whatsoever to see. No content, emptiness as it were. Paradox again. Though nonsensical I am being dead serious here.

Everything just is. This is the "suchness" of life Zen guys refer to. Yet clarity abounds. And the view is indeed crystal clear. It has never been anything but. Have I managed to fail eloquently or quite miserably as I first feared?

I know you are a fan of Mooji, but I wonder if he sometimes muddies the water with statements like "find the one who is aware" or "the one who is Self-aware knows." Just who would that "finder" be? Who is this "knowing self-awarer"? And what in fact does this character actually "know"? Love to get all the juicy details. I am out of the loop because I don't know a damn thing. Have to hook up with Mooji sometime and maybe get him to spill the beans.

Cheers,

DJ

∞Chapter 9∞

July

July 2013
To: DJ

Good day, DJ, I wasn't clear about what you were actually saying regarding the "clear view," but now you have clarified it as much as possible perhaps, and your deconstruction of the objective attitude to seeing and experiencing seems right to the point.

Some impressions and seeings that arise in contemplating this follow. Your suggestion that the "normal" way these things are understood and spoken of collapses at the point where objectification ceases, and we then enter the realm of paradox where the truth of what is being examined can only be known in a non-objective, nonphenomenal way.

Of course, the paradox is only such to the mind and doesn't exist in "what is" or the "Suchness." You have failed in your exposition only to the extent that words can never capture the reality of non-dual "knowing" or "not-knowing." The very desire of the mind to know and be certain of anything is an aspect of the ignorance of objective thinking, is it not? It may have a place in the manifest life, in science, and so on, but is ultimately not of value in the realm of "Truth." Even in science it seems that anything stated to be true is more a hypothesis or possibility and usually gives way to a more subtle truth before long.

Self-inquiry means looking ever more deeply into the nature of self, mind, consciousness, and so on. A significant aspect of this becomes the knack of collapsing or dissolving the subject-object duality and seeing without a seer or a point of view. This kind of "seeing" has a quality of "truthiness" which is its own confirmation without being a certainty or knowing in the conventional sense. There seems to be paradox everywhere, but only for the mind. As for Mooji, I'm pretty sure when he says something like "find the one who is aware," he is recommending such investigation precisely because that "one" will not be found to have any phenomenal or describable characteristics; it will not be a "one" at all. The inquiry will dissolve the inquirer.

Have a good day even though there is no one to have it and no day to be had!

David

9 July 2013
To: David

David,

Your last letter seemed to be right on "trackless" track vis-a'-vis "Beingness" versus objective conceptualization. See comments below.

First, I want to share a bit of the old life with you. The following example of how life unfolds presently may give you an inkling of how it is here. It's good to remind ourselves from time to time that this awakening thing is first and foremost a "lived reality," whatever that means, rather than metaphysical speculation as most seekers would have it. In a sense I guess what follows demonstrates how ONE may be "in the world" but not "of the world" post enlightenment. Yet, there is not detachment. Rather, there is a vibrancy and immediacy to life that was never apparent before. Again it's a paradox. Not in and not out but something else. Non-duality.

My housemates occasionally invite me to share my life with them (but only superficially so), and they ask me to tell them how I am doing these days. How does ONE answer that? I've yet to formulate a reply that satisfies both parties. I've never engaged in talks with them like we have in this forum. Why bother? As you have probably discovered, direct unabashed truth telling doesn't usually go down very well. Questions, as above, prove difficult. When you stop to consider it, isn't that a most bizarre question:"How are you doing?" Of course, "doing" is of prime importance as we are "human doings" after all, aren't we? Never once have I gotten a, "How are you being?" Of course that kind of question would never arise from the dream state. We may pay lip service to Reality as it truly is with the use of "I am a human being," but in actuality *almost no one is*....a "being" that is. So, "How do you do?" will remain the question of choice upon first meeting, as well as serve to gauge a person's well-being...er, I mean well-doing, later on in time.

Every Sunday we have a check-in at my shared house where this kind of sharing is expected. Of course, I can't do it. It's not that I don't want to. Rather, there is no "doer" available to comment on how the "doing" is going. So such questions are rather awkward for me and the gang is never pleased with my lack of earnest participation.

Generally, my housemates seem most animated by weekly recaps that stress turmoil, discord, and the "poor little me" story. Here none is ever forthcoming. The better moments people may report on seem to draw much less interest (why is that so, do you suppose?) Of course, I have none of those either. So what to do? What to say when life is simply living itself? How to explain that there is no one available to make any comments about life's low and high points? That the view here simply affords none. That at best all I can say is everything is peaceful and utterly ordinary and seems to be right on trackless track. That a sense of low-grade background joy and "okayness" is eternally present, but seems to be a function of reality itself rather than something created by "me."

I bring this up because a few minutes ago, just before I set about to write my weekly response to you, someone asked me at the dinner table to speak of an "awesome moment" I might have had today. I thoughtfully replied by asking them to consider what "awesome" really meant. I brought up the notion of awe-filled or awe-inspiring experiences. I then explained that those kinds of moments had actually been very few and far between in my life. Presently, I explained, "awe-some" moments were not even possible (or if I had cared to, I could have tried to explain that actually the whole darn thing was perpetually awesome if they but cared to truly have a look). I also stressed the fact that great joyful highs were incapable of being felt, as were opposing depressing lows.

This did not go down so well, so another person persisted with, "Ok, so what 'good thing' happened to you today, DJ?" Of course, I went blank on that as well. How to respond? I said nothing good happened today, nor nothing bad. In fact, nothing good or bad ever happens (unless the mind informs otherwise and in turn it is accepted as so). Of course, the ego cannot abide this kind of baldfaced truth telling, so again the question was slightly modified in hopes a positive reply might be forthcoming.

How about anything "cool" happening to you today? To appease the questioner I responded that my dear friend David had sent me an email. That sufficed and they shut up. Of course, your letter didn't "make me happy," nor cause an outbreak of "awesomeness" to overwhelm. (This term is important to these folks. They often refer to themselves as "awesome people," and I once could not hold my tongue any longer and assured them I was certainly not awesome in any respect).

Fact was your letter will certainly be the most relevant thing that passes the radar screen this week and, as we have spoken of before, the TRUTH does seem to enjoy revealing itself to itself.

As I said, I have not tried to explain what it is like to live life without a centre with this group. Truthiness is not part of their reality tunnel, so in all likelihood it would only portray me as some kind of weirdo or worse. Irony is, one of these "roomies" identifies with Buddhism and is an avid Thich Nhat Hanh follower, but it seems that more often than not TRUTH is the last thing she really wants to hear about. The best tact I have is to remain as silent and unobtrusive as possible, which is actually exceedingly easy. It's the damn "personal" questions I find tedious. They probably think I am just being evasive. They don't know the half of it. I am obscurity itself. So far gone that I can't even claim to support Plato's dictum:

> "This man, on one hand, believes that he knows something, while not knowing [anything]. On the other hand, I – equally ignorant – do not believe [that I know anything]."

Though that saying hits close to the mark, in truth I can claim nothing. Silence. I neither know nor know not. Muni told me that a seeker once asked her whether she "knew." I gather "knowing" here meant one was spiritually hip, in the "right" view, or awake. So, "Yes," she said, "I know." I was a bit confused or taken aback that she could actually say such a thing but remained politely silent. That seems the best and most truthful thing we can do. And what do I know anyway…maybe she did know. Though surely I don't know what that could possibly be or mean. Nor do I care. Truth be told, I don't seek nor not seek to know and that has made all the difference.

If you were to ask me if I "know," I might turn it around and ask you "Who is the one who wants to know that?" Ramana had terrific success with that one, didn't he? Or at least a little peace and quiet, as they tend to pretty much shut up after that "Zen bitch slap" momentarily shocks them to their senses, if applied using "clever means".

That is not to say that there is not recognition. When dreaming ceases to the extent that the "I" no longer has any apparent reality, then there is indeed a profound sense of familiarity. And a great "AHA" erupts, but in that "aha" moment nothing is grasped. There is just a profound aha with no objectification attached to it. AHA recognizes only itself. But what is there to know…or know not? Who knows…? God only knows. Is that true? Perhaps time will tell, but unfortunately that does not actually exist.

Objectification ceases and we then enter the realm of paradox where the truth of what is being examined can only be known in a non-objective, non-phenomenal way.

That point above is worth considering again. Can the truth of what is being examined actually be known in any way? I often say I went looking for the "answer" and was astonished to discover that that was precisely what I was (but, of course, it is unspeakable so turned out to be the last disappointment for the ego). When the MIND in a sense casts its gaze upon itself, "knowing" and "not-knowing" disappear. Certainly this duality is still quite applicable if egoic identification remains. The one that can know (David) finds out that he actually doesn't know a darn thing. Might you agree that the "truth of what is actually being examined" as you put it, is none other than "you"? (the not-two or emptiness).

Since you can only know something external to yourself, knowing or not-knowing what you are is simply not possible when things appear as they actually are. David, I know you have direct experience of what I am pointing to here. I just want to highlight it again and present it as a kind of preface to what you say immediately below.

Of course the paradox is only such to the mind and doesn't exist in "what is" or the Suchness." You have failed in your exposition only to the extent that words can never capture the reality of non-dual "knowing" or "not-knowing."

The very desire of the mind to know and be certain of anything is an aspect of the ignorance of objective thinking, is it not?

Yes, I do agree and this ignorance of objective thinking certainly prevents the realization that "the seeker is the sought" as good old JK put it. As you well know, when objectification ceases, so does the "I thought" and with that the veil of illusion that one was so desperate to rent apart itself vanishes as if it had never existed at all. Therefore, the endless seeking born out of the desire to know who/what you really are prevents the very thing from being revealed. Yet inquiry must go on until it doesn't.

If earnestness and wonder to get to the bottom of it all cease, I am afraid so does the possibility of making yourself "grace prone." Paradox again. Seeking is quite useless, but it seems like it is the only thing to be done. Then one day it ceases. Who can discern why the seeking stops and the "donkey" is dismounted, but Foyan would have it as such if realization were to unfold. What donkey, you say?

As I was pointing out above, so too the great Chan/Zen sage Foyan also notes (but more so through poetic metaphor) that only two kinds of spiritual sicknesses exist and these must both be remedied if awakening is to occur.

- Go looking for the donkey while riding on the donkey. (Sickness of perpetual seeking facilitated by doubt).
- Be unwilling to dismount once having mounted the donkey. (Be entranced by the allure of delusion.)

Realize you are and everything else is the donkey, or Snoopy as I would have it, and be astonished to find no donkey remains to be dismounted. When the two sicknesses are remedied and there is nothing left on your mind, Foyan says you find yourself rendered a "wayfarer" (liberty itself). Funny enough, a few weeks ago I asked an acquaintance "what he was" and he replied, "Well DJ, as near as I can figure it, I always reckoned I was a 'tourist'." I was really impressed by the honesty of his response. Echoes of Foyan indeed—and my own experience as well.

> It may have a place in the manifest life, in science, and so on, but is ultimately not of value in the realm of "Truth." Even in science it seems that anything stated to be true is more a hypothesis or possibility and usually gives way to a more subtle truth before long.

So true about science. In fact, this week I was pointing out to someone that nothing in science can, in fact, ever be proved. This chap was rather dubious about my assertion. Like you say, a hypothesis may give way to a theory if data supports it, and with even more data we may label such and such a law, like Newton's law of motion. Yet despite the number of tenets derived, we still have only a model. Models may fall at any time if new data arises to disprove them. In fact, science never claims to be able to "prove" anything. So nothing in science is held to be inherently "true". A model only lasts if no contrary evidence pops up to reshape it or abolish it entirely. Take the law of gravity. Another model, though many would not assume this. A strong one, no doubt, but it has never been "proven true". There are no absolute truths in science since there is always the possibility that novel data may arise someday to shed a new light on the situation. A very good point you have brought up. Have you found that as you investigate further and further it seems more and more apparent that nothing is ultimately "true"? If everything is relative who is to say, right? Scientific empiricism lays no claims to the truth. Fundamentally it admits its own naiveté. This may come as a shock to those who hold it out to be the last bastion of reason. Even science admits it can never ultimately know for certain what the heck is really going on!

As some sages note, The inquiry will dissolve the inquirer.
Here's to dissolution indeed!
DJ

He that findeth his life shall lose it; and he that loseth his life for my sake [the sake of TRUTH- DJ] shall find it.
    Matthew 10:39

The best way to find yourself is to lose yourself....
    Ghandi

12 Jul. 2013
To DJ

Hi DJ,

    I found your letter very interesting and relevant to my own experience. Your words regarding detachment and vibrancy ring true for sure.

    The story about your housemates is something I go through on a regular basis in my own way and for quite some time now have had difficulty with such questions as "How are you doing?" or even, "How are you?" There often seems to be difficulty in locating this "me" that I'm supposed to report on and also in ascribing to it any particular qualities of experience or specific concepts to describe what feels more like an undifferentiated presence of something indefinable or empty of definable characteristics. The feeling is kind of like I am nothing and everything, so how can I report on how that is? It's like asking God how he's doing today. He/she is everything and can't be narrowed down to one or two feelings or concepts. It always feels a bit jarring when this question is asked, but then I suppose I could ask what it is that feels jarred. I find it right on the mark how you describe this demand for objectification and identification with the body, mind, and emotions and I find your description very funny, too.

    I was talking about the exact same thing with Meghan the other day and she said that part of it is just people wanting to connect and that's the way they think they can do so. Yes, this is the usual explanation. Social niceities are ceremonial language to acknowledge the person's presence. People don't really expect an answer about how you are feeling and usually don't want one; it's more like I see you. I agree with that and can see that just acknowledging the desire to connect and responding to it on an energetic level to begin with can be somewhat "real." Perhaps if you are willing to contact them as they are, they may be more interested in exploring your perspectives (or non-perspectives) on life. But that just may not be how your Beingness is "wanting" to respond or express. I suspect your responses are mostly unpredictable and without reference to social conventions. Anyway, at least "I" was able to enjoy your sharing...

    The rest of your words on the subject of "knowing," objectification, and so on, seem to me to be very "truthy" and actually seem to leave me with nothing to say for the moment and a sense of not knowing anything, as you mentioned. I do find these days that often when I consider some kind of contemplation of a question or spiritual issue there is really a feeling of not having any reference points to resort to and having to begin completely from scratch, with a sense that there's no point in even beginning at all! There's nowhere to go.

At other times I notice that (my) mind is quick to assert some kind of knowing in contradiction to another person's assertions about life, self, truth, etc., especially in group "dialogue" situations such as happen at the K centre. The desire to sustain and promote the self runs very deep it seems, and yet it does all seem to become more and more insubstantial and insignificant, leaving the sense of "vibrancy and immediacy" that you mentioned in reference to your own "state."

I guess that's it for today
David

13 July 2013
To: DJ

Hi DJ,

I was pondering for some moments on your question about people seeming to find positive or non-dramatic reports about their or other's life experiences less interesting than more "negative" or dramatic descriptions. I imagine you already have some good understanding of the phenomenon but thought I'd pitch in with my two cents' worth.

It seems that when someone has a problem or misfortune then the ego of the listener is affirmed in that it can feel and think that it is in a better or superior state. One can feel that one is in a position to empathize and offer some help or consolation. The ego loves to get in there and help out, especially from a sense of having things more together than the other. When someone speaks of feeling well or having a positive experience the ego of the listener can't feel so superior and may even question whether he or she is having as good an experience. The ego is not fed but rather may even feel diminished and insecure!

Also, it seems that the ego thrives on drama and gruesome stories of suffering. As Eckhart Tolle has said, the pain body in each of us feeds on pain and finds joy thoroughly indigestible. Misery loves company, as the old expression goes...Negativity seems to the ego self very solid and real whereas more joyous or neutral emotions and thoughts are felt to be less real. Whatever helps the ego to feel more stable and solid is welcomed and whatever shakes the foundations of the separate self is avoided. Strangely, dramatic stories with a good dose of suffering make the self feel better about itself, as in the evening newscasts and daily newspapers.

This tendency of the mind can be seen and understood as it arises, but its appearance seems to be quite subtle and unnoticed much of the time. What say you my friend?

David

14 July 2013
To: David

Your last musings were very informative and well considered. I have nothing to add. Damn, if only I could think of something contrary to say, then we would be off to the races, eh? LOL

This tendency of the mind can be seen and understood as it arises, but its appearance seems to be quite subtle and unnoticed much of the time.

Yes, you have to be really aware to catch it. I remember quite well how I forcefully and with determination had to avert my eyes from gawking at car crash scenes. How I so longed to take a peak. With equal determination, I had to unplug from the media. Post enlightenment there was still a lot of conditioning at work pushing to continue "helping" people as you put it. Another term is "minding other's business." It seemed very programmed into the system, but lucidity of being overruled this compunction, so it disappeared over time.

I am working on a new letter for you. I think it will prove interesting but apologize in advance for its length. Here is something I stumbled upon today which will serve as a good teaser. Can you guess what territory I will explore next?

In 2003, Russian mathematician Grigori Perelman solved the seemingly unsolvable Poincaré conjecture, a 100-year-old problem, to prove that any shape without a hole can be formed into a sphere. It took until 2010 for a team of mathematicians to validate his results. The *Poincare' conjecture* was one of the seven listed on the Cambridge, Massachusetts' Clay

Mathematics Institute's Millennium Prize list. The bounty on such a solution is one million dollars and the Fields Medal, math's equivalent of the Nobel Prize. Not bad at all, right? However, right after being offered the prize, he turned down the offer. The genius refused the prize, claiming the knowledge gained to be worth more than the financial reward. "I'm not interested in money or fame," Perelman stated.

"Emptiness is everywhere and it can be calculated, which gives us a great opportunity. I know how to control the universe. So tell me, why should I run for a million?" he told a local newspaper. The 45-year-old genius still resides humbly with his mother and sister in his hometown of St. Petersburg.

Love,
DJ

15 July 2013
To: DJ

I imagine you will take up the issue of emptiness being calculated and the idea of controlling the universe. Should be fun!

I had a few more thoughts about the tendency of some people to use the word "awesome" abundantly. It seems like a very effective ploy of the ego mind to make everything seem just hunky dory and nothing to be concerned about. It's an example of super-positive thinking which is extreme enough to blot out any insecurity the speaker might be feeling and patch it over with loud and confident exclamations of "we're awesome people," and so on. Some seem to actually convince themselves of the truth of these congratulatory self-evaluations. But do they really? And of course if you fail to support this idea of awesomeness, you may not be considered so awesome!

So you couldn't find anything to be contrary about. I'm sure it won't be long before there's something you can take a good shot at.

Bye for now,
David

16 July 2013
To: David

You said: I imagine you will take up the issue of emptiness being calculated and the idea of controlling the universe. Should be fun!

Good try, but actually it sort of refers to something in your past letters of late as well as something from over a year ago. I want to touch on my disinclination to seek approval, power, fame, and money—that kind of thing. And by wider abstraction how this natural tendency is reflected in the drive of SELF-realization. That's the gist, though it will also cover a bit more territory as well. Basically, it's about how TRUTH overshadows all else.

I had a few more thoughts about the tendency of some people to use the word "awesome" abundantly.

Good points on the inclination to proclaim "awesomeness." Though if one is abiding as delusion itself, I guess you might as well tell positive lies over less savory ones (as in I am a loathsome fuck-up, etc.).

Obviously, I told them I was not awesome, as I am not anything at all. Playing the charade is of no interest, so I politely informed them of such. Your observations on how the ego utilizes ploys of self-aggrandizement to help define and sustain itself are most astute.

It's like what passes for most forms of "spirituality" these days, myriad forms of "mutual delusion clubs" abound. It's all in good fun, isn't it?

Cheers, DJ

22 July 2013
To: David

You can only receive realization if you don't deceive yourself!
Chan/Zen Master Foyan

I offer the following as an "answer" of sorts and hope it proves satisfying in some way but ultimately wonder, "What use is such babbling?" Waking up is cessation of thought, and here I am throwing more at you. Perhaps it's as one would enjoy a good wine, savor it in the moment, and then throw the bottle away.

It is about as "personal" a discussion as you will ever likely see from me, though I did shine the spotlight on "you" as well from time to time. Hope those parts don't irritate you too much. I guess brevity is not my strong point, so once again I apologize and offer gratitude for your forbearance. If you are at the library and it seems too daunting to digest this in one go, why not print it off and bring it home and cogitate over it for a while? Or not...it's all good.

If we are to believe the lore concerning outlaw cowboys or sheriffs of centuries past, then apparently several types of prevailing gun-play existed. For example, there were the quick draw artists who shot from the hip (faster but usually less accurate) versus those fellows who were "straight shooters" (poised, measured and a dead aim, though less quick off the mark). If you investigate the origins of the word "to sin" you will find it simply meant "to miss the mark," much like an archer misses the center of the target.

I would suggest that if sin is to be avoided, if the spiritual bulls-eye is to be pierced directly, then what the realm of spirituality needs in greater abundance is sages dedicated to inspiring us to be straight shooters ourselves, rather than those teachers who tend to ignore, or in some way even condone, the immature seekers' proclivity for being impatient, unmeasured, prone to a lack of discernment, and quick to believe the first thing that pops into their heads. My new favorite, Chan Master Foyan, defines such seekers as those who pose questions at random and answer "with whatever comes out of their mouths making laughing stocks of themselves."

Someone who usually shoots from the hip is likely, more than not, to be leading a scattered, unexamined life, prone to believing egoic projection and hubris (i.e., their own bullshit). They are also the ones who invariably shoot themselves in their own foot from time to time when scrambling to unholster their "firearm."

In contrast, a straight shooter has a much better chance of hitting that all-so-elusive-mark since his or her attention is so much more focused and unencumbered. I think most would agree that a straight shooter embodies certain ideals such as truthfulness and integrity. If hitting the mark dead centre is considered to be truth realization itself, then it follows that a straight shooting, truth-telling maverick (I use the term *maverick* here to describe someone like NSA whistleblower Edward Snowden who lives in an age where telling the truth is regarded as a revolutionary act) is probably our best role model. This was certainly found to be the case when I laid eyes upon the likes of Adyashanti and Jac O'Keefe. I am a great fan of straight-shooting sages who point us directly toward our true nature as expediently as possible. If waking up *is* one's sincerest desire, then surely the "straight shooting" direct path has a lot going for it.

I'll take Ramana over Sai Baba (of Puttaparti), a true Zen/Chan master over a Tibetan Crazy Wisdom Master, or UG Krishnamurti over Osho any day. Why UG? I think you would agree that there is something inherently trustworthy about the man. UG never had a huge following precisely because he rarely, if ever, spoke anything that pandered to egoic wishful thinking, hopes, dreams, etc. He was the consummate straight shooter and some may say he suffered because of it. If he had only toned it down a bit, the accolades would have come pouring in, and he could have died a rich and famous guru. Instead, he chose to tell it like it was. I heard him say a few weeks before passing that, "When I am dead and gone, just dump my body over the fence." That's how little he cared about worldly matters.

For my money I say that there was a man who had definitely seen through the veils of illusion. Silly old fool. Precisely! UG's mantra was always, "I have no message for humanity," and I loved him for it. What we need are a lot more straight shooting codgers like him, Jed McKenna, or Bernadette Roberts, and a lot less characters who pander to our egos (or try to subjugate it through force of their own huge presence). People like Cohen and Chopra, while undoubtedly famous, seem to me to rarely, if ever, even get near the mark.

That, then, will serve as an intro for the topic at hand.

I want to address matters concerning my "motivations," style of imparting the Dharma, and seeming inability to sacrifice "truthiness" at the expense of personal gain. These points, in one form or another, have popped up from time to time in our correspondences, so I thought I would finally address them all in one fell swoop.

First, reflect back again to the genius mathematician who seemed to give up the big prize in order to continue living the simple life. He knew that the carrot they tried to dangle in front of him (one million dollars) was a paltry trinket and of little value. In what follows I will try to explain how this is because I think I know what makes that mathematician tick. In his own peculiar way I think he chanced upon the emptiness of Zen and gained the whole world for it. When you are the ALL, what more can be added unto you?

You told me that:

> Meghan said that part of it is just people wanting to connect and that's the way they think they can do so. I agree with that and can see that just acknowledging the desire to connect and responding to it on an energetic level to begin with can be somewhat "real." Perhaps if you are willing to contact them as they are, they may be more interested in exploring your perspectives (or non-perspectives) on life. But that just may not be how your Beingness is "wanting" to respond or express. I suspect your responses are mostly unpredictable

and without reference to social conventions. Anyway, at least "I" was able to enjoy your sharing...

Yes, I can confirm your suspicions above. I have no interest in connecting with people so that we can chit chat about spirituality while treating it as a relative truth whereby each and every viewpoint is considered equally valid. That is what got us in trouble in the first place. It's called delusion. I am terribly interested, though, in having truth reveal itself to itself. If that involves an earnest seeker in some regard then how wonderful.

Remember what Dogen said:

> Learning the way of enlightenment is learning selfhood.
> Learning selfhood is forgetting oneself.
> Forgetting oneself is being enlightened by all things.

Dogen clearly points to the primacy of transcendence of self. I can't help repeating the same mantra as well just like a parrot on meth it seems...must go with the territory. It is not, I repeat, NOT about accommodating the ego's desire to find other egos that resemble itself so that it can continue to wallow in its own self-delusion. I call this a mutual delusion club, and it seems many so-called spiritual gatherings often serve this function. For Buddha's sake, when are things ever going to change? When's it going to end?

David, you've been at it for over forty years. When is enough, enough? I guess precisely when it is and not a minute sooner, eh? Tell me exactly how is it that "acknowledging the desire to connect" is going to eradicate the little me such that SELF blooms? How does this support Dogen's supposition of learning self-hood? Doesn't "connecting," as you put it, merely reinforce the illusion of other, of duality? That's a rhetorical question as I know darn well it does. As you know, I made it a point to visit all kinds of spiritual groups and traditions post-awakening, and I found few if any seekers whom I considered much inclined to transcend self. Personally, this inclination was simply not good enough for me: I HAD TO KNOW.

"Seeing through the doings of the vain and suggestive ego makes it possible to be immune to its seductions." That is from Thomas Cleary's *Kensho: The Heart of Zen*. "Seeing through the doings," as it were, is not something I often see welcomed in group meetings or satsang. Sure, lip service is paid, but point out a "bit of doing," a "spot of delusion," to someone – or, better yet, invite them to rout it out themselves — and you are sure to raise their ire. My experience in meeting folks as "they are," as you put it, feels very akin to those occasions when I had to interact with schizophrenics, save for the one fact that those folks tended to make a hell of a lot more sense. Just kidding☺, though I know you get my drift here. Perhaps you embrace the adage of best to "go along to get along"; but where is the radical in that?

Foyan says, and I quite agree, that on the topic of inquiry, "You have to know HOW to ask before you can succeed." JK says the same. Knowing HOW made all the difference, and it sure didn't involve fraternizing with a deluded peer group. It involved shutting the fuck up. It involved being wrong over and over again and accepting this as part and parcel of the journey. It involved acknowledging that everything I ever believed in, or thought, wasn't actually based on reality as it truly was. This was very heavy stuff indeed. Meeting new friends was the last thing I had on my mind. Surviving the whole ordeal in one piece was much more relevant.

Here's another martial analogy for you to consider that may help illuminate what I am pointing to here. This is not so unexpected, given my lifelong passion for warrior-ship. At first glance it may seem out of context given the topic at hand, i.e., determining one's position in the spiritual marketplace, but I assure you it is most relevant.

David, I suspect you would not disagree that my style of imparting the dharma is often a "take no prisoners" or "give

Chapter 9 | July

no quarters" (quarter here referring to housing enemy soldiers) approach. You and others have said as much directly to me. Obviously, the origins of these military terms derive from military code and are used these days when we want to describe someone's behavior as being "ruthless and stern." This code is sometimes taken to be figurative, but for the samurai it was something they actually lived, or died, by. They almost never took prisoners unless it provided some sort of tactical advantage and considered personal surrender a truly horrendous act of cowardice which brought huge dishonor to themselves and family.

To be a *Bushi*, or samurai, one had to embrace death at every instance. Death was a foregone conclusion once the decision had been reached to serve one's lord and master. At this point a warrior's life was rendered irrelevant as all motivation was now directed towards serving the master most diligently and honorably (in a similar way that I presently serve my master - TRUTH itself). To be taken prisoner was something to be avoided at all costs. I assure you that this is not an exaggerated or idealistically romanticized portrayal of Japanese warrior-ship. Research, as well as experience of this ethos directly (obtained when I studied the way of the sword in Tokyo under the tutelage of a traditional Japanese sword master), has proven to me that these guys were hard core to a fault.

This mindset is not the way of the western military man. For them, surrender is always an option. This act is abhorrent to the traditional Japanese warrior and demonstrated, amongst other things, a profound weakness in spirit. Not surprisingly, Zen was often embraced by the Bushido (for it tended to cultivate a similar sense of single-minded dedication to cause) and was often reflected in Bushido (the warrior code). I think the Japanese outlook here towards warrior-ship is a most sane approach. If you are fully engaged in defeating your enemy, then this practice is unavoidable. I suspect you know what I am driving at here, having been a top-notch national class skier yourself once upon a time.

Full attention is unwaveringly focused on attaining the goal at hand. As that great Wisdom Master Yoda, of Star Wars fame, once said to young protégée, Luke Skywalker, "Do or do not. There is no try." Kill or be killed. There is no giving up. To be taken prisoner is only "to try"—and quite possibly not bloody hard enough either. Adyashanti has often called waking up to reality a great big "bloody mess" that must be endured until transcendence occurs. Die or die not. That doesn't really leave much of a choice does it?

If a seeker is determined to vanquish delusion, then a ruthless and uncontrived earnest mindset is required. Certainly the case for me, as over time an increasing "bellicose stubbornness" arose to see this thing through to its natural conclusion. I am speaking here of the single most important matter that can ever confront someone, namely, life and death. And if a seeker were reading these words then that would be YOURS. You need to die.

Here is a snippet I wrote (below in italics) from a recent email I sent to a seeking friend which helps to demonstrate the kind of fortitude I found I required to awaken. Spoiler alert. No bullshit here, David. Just telling it like it is. If the thought of assisted suicide makes you at all squeamish best to skip this next part. And, if that is the case, why are we corresponding at all? LOL
DJ writes:

If it's assisted "die before you die in order that you may live" kind of thing that you are after, if you are looking for a spiritual "Dr. Kevorkian" of sorts, then I dare say I am your man. If you'll accept nothing less than that, then I'll point you

Chapter 9 | July

in the direction of the syringe, but you gotta push the plunger yourself. "Push the plunger you say"...what does that mean?

Little anecdote. Met a guy last year. Seventy-five years old. Said he was serious about waking up. Said he helped bring Gangaji to his town for the first time, was looking for a teacher for a long time, and was super glad to have stumbled upon me. I asked him if realizing his true nature was the most important thing in his life. Sure was, he assured me. So we started to look into the nature of BEING.

Problem was waking up wasn't as important as he thought. His actions (or lack thereof) talked way louder than his words ever did. Pointed this out to him. Later agreed that after a second look, probably was not so important to him. Took off on a month-long vacation to Peru. Never saw him again as I left town before he returned. Moral of the tale....many seekers are lying to themselves. Or they are utterly deluded. Probably the same thing eh? So, yeah, he really wasn't at all interested in pushing the plunger. Just talk. All talk. The ego loves it.

As Krishnamurti once said, "Don't take me for a spiritual entertainer." That's what that guy found out. I am not an entertainer, but, of course, I prefer humor to a blow on the side of the head when it comes to imparting the dharma. Huang Po (Chinese Zen guy) was famous for hitting and yelling. Not my style, though I may occasionally impart a metaphorical "Zen bitch slap" if the occasion arises. I have a real soft spot for sincere seekers, for I know so well how tough it can get. Poseur? I could care less.

So, as I intimated above, it's no more complicated than that. Just die into being. Be ruthlessly honest and meet "fierce grace" head on in a kamikaze death plunge to oblivion. This requires a sincerity or earnestness that few seem able to muster or, if they can, keep it up over the long haul. Tirelessly disengaging from egoic identification and ferreting out delusion at every turn, is surely found to be an intolerable bore for most who take it up for any length of time. Just look how fast they scramble to get into their cars, hit the accelerator and get the hell out of Dodge at retreat's end. I have used the term *radical honesty* before, but *ruthless sincerity* seems just as apt. For me it meant, both during the journey as well as presently, not being willing or able to sacrifice the truth for anything else on offer.

As I tried to explain to Harvey on the day I decided to no longer come out to the centre, "sugar-coated truth is not the truth." Truth is truth. If it's sugar-coated, it is something else. Just like Fruit Loops or Lucky Charms is something else (I call it dessert), when compared to a wholesome breakfast cereal such as muesli or granola. If I don't choose to make compromises regarding my selection of a morning meal, why the hell would I do so when it came to something far more important like discovering or talking about just what the fuck was actually going on?

But heh, that's just me. To each his own. If a seeker wishes to be coddled, and have "Mommy kiss the boo boo and make it all better," then so be it. Everything is allowed. What the heck, sounds like it could be fun, but let's not kid ourselves here: this inclination usually has precious little to do with Buddha's admonishment that we can indeed awaken to our own true nature in this lifetime. As I said above, it seems to me that direct-speaking, forthright guides are far more spiritually valuable, at least as far as awakening goes, than those that tend to pander to our baser instincts. If the Lama, guru, or new-age savant is promoting a free-sex lifestyle, asking for your money, has a huge collection of luxury cars or numerous real estate holdings all over the globe, it is probably best to eschew such individuals. If you want to have a rollicking good time, then why the hell not, eh?

Of course, it all boils down to what motivates you. For me it was the battle cry of "Sapere Aude"- daring to know for myself, by my own wise judgments, just what was what. Which meant discerning fact from fiction and routing out delusion. NOT figuring out correct beliefs, accruing "teachings" from all over the nation, as one would accumulate prayer beads on a mala, or indeed befriend spiritual buddies. In the end, none of it matters. Even teachers matter not a whit. You become alone in the world. Your true nature is aloneness itself.

I realize that this letter is getting on a bit, and I do apologize once again. In a sense, though, let it serve as the answer I forestalled giving you last year. Remember my short reply to a memorable message you sent me:

Thanks for your thoughts. Most appreciated.

I can't seem to formulate a meaningful reply save for one point: I am a fool through and through. Everything I say is nonsense. Why consider any of it? Rubbish I say. Bullshit, as you so wisely point out. Fortunately, there remains the great silence. In that, "stillness speaks" as Truth.

Cheers

DJ

At that time it seemed best to remain as stillness itself. Now it seems something stirs and this present email formulates itself as a kind of echoing response to your letter of a year gone by in which you may recall you penned the following:

> ...you have been at times very judgmental towards me and others in a way that doesn't feel supportive of true inquiry and a freedom to look into the nature of things or into myself. We've had some great conversations—very meaningful to me—and then some of the conversations have just seemed kind of nasty and

pushy. The puzzling thing to me is how you seem to feel justified in making disparaging, highly critical remarks about those who you consider not to be "awake." You've done this in the context of the meetings at K centre and other places and times.

Adya doesn't make these kinds of distinctions or criticisms at all and says so sometimes in his talks. Other teachers like Mooji also sometimes say they don't see any ignorance—only consciousness expressing itself in a myriad of ways. Maybe they speak sometimes from other perspectives also, but rarely if ever with condemnation or judgment, as far as I remember. I suppose you could argue this point in some ways, and no doubt will, but the issue for me is that it just doesn't appear helpful when inquiry contains this kind of criticism. I think you would get a much more receptive and open response from people if you were not so critical. And if you really want to help people, I think it might be something to look at.

How many people have responded openly to your absolute statements to the affect that "I know and you don't" or "I'm awake and you're not"? I've mostly seen people just closing down and avoiding any further conversation. Perhaps you are suffering from what Adya calls one of the last delusions: "I know what's true," or "I'm one who knows." The identification as the knower, perhaps the last stronghold of the spiritual ego. In my case I've sometimes, as you know, felt a reaction to fight with your apparent attitude rather than consider the truth of what you are saying. Of course, in the big picture it's hard to say what is needed and what is effective.

Anyway, I don't know what value this will have to say these things, but it just feels like I need to do it. I appreciate what we've shared and am open to continued exploration and friendship if you want to discuss from this point. These are thoughts that have surfaced and not the final word on anything.

I look forward to your consideration and response.

When you say (or said), "Adya (shanti) doesn't do or think so and so," my reaction is, "I couldn't care less what the man does or thinks." Again, it is only my own clarity, or lack of discernment thereof, that concerns me, not that of others. Though I have said, and will likely continue to say, that from the view afforded here it sure seems apparent that some teachers are "clearer" and have a lot less "agenda" on hand than others. You have articulated this point in the past as well. But if Adya's "spiritual GPS" points the way towards truth and freedom, then that is well appreciated, I assure you. It simply has nothing to do with my own awakening.

You said,
> Other teachers like Mooji also sometimes say they don't see any ignorance - only Consciousness expressing itself in a myriad of ways

That's well and fine, David, but, again, who cares? What do you know? Is this the absolute bona fide reality for you moment to moment? If not, then who the fuck cares? Let's talk about this when it is! When it comes to pass that for certain, beyond any shadow of a doubt whatsoever, it is utterly apparent (not to you - just apparent) that you are NOT and all that is IS, ALL simply is is-ing itself, and that there is no way to make any distinctions anymore that are actually perceived as real, then and only then will you know for certain that Mooji's statement is quite correct. Until then, it might be wise to stop using others to do your dirty work for you. If you were to presently tell me that you don't see ignorance at all anywhere, that everything is simply consciousness, then I would conclude either:

1. You were lying.
2. You were mentally ill.
3. You have naively confused a conceptual understanding for real recognition.
4. You were deluded
5. You were NOT, i.e., Truth or Buddha nature had realized itself and there was no going back.

I expect, though, that you would say nothing of the sort at this stage of the game, would you, as I bet none of those criteria apply in your case. If I am wrong, let me know. We will then have very much or very little to say to each other. So, again, perhaps it is best not to quote others until you directly know of what they speak for yourself. Just sayin'... Of course, that was how you felt last year. How about this one?

I would like to state that, contrary to what you believe (or at least felt last year...???...everything truly is in flux, isn't it?) Adya clearly DOES often make distinctions that point out egoic projection in a most direct and no nonsense fashion, such as, and I quote, "Step out of your dream of being a deluded person," or "You are insane," etc. Emulating another teacher's "shtick" interests me not. If I don't come across as being "Adya- like," so what? But are we both telling the truth? Aye, there's the rub. The goal is not to emulate Buddha but to realize Buddha nature yourself.

You know what else doesn't interest me? The things you suggest I may be "missing out on," like where you said, "I think you would get a much more receptive and open response from people if you were not so critical. And if you really want to help people I think it might be something to look at."

Obviously, cultivating receptive audiences, currying favour, "helping people," and accruing wealth, power, and prestige are things I don't seek (I've yet to even put my book up on Amazon, and it's been finished for years now - that's how little I care) since waking up is the end of all seeking. And how do we know this to be true? By the simple fucking fact that DJ don't want any of it. He simply don't want - full stop. Freedom is all there presently is. It's not that I am doing this "imparting the Dharma thing badly" and could use a few pointers or a helping hand to tweak the rhetoric and overall appeal of the message a bit, like one would employ a speechwriter or body language coach to improve his or her political image.

I very well know how to play the game, manage and manipulate people very skillfully, just like anyone else does. I once used to be in charge of a whole freakin' prison, for God's sake (position was actually known as IC - In Charge). The fact is, all that is over now. I well and truly received my wayfarer walking papers quite some time ago.

The book I just finished on the teachings of Zen revivalist and Song Dynasty Master Foyan, says it just as plainly when it speaks of this wisdom master's penchant for fostering autonomous thinking in his students and invigorating their practice at every turn.

Foyan was a rare master completely free of any desire for fame and followers. He made no attempt to recruit disciples. All he wanted was for people to open their own eyes and stand on their own two feet, to see directly without delusion, and act on truth without confusion.

If I were to claim to want anything at all, then let that stand as my testament as well. Yet it is not testament but bearing "fruit" that really interests us here, right? Sometimes it is sour, I agree. Sometimes the medicine is bitter, but while the mouth may object, the soul says " Yes, yes, yes." Silence really does sing...if we but have the ears to hear it.

DJ

Matthew 7: 15-20
New King James Version

You Will Know Them by Their Fruits

> Beware of false prophets, who come to you in sheep's clothing, but inwardly they are ravenous wolves. You will know them by their fruits. Do men gather grapes from thorn bushes or figs from thistles? Even so, every good tree bears good fruit, but a bad tree bears bad fruit. A good tree cannot bear bad fruit, nor *can* a bad tree bear good fruit. Every tree that does not bear good fruit is cut down and thrown into the fire. Therefore, by their fruits you will know them.

The Clothes Have No Emperor

24 July 2013

To: DJ

Hi DJ,

   Well, that's a pretty long letter and will need some time to be fully considered. There is just one thing at the moment. I did use Mooji's statements about no ignorance because "I" have seen the truth of it. It was a direct experience that arose during an Enlightenment Intensive (EI) and lasted in its clarity of "knowing" beyond mind for some hours. It was absolutely clear without a doubt that there is no such thing as ignorance. It's not something that can be true for a thinking mind—that could only be a concept—so, since the "knowing" faded and was a passing experience, I no longer assert it as a truth that I know for sure in the present. I don't take it to be untrue either, and it seems, more accurately, that I have no position on the matter and don't feel qualified to take any position. Memory tells me that a direct knowing of no ignorance existing is possible and in that state of knowing it is true. But perhaps most true at this point is a not knowing.

   Your point about the uselessness of quoting others if there is no direct understanding of what is being pointed to is heard. And if there is direct knowing, then why quote others anyway? Others may perhaps be quoted as a stimulus to look into an issue, as you yourself seem to do. That's it for now.

   Much more to consider...
   David

24 July 2013

To: David

You said,"..no position on the matter.... and not knowing..."

   Bravo! I enjoyed your initial response very much. Hope more like this is forthcoming. Your reminiscence about "momentarily seeing though ignorance" and your analysis of it and explanation of how it was a memory yet in a sense still informs your present experience was illuminating. Looking forward to your next letter.

   Cheers, DJ

∞ Chapter 10 ∞

August

1 Aug. 2013
To: DJ

Hi DJ,

Sorry, life seems to be very full these days, and it just hasn't happened to write you. Hopefully, some communication (more than this) will take place soon!

Hope all's well,
David

2 Aug. 2013
To: David

Sure, no problem. I'm cogitating over the principle that "great doubt and great faith" come hand-in-hand with awakening. You brought up the doubt part in passing long ago. It's something worth investigating further, so I am taking a shot at it. We'll see what comes of it.

Cheers,
DJ

The Clothes Have No Emperor

2 Aug. 2013

To: DJ

Hey DJ,

 One of the reasons I've been short on material to you was that the few times I felt inspired to write I was engaged with a member of our "Meditative Inquiry" group from the K centre and wanted to respond to a couple of questions he has posed. So, I think the material is relevant to our discussions and am forwarding it in two parts. I will still get back to your letter but not till next week as I'm busy at the K centre all weekend and Monday is a holiday with the library closed. Have a good weekend.

 Love,

 David

Subject: Written Inquiry
Date: 21 July 2013 18: 38: 23 -0700

Greetings Fellow Inquiry Group Members: Message from Rick

 At today's session we discussed how sometimes our thoughts can be untrustworthy---in other words, although powerful, not true.
 The questions arose: (1) How can we know for sure what *is* true in our experience and trust totally that it is true? (2) How can this knowledge improve our ability to communicate and facilitate the creation of harmony, peace and compassion?
 I have volunteered to compile your written responses to these questions, subsequent to your own personal inquiry, to:
- enhance continuity between our meetings
- support us in starting and continuing inquiries that could impact daily life
- maintain a written record of our work so that we know what we have been doing, as time passes
- offer any guests a written record of what the work of our group is about
- share the insights we are having while not physically present in the group

 If you would like to pursue an inquiry into these two questions and make written comments, please feel free to email them to me so I can put them altogether into one document.

 Peace!
 Rick

Subject: RE: Written Inquiry, David's response
Date: Fri, 26 Jul 2013 12: 21: 19 -0700

Hello Rick,

You never know what's going to happen it seems. At our last meeting I seemed to have some resistance to taking time in the summer to write up a response to your worthy questions (see the questions at the end). But while sitting at Thetis Lake yesterday, a fairly lengthy response arose, so here it is, my stab at the issue. It only addresses the first question, so another response may be forthcoming for the second question.

How can I know for sure what is true in my experience? What first arises is that thinking about any issue on which clarity is sought will be very limited. Thinking is usually mere speculation. It is not reliable as it is conditioned and is not direct experiencing or knowing. So what else is there? How about looking directly into my experience? Some teachers say "Look, don't think." They pose a question and then remain quietly open to how awareness will respond; this seems much more powerful than initiating a thought process. Direct seeing or insight may arise, a sense of a deeper, truer knowing. Is this seeing or insight dependable? It may not be the final word. Further, looking may reveal a more subtle truth or a new seeing of how it is. There must always be an openness to further revelation or unwrapping of the issue.

It seems to me that when looking for the truth, the question must be asked, "Who or what is doing the looking? " Any thought-created entity or observer will be conditioned or biased as a "me" with vested interests, a lens through which the looking is happening and which will distort the seeing. For any real clarity to be present this observer or "me" must be noticed or seen through.

What are we looking for? The truth of what is here? The truth of what we are? It is seen that any concept or thought about what is truly here, what is reality, is an overlay or imposition on something prior to thinking about it. It is seen that thought is always about reality but is not directly experiencing it. Thought creates a veil over reality so that seeing is muddied, obscured. But this, too, can be seen!

As all this is looked into and understood, it becomes clear that reality cannot be known by thought. All thought falls short of accurately perceiving what is. Even our perceptions, which we take to be truer than thinking, are often not trustworthy. For example, my mind's conditioned default perception is that the unknown is threatening. Death or dissolution is unknown and, according to my "normal" perception, is something to move away from, to be avoided. At a subtle level of thought the mind (thought itself) is creating ideas about all that it doesn't know—the unknown aspects of moment to moment experiencing, like what will happen the next moment—and retracting from being fully present. Thought actually believes that its interpretation of reality, of the unknown, is true, that the unknown is actually threatening, something to be avoided, a kind of black hole which will swallow me up, which I will not survive. In this instance, thought is creating an image of reality which is not at all true and calling it my perception. The unknown is not in fact threatening: It is merely unknown. It is not to be avoided; it is a truth of life. When there happens to be a letting go of resistance to the unknown, the experience is usually, in fact, one of joy, beauty, wholeness, and love.

So all thoughts and even perceptions are deeply flawed at times and probably always limited. When seen, this in itself is a great "truth." How can I be certain of its truth? It is not arrived at by thinking - or not by thinking alone. There is a clear seeing into these issues where no thought is interfering and there is a sense of knowing beyond speculation or analysis: A seeing with total attention. Again, though, this cannot legitimately become a conclusion. Any concept sustained after an insight immediately establishes a "tradition," a dogma of knowing the Truth

Can any truth be the final word? There is always the possibility of seeing more deeply, more widely, from slightly different angles, or in a new way all together. As soon as truth is known, it has become a limited concept about truth. Instead of believing that we can know anything for sure, how about being in a not-knowing openness? This seems more true and real than any knowing. And then the kinds of knowing that arise from this quality of presence or awareness are more likely to be informed and imbued with truth or reality. Of course, provisional knowings are necessary for functioning in the world but, as science now tells us, these are not accurate representations of what is actually here—which is at bottom a mystery!

Some spiritual teachers suggest that any assertion about what we are or what reality is, is only a concept and as such its truth can be argued about or challenged. There will always be at least two sides to any idea. They say the only thing we can know for sure is that we exist, that "I am." I am present. "Present as what?" gets more subtle.

For fun and interest I would like to inquire into this idea that "I am" is something I can know for sure to be true, but that will be the next installment.

Wow, once I got started on this it became quite lengthy. Words seem to be so cumbersome at times!

Enough for now,

David

2 Aug 2013

To: Rick

Subject: RE: Written InquiryDate: Fri., 2 Aug 2013 17: 01: 31 -0700

Hi Rick,

I'd like to continue with my answer to your question below on the topic of what is true and how we can know anything for sure. This will be going into subtle territory which many may not appreciate, but it seems interesting to me, so I'll now enter into an exploration of the idea that the only thing I can know for sure is that I exist or "I am." As far as it goes, this seems to be true and appears to be a solid foundation for self-inquiry and meditative practice. Nisargadatta recommended staying as the "I am" as much as possible. And yet he also said that staying as the I am will take "you" beyond it, and this is what I'm interested in exploring here. Rupert Spira says we are "awareness" and "presence" and, again, these are very useful pointers to our true nature and to freedom from the thinking mind and its projections. Not in opposition to these statements but as a further exploration, I would ask how I can even say that much unless thought is saying it. If there is no movement of thought, even the subtlest movement into subject and object perception, "what do I know about myself?" Do I know that "I am" or that I am Presence or Awareness? How do I know this and in what way? As an object of perception? If the mind is not objectifying, what does it know?

Can we ultimately confidently be sure of anything? Do we need to be? What about deep sleep where there is no awareness of presence or awareness? Awareness can be said to be present by logical deduction as something is aware when there's pressure on the bladder, for example. Some have said that they have experienced being aware in deep sleep and that would introduce a new factor into the exploration, but for most people there is no knowing of anything. Does not this state of deep sleep also happen when awake, a state between awakeness and sleep but neither of them, as in deep meditation and perhaps otherwise more often than we recognize? A state of not knowing anything but not being asleep.

This actually seems to be the natural state. Who or what am I then? Nothing can be said about it! No definition is possible. A definition or even recognition of anything as an object of perception requires a splitting of the mind into perceiver and perceived, observer and observed. This duality is the only means for identifying anything as being present, and thus it is a part of the functioning of consciousness in the manifest world, a necessary and legitimate aspect of the functioning. And then for some beings there may be an interest in exploring beyond the subject-object way of knowing. I find that when I follow such an inquiry, pay attention to how the mind is creating duality, there is often a shift in perception wherein there is a "knowing" but no information, nothing to be known. As soon as the first subtle movement of the mind arises, then I find words like Awareness, Presence, Wholeness, Love, Beauty, and so on are the closest descriptions of THAT (or THIS). Another word that seems to carry a resonance of that which is beyond conceiving is "mystery."

I hope all this is of some interest, but if not, it has at least been an interesting exploration for "me."

I would also like to explore the second part of your question, so here goes...

All the problems of human beings beyond, and probably even including, physical survival and security appear to be created by the belief in a separate "me." When the separate self is given belief and importance, immediately it must defend itself and seek its own continuity, often without consideration for the needs of others or the environment. The separate self is driven by fear as it is not in itself real or substantial but is a mere concept of thought, always unstable and insecure. Actions motivated by fear are rarely harmonious with the needs of the whole, of the total situation, and conflict is the result.

Asking what is really true about how I am conceiving life, the world, and especially others and myself, is, therefore, getting to the core of what is creating suffering and conflict in ourselves and the world. Looking into the nature of mind and thought, exposing the beliefs and assumptions behind how I function in life, has the power to weaken or dissolve the patterns of thought and belief that shape experience. When I function through the filter of the "me," then conflict is the result.

However, when the me is seen through, what remains is the spontaneous action of love and compassion, action which is attuned to the whole rather than just the perceived needs of the separate self.

How do I know this is true? My capacities of looking, feeling, intuiting, perceiving, and conceiving take me as far as possible in knowing the way of things in the world of relationship and manifestation and deliver the truth as far as the mind can presently perceive it. Beyond that there is, as explored above, a different kind of knowing or not-knowing.

And this is all, as always, subject to ongoing exploration and inquiry. From another perspective it may sometimes be seen that, in fact, there is no problem at all in this life, that everything is always in harmony and the whole is always nothing but itself, absolutely complete. But to directly experience such an understanding would seem to involve a transcendence of the thinking mind and the conventional way of seeing and knowing the world. Merely to believe it as a concept wouldn't have much value.

I trust our contemplations and dialogues are on track and serving us in our ongoing investigations of self and life.

David

2 Aug. 2013
To: David

"Seeing through the doings of the vain and suggestive ego makes it possible to be immune to its seductions." That is from Thomas Cleary's *Kensho: The Heart of Zen*. "Seeing through the doings," as it were, is not something I often see welcomed in group meetings or satsang.

If you recall that's a passage from the last thing I sent you. My first reaction to your latest sharing is gratitude for stepping up and taking a kick at the can. As I said, real truth telling happens infrequently but there are exceptions. Your material is a case in point. I hope that sometimes these days you dare to directly engage in similarly frank and sincere dialogue at the JK centre despite Harvey's (and your own ego's) misgivings. Back in the day, I never much saw this kind of thing welling up from you. Though as Dylan and the Buddha said (and you note in your own writings just sent) *"The times they are a changin'."*

Of that fact, impermanence, we can be assured. I read all of your material over a good two or three times. An absolutely brilliant piece of writing. Wonderfully structured. You hit most of the key points. Every single thing you spoke of concurs with the experience here. I think what I just read was very "skillful," as in the Buddhist ideal of using "skillful means" when imparting the Dharma. For what it is worth, my "bullshit detector" never once went off - and that was most surprising. Your part about what Spira had to say was terrific. When Rick asked, *The questions arose: (1) How can we know for sure what is true in our experience?*, I really appreciated how you turned that quote above around and asked "Who or what is doing the asking?" That happened pretty quickly in our inquiry as well, didn't it? We agreed that we both found it to be a terrific tool for sussing out the truth, didn't we? Reading your words today was like looking into the mirror. What do you suppose I saw? Thanks ever so much for sharing.

Namaste. I believe that this is the first time I have ever used that particular salutation. For some reason it presently rolls off my tongue very naturally and feels totally sincere in its expression.

Love,
DJ

PS If you do happen to feel inspired to offer some feedback on my last letter, I would surely welcome it. If it seems not to warrant it, then of course I welcome silence even more. If there is something else on your mind, let me know. As I indicated, I am looking into doubt and faith. Maybe something will come of it...

7 Aug. 2013
To: DJ

Chapter 10 | August

Hello DJ,

It's "nice" that you enjoyed and "resonated" with my latest writings. After sending them I was expecting you to punch a few holes in some of it, but when you replied and I read over again what I'd written; it did seem indeed quite clear and to the point. Imagine that! But I shouldn't get too self-congratulatory as I'm sure it won't last.

So now, looking again at your long letter of July 2 I'm first impressed by how you talk of "straight shooting." Very good analoies! And you certainly do seem to place yourself accurately on the spectrum. And the letter continues with so many telling points about directness and integrity. After first reading the letter, I thought I'd have a few challenges to present, but on reading it again just now those seem to have fallen away.

Some of what you wrote sounded at first like a bit of an advaita fundamentalist rant, and it seemed that maybe you were taking a position against what you describe as a kind of human weakness or failure to fully step up to the plate, implying that there is a doer who can by strength of will produce the results he desires. Taking any position is only something that can be done by a divided mind, isn't that correct? And doesn't it preclude compassion? I do realize that compassion can indeed show itself in the sword that cuts away delusion. Anyway, as I say, I now see nothing to take any position towards myself, more just a sense of listening to what is said without any conclusion and being open to the import of it, more of a question mark than any other form of punctuation. And, as I say, I find your expression to be direct and definitely potentially of great "value" when heard by ears that are in a readiness to hear.

You ask when I will wake up, "When is enough, enough?" and then you give the answer: "Exactly when it is." I must say that there's a sense of helplessness when this kind of question is asked by me or another. For sure the suffering of the separate self still arises or exists in this body-mind organism, but there is a seeing that in a very fundamental sense I can do nothing about it: Anything I could do is only the I seeking to continue, to avoid the Void. And I think that seeing is a truth. On the other hand, any strategy of mind to dodge the issue is a holding on to delusion.

You say I must die. Maybe we could look into this further: What does it really mean to die? What is it that must die and how does this happen? If there is in fact no I or separate self and it is only a mistaken idea, then why does that which doesn't exist have to die? Yet many have described different kinds of intense experiences of ego death. Others have said the idea of the "I" only needs to be seen through. I see through it but seem to have absolutely no control over the results of that seeing. There seem to be some other factors that are at play here. And is it in fact a problem at all, or is that only an idea of the divided mind? And who is saying that? Perhaps some fruitful questions for investigation.

Ok, enough for today...

David

7 Aug. 2013
To: David

Hi David,

Thanks so much for your reply.

Very good questions you have posed. I will take a crack at a few of them shortly. I am just finishing cogitating over a rather tricky topic.

The results of my labor feel truthy and relevant. I'll get them off soon to you and await feedback.

Cheers,

DJ

PS What was the gist of the reply from the chap you sent your terrific "pointers" to? Was your truthiness mostly lost in translation?

8 Aug. 2013
To: David

Hi David,

I recently purchased a several-hundred-years-old, antique Japanese calligraphy scroll drawn by famed Zen poet, hermit monk, and all around cool guy, Ryokan. I admire his wisdom and directness of approach, which he often put down in verse. Here is a snippet of something he wrote which encapsulates the content of the last long letter I wrote. You may agree our outlook appears similar in some regard:

Chapter 10 | August

> If someone asks what is the mark of enlightenment or illusion,
> I cannot say–wealth and honor are nothing but dust,
> As the evening rain falls, I sit in my hermitage
> And stretch out both feet in answer.
> The ridicule or praise of worldly people means nothing.
> This is an old truth; don't think it was discovered recently.
> "I want this; I want that"
> Is nothing but foolishness.
> I'll tell you a secret:
> All things are impermanent.
> I have nothing to report, my friends.
> If you want to find the meaning,
> Stop chasing after so many things.

The last email concluded with the reminder that "fruits" were the outcome desired when it came to spiritual awakening rather than the production of any number of words/concepts or "chasing after so many things," as Ryokan's passage above reminds us.

It's actual detachment from illusion, and transformation of self that demonstrates the nature of the fruit born. David, we both recognize that awakening has nothing to do with philosophical speculation, the adoption of new belief systems, or the rejection of old. That nonsense bears naught but more confusion. So what attitude then facilitates clear viewing? The following is what I discovered, and it involves an aspect you mentioned previously.

When I reflect back to how my journey unfolded, the Zen saying, "Having great faith, great doubt and great determination" (sincerity could be substituted for "determination" here quite easily) comes to mind and reminds me how these attitudes formed the nexus of the awakening process. This "truthy trinity" naturally welled forth in equal measure and helped create an environment favorable to radical transformation. I wonder, David, if you feel like speaking about this kind of thing in your own practice. You once brought up the subject of doubt (something about doubting the possibility of awakening as I recall), and I invited you twice to elaborate on the topic but you declined. I am most interested to hear what you have to say about it. Here are a few of my thoughts.

I think my last letter addressed the sincerity and determination aspect of the trinity pretty well. The fact that my own journey entailed totally uprooting myself from all that I held dear and adopting a steadfast inclination to accept nothing less than full realization of Self, or alternatively discover that spirituality was really nothing more than a canard, surely demonstrates my own sincerity and determination to get to the bottom of things. I have learned that if one sincerely wishes to awaken to the exclusion of all other desires it will by necessity become quite unavoidable.

It's not really all that hard to stop dreaming (the amazing thing is discovering just how much deceit and energy is required to keep the pretense from collapsing in on itself). But why would anyone want to awaken in the first place? That seems to explain why the masses slumber on. Awakening is a totally irrational act. How this drive gets going is still a mystery.

You may recall I wrote in *A Fleeting Improvised Man* about my penchant for looking into conspiracy in order to figure out how power was accrued and wielded. I also enjoyed investigating the paranormal and other matters of "high strangeness" like quantum mechanics, UFOs, and telepathy, etc. I had doubts that the ordinary, mundane representation of worldly affairs commonly presented in mainstream media really told the whole story. By deeply investigating the supernatural (which is entirely natural save for our own ignorance), the occult (the word itself simply means hidden from plain sight), as well as learning how the real power brokers in the world operated, I slowly discovered things were not at all as they appeared. But these realizations didn't go far enough. As old-time radio show host Paul Harvey always promised, I too wanted to know "the rest of the story."

Chapter 10 | August

In order to discover "the whole truth and nothing but" my position had to be that of skeptic (the Zen beginner's mind of "show me") but never cynic (don't bother me with the facts: my mind is already made up). Buddha speaks of this healthy attitude in this way:

> Now, Kalamas, don't go by reports, by legends, by traditions, by scripture, by logical conjecture, by inference, by analogies, by agreement through pondering views, by probability, or by the thought, 'This contemplative is our teacher.' When you know for yourselves that these qualities are skillful, these qualities are blameless, these qualities are praised by the wise, these qualities, when adopted and carried out, lead to welfare and to happiness — then you should enter and remain in them.

The Kalamas, Buddha's nearby countrymen, were confused by the multiplicity of teachings they heard. They asked of Buddha, "Which of the visiting venerable Brahmans and contemplatives were speaking the truth, and which ones were lying?" They were a doubtful people and wanted to hear which sages they should trust. Buddha wisely explained it was not a matter of belief but rather a process of determining for yourself by your own experience just what was true and what wasn't. David, I know you are familiar with this quote, but I like to reflect upon it from time to time as it is an astonishingly truthful thing to say... and an even greater profundity to realize for yourself.

This is the kind of skillful, healthy doubt I engaged in, not the cynical, "foxy doubt" Chan master Foyan advises us to avoid at all cost. David, when you spoke of doubt regarding the possibility of awakening, I wondered if that pondering stemmed from egoic foxy doubt or was perhaps caused by something entirely different. The so-called foxy doubt I am referring to here is a highly conditioned, mechanical, knee-jerk reaction the ego uses to resist or discount the possibility that one can awaken to true self (for to do so will unavoidably cause its own demise) or indeed, even more pointedly, can discover that presently I am already THAT. Now them's fightin' words!

Of course, most spiritual aspirants learn at one time or another from some learned sage or guru that enlightenment is utterly impossible, for who would remain to claim this enlightened state once the self had dropped. Good point, but clearly the dream of me or the inclination to "self," as Paul Hedderman puts it, can indeed cease for all intents and purposes. So I say that if one says, "I doubt awakening is possible," this statement is factual for them, this is how they feel about it, but I assure you it is not born out of truth realization.

Instead, of being born out of truth realization, it is delusional and is merely a product of foxy doubt. Clearly, Buddha and other awakened sages state for the record that they are indeed awake, or more accurately still, no longer entranced by the dream state. Rather than treat enlightenment as a speculative point of inquiry, wake up to your own true being fully, and then let's speak of doubt again in passing. I assure you we will have little to discuss.

Again, David, what kind of doubt were you pointing to so many months ago? Was it that kind embodied by the ever skittish, distrustful and wily fox/ego or rather that stemming from an aspirant driven to shed a false persona once and for all? Maybe it was neither. If that is the case let me know.

Ordinarily, we envision faith and doubt as mutually exclusive concepts but this was not the case in my journey. Great faith and great doubt were not held in opposition but rather supported each other in mutual benefit. Without doubt there is no faith, without faith no doubt. Doubt here is the kind of healthy spiritual investigation Buddha suggested the Kalama's might be wise to engage in.

During my journey healthy skepticism came very naturally for the reasons I already articulated above. I was surprised, though, to find faith naturally welling up as well. This is the inclination to trust the gut and let things be as they were, to trust that things would naturally work themselves out by their own accord. This feeling/realization was both consoling and a little scary at first. I imagine the feeling might be a bit like letting go of the tiller of the sailboat I once piloted years back and then discovering that the darn thing didn't need a helmsman in the first place. It could navigate quite well all by itself. Weird!

True spirituality demands faith but not the kind religious nutters…err…"persons of faith" engage in. That is blind and requires rigid adherence to dogma, doctrine and policy with an unquestioning obedience. Where some schools require us to believe in saintly miracles, divine beings, and future realms to come, despite presenting not a single shred of evidence, Buddha tells us to question everything. Of course, that would include the very words he speaks. I find this honesty just as refreshing as when I recall Lao Tzu telling us the Tao that he can speak of is "not the real Tao." Faith is not simply taking someone else's belief system and accepting it for the "gospel." That practice is better known as delusion. Faith is trusting in your own ability to discover what is wise, truthful, and relevant via means not typically involving the rational movement of conceptual mind.

So it is that faith, doubt and determination work together in a kind of symbiotic relationship much like the constituent parts of blind Japanese swordsman Zatoichi's staff do. Zatoichi has the soul of a monk and the skill of a samurai. He lives in dangerous times full of intrigue and banditry.

Forever in his grasp is a walking stick cum sword, but here for the sake of metaphor I will call it a "spiritual staff." He relies upon it to help him wander about the world. It points the way ahead with the promise that things will end well. The handle of the staff is always grasped with great determination in order that it is never relinquished.

The other end of the staff represents doubt which he uses to cautiously poke about the inky black void in front of him.

Faith is represented by the concealed blade. He trusts that this unseen blade will always keep him safe and lead him to salvation despite the harrowing circumstances he encounters along the way. His enemies never realize until it is too late that the faith he has in skillful wielding of sword will always vanquish them. Zen literature speaks of a great sword as well, and it, too, vanquishes delusion at every swing.

Like Zatoichi's staff, we too need to discover the rod of great doubt and faith if we are to ever wander the world freely ourselves. Of equal importance, great determination is necessary for it is what allows us to pick up the staff in the first place. Once the rod is firmly in hand, tremendous fortitude allows it to never be dropped. For me this meant absolute unwavering orientation away from delusion. If any of those three constituent elements are lacking, I don't think the prognosis for awakening is very favorable.

When I speak of faith I am pointing to something entirely different from what the dogmatists and absolutists usually suggest we embrace. My faith was not comprised of conceptual certainty of belief but more like tacit trust in self and the world at large. A trust born of "fruit." Here I am in part speaking of trusting the guidance of others. And this became easier and easier for me since what the spiritual guides I admired most were speaking of, little by little, became my own reality as well. For example, a teacher might talk of non-doing pure Beingness or use the term "spacious awareness," and I would know exactly what they were talking about. It was very easy then to entertain the possibility that some other pointer they were using, though still unfamiliar, might be worth considering or investigating. This trust is couched in reality and is aided by healthy skepticism. I knew certain teachers were telling me the truth because some of the stuff they were saying was already my experience.

Similarly, there was a trust in the intuitive self to know what was best. Great faith became ever more present as the journey unfolded. Trust that the more "I" stepped out of the way and let this thing (the ineffable mystery) propel itself forward on its own accord, the better the chance TRUTH would be realized all by itself. This form of faith or trust was not something I was very versed with since ego tends to be reticent and wary of anything it doesn't understand.

Once embraced, though, trust and following intuition (the small quiet voice we rarely pay much attention to) was recognized to simply be part of the natural way of things. Again, faith and doubt are not found to be mutually exclusive since they merely mark the path of the middle way when embraced in equal measure. I might add, too, that since fear was always a constant companion, faith was the antidote to what scared me. I guess it had to be, since there was nothing else to console me. Not very far into my journey I was one day informed exceptionally clearly during a direct wakening experience that I should be "careful what I wished for, since it would definitely come to pass."

This "knowing" was both consoling and frightening at the same time. In fact, it so unnerved me that I went to the Lama to discuss whether or not this awakening thing was the kind of enterprise I really should be looking into. Thereafter, I had faith that this thing would see itself through to a natural conclusion of sorts. Later, when I learned that what this entailed was the complete dissolution of self, I naturally became quite distraught for a while, but always in the background a certain tacit faith held things together.

More and more the "beginners mind" or "don't know mind" Zen folks are so fond of mentioning came to the fore. Though at the same time doubt helped keep me on the straight and narrow avoiding the numerous spiritual cul-de-sacs of delusion I saw so many wander down. This was not the doubt of a cynic. That doubt is poison. Foyan advises that the antidote to that is "wonder." Another wise teacher said, "Sell your cleverness and buy bewilderment." I once recall hearing that great altered statesman of the psychedelic experience, Terence McKenna, say upon being asked if DMT caused a dangerous state: "Only if you fear death by astonishment." Astonishment doth hath power to cause miracles if we only have the faith to "look." Here I mean the element of trust required to peer into the void, the faith necessary to gaze into the mirror of SELF, to not turn away, and thus to let the astonishment carry you away once and for all. Anything less simply won't do.

    Love,
    DJ

13 Aug. 2013
To: DJ

Hello DJ,

    I have been contemplating my own questions regarding seeing through the sense of the separate "I" and what is it that has to die. Thought I'd share a few perceptions. The insight that there is, in fact, no separate I and that I am nothing but a thought or projection of mind and have no substantial reality seems to be a crucial aspect of inquiry and "awakening." From this perspective there is no I or ego that has to die; it was only a mistaken belief in the first place and never actually existed. It was only necessary to see through the idea that I exist as an independent entity.

But then comes the other aspect of this "process." This idea of the "me" has been present since early childhood and has been reinforced millions of times since then in almost every interaction and experience. In other words, there is a very strong conditioned and unconscious belief in the reality of "me." Even though the me idea is seen through, it seems to persist as an energetic and mental reality which affects the experience of living in a palpable way and continues to create suffering. (The suffering, however, is substantially weaker and the I is not given anything like the same reality it had before.) It is this lingering concept of the I that has to die. It may gradually wither away as it is seen again and again to be no more than a thought or there may be a more dramatic event where the ego seems to go through a death, leaving the being radically free of the limitations of the "I" sense.

Even these dramatic self dissolutions don't appear to always (if ever) mean that a sense of a "me" never arises again. Apparently when Ramana Maharshi was asked if the I thought ever arose for him, he replied something like, "The I thought arises, but I see it for what it is and it does me no harm." The dissolution of the I as an energetic reality seems to happen at its own pace and to be beyond the control of the apparent individual. The effect or impact of witnessing the I concept as it arises and inquiring into its reality is felt, but there seems to be no way to control the process so as to bring a total dissolution. It would seem that the more attention (described as vigilance by some) one gives to the seeing through of the I, the more powerful the dissolving would be. And yet, as I say, there is the sense of helplessness in ultimately having no control. The helplessness seems to be a significant experience, inviting a letting go of all strategies for change or attainment of anything. Helpless before God has a different sense to it (than helplessness before other humans or an uncontrollable life).

What is your experience in relation to what I've written here?

Over to you...

David

PS The fellow who initiated the discourse on what can be known for sure seems to be a pretty deep inquirer and to be genuinely looking into all this.

13 Aug. 2013
To: DJ

I just realized I haven't yet read all of your "trinity" letter and even more so have not replied.   May take a few days at least...

David

13 Aug. 2013
To: David

Geez, and I tried to make that last letter extra short...LOL

> I will respond to your thoughts very shortly. Thanks for getting the ball rolling on this one. Good starting points. I'll expand on some of it and add several other ways to look at this challenging topic.
>
> Cheers, DJ

16 Aug. 2013
To: DJ

Hello DJ,

Your letter is definitely not short, as you (humorously) claim!

You say I declined twice to respond to your question about my doubts concerning full enlightenment. I'm pretty sure I did respond some time ago with something like as follows. My doubt was about any claim that a state of "perfection" is reached where one is infallible or no longer subject to the tendencies of being "human" or expressing as "ego," in other words, the idea that all ego is wiped out and never is a factor in behaviour or vision. I have seen a number of so-called enlightened beings claim that their enlightenment is total and irreversible only to then display actions and attitudes that seem far from enlightened.

Some cases that come to mind are Osho, Adida, Trungpa, Andrew Cohen, perhaps Krishnamurti, and I'm sure many more. It looks like maybe their idea of a full and permanent enlightenment was a delusion and fraught with arrogance. And my question was about whether or not one can ever say there is no more delusion on any level or no more active tendency to express as a (small) self. You say that the "fruits" of realization are what is important and include in them "the transformation of self." You seem to be pointing to the issue of action and expression. Even if you just mean the dissolution of self rather than the transformation, still I wonder if that dissolution can be said to be complete if the individual is displaying obvious or subtle egoic tendencies. And then there is the question of how can we or how do we judge or discriminate. Which leads to the next statement below...

I also replied that I no longer have any fixed belief about the matter but more a curiosity. It never meant that I doubt the possibility of authentic awakening. I just wondered, and I suppose still wonder, if I think about it, what that actually means in terms of how it manifests in

Chapter 10 | August

daily life and interactions. Are the claimed enlightenments always as real and far reaching as claimed?

I'd say that your words on doubt and faith do mostly match my experience as far as it goes. You may have gone more deeply into the actual import of the words by whatever means - I would say by grace or the intent of the Whole.

Note: It has become a point of question and observation lately to look at how the mind slips out of fully confronting its own subtle or not so subtle escape mechanisms and can use true sounding non-dual-like concepts to support its own status quo. It seems a "fruitful" inquiry.

That's all for now.

David

18 Aug. 2013
o: David

Let's attempt to examine what it is that actually dies...or dies not...but first...in Zen, they say something to the effect that "If you speak, you're wrong from the start. If you don't speak, you're deeply confused."

Damned if you do, damned if you don't. Furthermore, as I said awhile back, I had to come to terms with being wrong over and over again as Truth inexorably revealed itself to itself. Admitting that one has erred or more precisely realizing your very nature is error itself, can't be avoided forever. Of course, that's the way it is. Quite predictable really. That's what happens when you discover you are utterly deluded. Eventually there was an openness here to simply see things as they were. Resistance was found to be quite futile.

"The mind is the Buddha"—this is the medicine for sick people.

"No mind, no Buddha"—this is to cure people who are sick because of the medicine."

Seems like another pertinent Zen pointer well worth considering and is certainly germane to what follows, though in the end no amount of medicine actually "cures." The hope is that the patient expires as quickly as possible regardless of the treatment administered, unlike the case with conventional medicine.

I have broken this letter into 2 parts as I expect the last one was tedious, and this is lengthy as well. The next part I will send once I return from my ramblings down the rail trail and beyond. To get to the lake on foot should take the better part of a week, I reckon. Talk to you again when I return.

You said:

>...there is a very strong conditioned and unconscious belief in the reality of "me." Even though the me idea is seen through, it seems to persist...

David, I completely understand what you mean about the conditioning centred around self. I do sympathize with you but, again, I wonder what you mean when you say "see through" and further wonder of what "value" this has been in practical terms. Is spirituality a results-oriented enterprise, as Adya suggests it should be? Could the following serve at least in part as your answer?

(The suffering, however, is substantially weaker and the I is not given anything like the same reality it had before.)

If so, then, to paraphrase, would you conclude that Maya still very much rules the roost...just to a lesser degree than previously? Self-ignorance may be diminishing, endarkenment becoming less prevalent, but David is still fundamentally a deluded fool, right? I have never heard you describe yourself in such candid terms. Have you ever entertained the possibility? This is not a personal attack, for that was how I viewed myself while awakening. As I was still dreaming, naturally I had to conclude that I was very confused. Does this outlook seem peculiar to you?

> Explaining a dream while
> in the midst of a dream
> in broad daylight
> Mahaprajnaparamita Sutra

That pretty much describes how the situation is in so-called normal (anything but) consensual reality. Realizing this, I also recognized that this dream is a particularly wacky state of affairs to be dwelling in. If not a confused dream character, then who or what are you, David? For most seekers the ego seems exceptionally reticent to take itself less seriously and make such truthful pronouncements, but if one is in "the view," I daresay it will become unavoidable. You probably feel I am being pushy here. Perhaps you feel I have gone too far, but certainly my intent is not to insult. All I can do is encourage you to consider the wisdom of Chuang Tzu's words below; he knew a thing or two about dreams:

> It is only after a great awakening that we know all this is a great dream.
> Fools, by their own accord, consider themselves to be awake,
> And go about in a knowingly fussy way,
> defining one man as a gentleman,
> and another as a rustic. How hard-headed
> is this!
> Confucius and you (DAVID) are both dreaming.
> And I, who tell you that you are dreaming,
> am dreaming, too. Even these words
> themselves may be called a great deception.

You said, "It is this lingering concept of the I that has to die."

Become extinguished, yes indeed.

"It may gradually wither away as it is seen again and again to be no more than a thought or there may be a more dramatic event where the ego seems to go through a death, leaving the being radically free of the limitations of the "I" sense."

This "withering away" business definitely seems to be happening as things unfold. Seems like progress is being

made, I agree. Perhaps an example of a "result" or indicator of seeming transformation going on. Though, of course, transformation is not what really happens, for there is no one left at the end of it all to claim to be renewed. But as I say, transformation is seemingly a possibility when one is deep in the throes of the spiritual journey.

Considering your feeling about "leaving the being radically free of the limitations of the "I" sense," I am inclined to say that nothing is "left," nor "not left." In actuality no being exists that is encumbered or later freed from bondage, though I would not argue that there may appear to be an entity when you take yourself to be a self. Pure Beingness yes, but no "being" in and of itself. The MIND or NON-MIND, take your pick, does not know itself. No objectification, no being, no noun; perhaps a verb at best.

Even these dramatic self dissolutions don't appear to always (if ever) mean that a sense of a "me" never arises again. Apparently when Ramana Maharshi was asked if the I thought ever arose for him he replied something like, "The I thought arises, but I see it for what it is, and it does me no harm."

I hesitate to say this but you are really muddying the waters here. Much confusion, I am afraid. If what happened to Ramana is the same as the abiding non-dual awareness here—and I have no way of knowing, but for sake of argument I will presume it is—then the experience for the both of us when the self dropped, the dream ceased, etc., was not a state that came and went. The SELF, or NON-SELF, is realized and that's that (though in a sense that realization begins another unfolding or deepening of sorts…). Therefore, I tell you with absolute confidence the "I thought" does not exist post enlightenment. If it does, you ain't ALL THAT!

I assume Ramana is speaking here of thoughts that have no power to entrance him so they are not "I thoughts" at all. They are not "I thoughts" like you imagine them to be. For "me," notions infrequently pop into "my" field of awareness unbidden but pass away just as quickly. They have no power to sustain themselves. I am quite sure that this is what Ramana meant. Before the ground of being appears and wipes all objectification away, thoughts revolve entirely around the little me concept. They can be ignored or suppressed for a short period through meditation techniques but invariably return, and there is an "I" present that claims ownership over them. If the clothes truly have no emperor, then are "I thoughts" possible? Wouldn't the prerequisite for having I thoughts be the existence of self? Do rocks and chunks of iron have I thoughts? No. Please consider me a rock, or a fool if you like, it's all the same to non-me. You might revisit Bernadette Roberts as she really does a fine job of presenting what non-self really feels like.

After self-ing no longer arises, thoughts in no way resemble what they once were. In truth I could say I no longer have any thoughts at all, since there is no one present to have them. You might imagine that presently my thoughts are somehow "emasculated" or "disempowered" in some way, but it is not like that. Thoughts associated with the so-called past and future seldom arise and are simply of no consequence when they do. To even say that they are unacknowledged lends them too much credence. With no "I" present there are no thoughts that get identified with, so in a sense there are no thoughts at all (sure, cognitions happen, but that is not what I am pointing to here). Of course, I am speaking here of thoughts that pertain to the so-called future or past. Cognitive ability is not impaired. Memories can be recalled if need be, problems solved, or plans carried to fruition just as before. The difference is no one is attached to any of it.

> The helplessness seems to be a significant experience, inviting a letting go of all strategies for change or attainment of anything. Helpless before God has a different sense to it.

This helplessness you speak of, "the one before God," as you so wonderfully put it, is really quite exquisite isn't it, and seemingly a necessary part of the journey? Really worth pursuing wholeheartedly if identification is still going on. Your feeling of helplessness seems to me to be an authentic reaction to the absurd proposition of "destroying the self to find the Self." Isn't it the case that from your viewpoint there is nothing but utter helplessness? I know you long ago discovered that you have no control over anything at all...or did you?

One can't even control such basic things as their own thoughts. In this clear seeing the seeds of freedom are born. I found out that I didn't make my thoughts so the idea of choice and control was found to be utterly illusory. Thoughts just appear unbidden, as we both know so well. I ask you, David, where's the choice in that? Pretty helpless, eh? Good for you. That's authentic. I say wallow in it. Better still, why not indulge in hopelessness too while you are at it? Stop trying to avoid reality. Come to terms with it. A good place to start is admitting your shortcomings and failures, but this is only the start. See how you speak untruths as soon as you open your mouth. Then go beyond even that. Get terribly confused. Lose your mind. It's all grist for the mill. Then, at long last say "fuck it all" and give up entirely. Et voila, absolute freedom.

For sure the suffering of the separate self still arises or exists in this body-mind organism but there is a seeing that in a very fundamental sense I can do nothing about it. Anything I could do is only the I seeking to continue, to avoid the Void. And I think that seeing is a truth.

Above you said, "I can do nothing about it." I concur. In truth you can't do anything at all, but it sure appears like you can until one day this is no longer so. David certainly "does" his best all day long, doesn't he? You have told me how busy you are this summer. Busy is the result of a "doing" isn't it? You own the experience don't you? The plain and simple fact is, David is a busy body. So I am at a loss when I hear people say, "I can do nothing about where my identification lies," yet they are only and always engaged in nothing else but "doingness" and active identification with self. Have you ever wondered what not doing really means? Not "I am not doing" but that of the eternal kind. If that doesn't give you pause, then you are not doing (is there no way to once and for all abolish this blasted word?) it right.

Seeking does in fact, just as you say, result in avoiding the void but not seeking results in the very same outcome. It's a paradox. What is required here is a "doingless doing." In my experience waking up to reality required a sense of great urgency but at the same time seeking no outcome. I desperately wanted to find out "the TRUTH," but I had no idea what that could be. Therefore, there was no concrete sense of a tangible goal. I never attempted to acquire spiritual jargon, learn chants, find my higher self nor appear spiritually hip. That would have been to engage in window dressing or "rearranging the deck chairs on the Titanic," as Adya is fond of saying.

To be sure "doing" occurred, but precisely doing what? For me it became an "undoing" of sorts, as I mentioned many times before. It's a bit like fishing with rod and reel. I have found that the best strategy to catch a whopper with hook and worm was to cast the bobber into the water as far as possible and do nothing... sort of. Letting the line float a good long time was the key to success so resisting the urge to reel it in prematurely was paramount. Still I had to be attentive. Sometimes a boat would float close by, forcing me to reel the bobber in a bit. Sometimes a gust of wind would force the bobber too close to seaweed beds. Maybe I would spot a jumping fish and tug the line a bit in the direction of the ripples. Keep incessantly reeling the line in in order to cast again and nothing will be hooked at all. Do nothing at all and you will lose your hook on a seaweed snag or half-submerged log. Same result. Non-duality "fishing" will assuredly hook the prize, though it will not be the trophy-sized keeper you expected. It's the booby prize of all booby prizes. You proudly put your "catch" on the scale and it weighs precisely nothing. How disappointing.

Has this "non-doing doing" worked in a similar fashion for you? Taoists refer to this practice as *wei wu wei*. Richard Rose called it "inbetweeness." It seems to run through all paths that lead to awakening. Obviously nothing new here, but I thought you might enjoy my musings.

While doership was still seemingly going on for me, and that was the case right up to paradigm shift, my strategy was one of shifting identification as much as possible away from delusion. Neo-advaitists wonder if undermining the ego is worthwhile or even possible. At the time it sure seemed to be an important part of my practice. As I say, why not be inclined to make yourself grace prone if that seems possible? If there seems to be a doer, then do well. If there is no doer, then you will be awake and the inability to do will be self-evident. I find the "doing nothing" position certain aspirants adopt to be contrived and likely tabled by the ego and, frankly, seeming a bit phony. I think some of these folks are operating from wily foxy egoic mind ""mantracism" (the repetitive endless drone of "there is no one here, there is nowhere to go and nothing to do, there are no students nor teachers, you are already that", etc., etc.) rather than healthy authentic abiding non-dual awareness.

Your co-blogger Josh's compulsion to write almost every day and perpetually quote others seems a good case in point. Man, that guy seems to almost have the religious fervor of a holy-roller sometimes and sure has a lot to say for someone who doesn't even exist! I mention this to demonstrate how pernicious and sneaky delusion can be. The question, "Am I deluded? " seems a pertinent one and should be revisited often. Whenever I found a self present, the obvious answer was "Yes." How about you, David?

You say I must die. Maybe we could look into this further: What does it really mean to die? What is it that must die, and how does this happen? If there is in fact no I or separate self, and it is only a mistaken idea, then why does that which doesn't exist have to die?

I wonder if you are in fact confirming the very thing you are trying to refute. Do you mean it is ok to tolerate or ignore the "I thought" since it doesn't really exist…? "not really"… kind of thing? Or, rather, do you mean that there is nothing to die as the little me does not inherently exist in the first place? If it is the former, then you are confirming your belief in doership and small "s" self. If the latter, it must actually be embodied, and then it is self-evident.

If there is a self, apparent or otherwise, it must disappear, evaporate and cease to exist. I have never felt inclined to use the term "apparent self." If the I-thought is "no longer" why would I use such a term? There is no "I" here presently, apparent or otherwise.

On the other hand, when I was "self-ing" that was precisely what was occurring—all the time. So to speak of the "apparent self" at that time would have been to contradict reality as it was, for there bloody well was a self back then. When the paradigm flipped there wasn't. It's really that simple. Just a small tweak in identification. Now you see me, now I don't. Finding true freedom does not involve keeping up appearances or trying to be spiritually correct, as Jed McKenna warns us. Distilled to its quintessential point, spirituality entails only waking the fuck up! No more complicated than that. All the rest is bullshit.

What a wonderful thought to end on for now. Talk to you soon. Really anticipating your reply.

Cheers,
DJ

24 Aug. 2013
To: DJ
HelloDJ,

I've been sitting in front of the computer looking over your letter for quite some time now. There is certainly a great deal worthy of consideration or inquiry or looking into and there are so many points I could respond to for further clarification in the process as not all you say seems at first, second, or even third examination to be quite the way it appears to me. (But then, as you say, I could no doubt be called a "deluded fool").

It feels a bit overwhelming and there's a kind of paralysis with the prospect of going into all the issues that are raised. I guess maybe it would be best to print it out and spend time at home with it, but so far I don't know how to do that as the computer doesn't break it down into separate pages for printing. Maybe have to break it down myself and create separate pages. But beyond that I feel a lack of motivation to pick apart all these seemingly subtle points and distinctions which may be sometimes a matter of semantics, but obviously sometimes not, and sometimes maybe a case of apparent dualities where there is in fact no duality. You suggested I get into hopelessness. Well, that's what I'm feeling at the moment.

As I said before, there have been many insights that the "me" does not exist as anything more than a thought, and yet a sense of me keeps arising. You say there is either a self or not, but for "me" at some moments there is the experience of a self and some moments not. There are so many paradoxes and contradictions in words and explanations. As you quote, "If you speak you're wrong from the start" and so on. It is seen that paradox and confusion are only in the "mind" or thought. We have previously inquired and found that the truth is beyond all concepts, so what meaning does confusion have and what is the need to clear it up? But I suspect you will question that statement itself. You seem to be continuously pointing to the fact that I am not directly experiencing the truth of no-self. I'm not claiming that I am. I'm experiencing whatever I am and inquiring into it. Will this kind of inquiry bring about the awakening you are saying has happened to you? Will my awakening be the same as yours? Maybe, I don't know...I do think that essentially there is indeed value in the exercise.

There seem to be so many things I could say at this point but to what end? Right now, I just don't seem to have the energy to get into it all but now have exerted energy to write this "complaint." I guess that's what there was at least some energy for, but it feels like a kind of venting and probably not of much value ultimately. And yet it's what is happening.

I wonder if it might be more helpful when you write to address only one or two issues at a time, otherwise it lately often seems like too much, and I tend to gloss over some of what is being said. If I read your words and they have an impact, then well and good, but I'm wondering what is the most effective way for this to be possible. I really don't know. This present "mood" will no doubt pass, and who knows what will occur next? Anyway, to sum up, there is definitely some resistance happening here and maybe the most productive thing is as much as possible to just let it be, be it, be the knowing of it, or however it would be described to not be a doer in relation to whatever is arising and to not try to not be a doer! We'll see what happens next...

Hope you had a good hike and are feeling well,
David

26 Aug. 2013
To: DJ

Hello again,

I was definitely feeling physically tired when writing my last letter; I'd had a poor sleep the night before. Will see if energy comes to respond more directly to your letter...David

26 Aug. 2013
To: David

Hi,

Just got back minutes ago from a week-long hike down rail tracks past Procter and back, all on foot. Giant loop: First rail then ferry to highway and back. Camping along the way. Quite exhausted. Walked five hours straight today. "Tired" – that makes two of us.

I read your previous letter with some interest. Mostly for what you didn't say. Wonder if, besides fatigue, your ego didn't enjoy the kind of investigation I was proposing. Perhaps too close to home.

Perhaps if you review my letter again and address the points you think are most salient. I am keen to see which ones you choose.

I include many points of inquiry as I have no way of knowing which ones will resonate with you on which particular day. And maybe the ones that don't strike your fancy have merit too.

I do hope you look closely again about the points regarding delusion, but it is entirely up to you.

Printing it out is a good idea. Maybe copy it and paste to MS notepad at library; then send to printer. Notepad is found in accessories.

You can use your home computer to formulate a response in Notepad as well. Then save on thumb drive...bring to library and copy/paste into your email.

Love,
DJ

26 Aug. 2013
To: David

Little extra point regarding admission that one is a "deluded fool." Do you take this to be a pejorative admission best avoided at all costs? I get the feeling time and time again that you do. For me this admission was just a fact but a very wonderful revelation indeed, like Ebenezer Scrooge seeing through his delusion and wasted years. In fact, I recall he sang a little ditty upon "awakening" from his dream about what a fool he had been with great compassion and glee in his voice and spirit.

Do you know Zen master Ryokan's full name means "broad-hearted generous fool"? The ego disdains such labels. I relish it. Jed McKenna has his "Wise Fool" press.

Lao Tzu in the *Tao Te Ching* says:

> Others have more than they need,
> But I alone have nothing. I am a fool.
> Oh, yes! I am confused.
> Other men are clear and bright,
> But I alone am dim and weak.
> Other men are sharp and clever,
> But I alone am dull and stupid.
> Oh, I drift like the waves of the sea,
> Without direction, like the restless wind.

Maybe you can get a sense of what I mean. The literature is rife with such descriptions if you go looking for them. I am using the term differently than you suppose. The "fool" knows nothing and knows that he knows nothing, and in that, freedom and great merriment dwell. I am a fool. This much is clear. If you ever come to recognize this fact yourself, know it intimately, then perhaps you will have occasion to recognize it here as well and honor me from time to time with the moniker "silly old fool." What a pleasure that would be.

Maybe then we could argue over who is "dumb and dumber." LOL

Cheers,

DJ

27 Aug. 2013
To: DJ

Hello DJ,

This is a surprising bit of information you've added. I did get the feeling, you are suggesting, I think, as a kind of self-projection, that you were being pejorative the way you used the words and this latest seems to be a sudden about turn, which is a little puzzling as the two senses of the words are very different. If I take myself to be a deluded fool in the pejorative sense, then I truly am one as any self-definition or self-image is deluded and not the emptiness that really is.

If I take myself to be enlightened or awakened I am then, too, a deluded fool, as they are just better-sounding concepts or self-images. To see after the fact "with great compassion and glee" that one was a fool is (it seems to me) very different than labelling oneself in a critical manner with the idea that such self-criticism will actually help one to become something better. Wouldn't it be just affirming the existence of an entity who is such and such, whatever it is?

And yet, as I have acknowledged various times, the tendency still exists to take myself to be my thoughts and emotions, reactions and beliefs that there is someone here to defend, etc. And this is obviously not full embodiment of clear understanding. I do my best, so to speak, to penetrate such tendencies as they arise, and you do your best to provoke me into the awareness of the belief in a somebody, it seems. I guess being called a deluded fool in the pejorative sense may have its value if it brings some awareness of the "foolish" beliefs that are living their own attempt at a comfortable life and attempting to be undisturbed. Your second interpretation of the term is, of course, something that I can enjoy...

David

27 Aug. 2013
To: David

Thanks. I enjoyed your letter. I think you got the point. If there is still a doer then foolishness and delusion must be part and parcel of the doer-ship. To acknowledge oneself as being deluded, or not, is resisted to the extent that egoic identification is still working. The ego hates such frank admissions. What's the problem with admitting this? If there is no one present, who cares? I found it helpful to undermine self at every opportunity.

Regarding post enlightenment one may also regard him- or herself to be a fool in the other way *I* suggested. Neither outlooks can be forced or contrived. We take ourselves less seriously, or we don't.

It is very natural to feel this way when you know beyond any doubt whatsoever that "life is but a dream."

DJ

Aug 30, 2013
To: DJ

Today your quote from Lao Tzu seems particularly apt. I realize that it very much describes how I often feel these days. Nothing seems clear cut and all concepts and explanations are questionable. Others seem to have some certainty, but I don't, except when I start arguing for beliefs and ideas which, if looked at more closely, I don't even believe in. I'm not saying I'm the same as Lao Tzu but only that I can relate very much to what he says here.

You also mentioned recently something about life being a dream. Last night there came a clear seeing of the truth of that statement. The "I" is truly only a thought, a concept imagined by "the mind." In fact there is nothing here that can be conceived accurately: It's all being made up by thought, whatever thought is. Thought seems to be dream stuff, image projection by who knows what (the Mystery). It's all a dream! How deeply this insight is allowed and lived as opposed to believing that the dream is real remains to be seen, I guess. There is felt to be an impact to this seeing but exactly what it is I don't yet know. Life usually seems like such a real dream, you might say a lucid dream. And can one still see it's a dream when faced with death or acts of violence in one's direct experience? And what are the implications? Does it deny compassion for suffering? Is it a very different quality of compassion than when the dream is believed to be real? In what way is life real and in what way a dream? All a dream and at the same time, real? One or the other? Both? Neither? Beyond the paradox of such dualities? Are these questions meaningful? They seem to be just arising in the moment with some curiosity.

Cheers,

David

The Clothes Have No Emperor

∞Chapter 11∞

September

3 Sept. 2013
To: David

The news from your latest letter chronicles several rare and marvelous developments indeed. Without a doubt, things are moving along very nicely. I really think these are great portents for the future. Thanks so much for sharing them with me. Such news really does warm my heart. And, as always, I wish to again let you know how much I appreciate the opportunity to engage with you in this investigation into reality as it truly is.

Your revelations really do hit the mark regarding the Lao Tzu quote. This is the kind of authenticity we are looking for. As results-based practice, this is how backing away from delusion really expresses itself. Just "not-knowing," but here I mean "being not-knowing itself," not merely thinking you are not-knowing, will take you very far indeed or indicate arrival itself depending on the kind and extent of not-knowing that is involved.

To be clearer, I suggest that authentic not-knowing has no "knower" that knows nothing but rather a Beingness that neither knows nor knows not – and it is present all the time. So it is really more an unknowing or a non-knowingness than it is a state where someone says, "You know what, I don't know a blasted thing." Authenticity is the silence prior to the thought

"I know nothing" and, if all goes well, that is how it is at all times...well mostly, anyhow, except when things like what I am doing right now, i.e. writing, happen. Still, there is a kind of silence in that as well. It seems to me that that is what we are talking about here, right David?

And this unknowingness is not a dazed, numbed, spaced out, lazy-minded, disengaged not-knowing but, rather, a vibrant, alive, immediate, intimate and loving way of being. So I say keep the faith, keep relaxing; all is well, as that truly is what you are: wellness itself.

I take it distinctions are becoming harder for you to entertain. Perfect! Just a lovely, naïve openness to what is.

Others seem to have some certainty but I don't - except when I start arguing for beliefs and ideas which, if looked at more closely, I don't even believe in.

Ha, ha, that line made me chuckle; so true and rarely expressed. Bravo!

You also mentioned recently something about life being a dream. Last night there came a clear seeing of the truth of that statement.

Great news. That's the kind of direct experience I love hearing about. A knowing that transcends conceptual thought and, I would say, endures in some regard or another, as well. Once Maya has been seen through to the degree you have just experienced, I suggest it will be rather difficult to reduce the significance much. I bet this realization really makes a difference. Wonderful!

Life usually seems like such a real dream - you might say a lucid dream. The dream of me having such veracity and immediacy...

I know exactly what you mean. The simulation is as good as it gets, isn't it? It has to be if it is to be believed in. But for the sake of transcending this so-called dream, let me ask once again... "whose life, whose dream?" There is quite simply none to be found if viewed from "lucid eyes."

Here I will touch upon your lucid dream analogy for a moment. When engaged in lucid dreaming during the nocturnal hours, I find whatever transpires to undoubtedly never be regarded as "real" in any sense at all. I don't need to ever question the veracity of what is transpiring if I am totally aware. It's simply always seen to be fake. (My) AWARENESS is just as lucid in this virtual dream state as it is right now as I write to you. I carry all my memories with me while lucid dreaming and know beyond any doubt that this dreamscape is a fabrication. Am I real, then? Hardly. I am a dream character.

There are no limits or repercussions to be found while engaged in this imaginary realm. No consequences for any moral transgressions or dangerous acts of any kind. You truly are an ubermensch, superman, or something almost God-like, during lucid dream-time escapades. But the more you engage in it, the less it fascinates, until sooner or later everything starts to feel cheap and tawdry. Truth be told, I no longer engage in the practice. Why bother? It's only a dream.

Death during lucid dreaming has no finality to it. It merely means awakening to find a mattress below your back. This dream stuff is just a projection of sorts. Not real in any sense but, curiously, the lucid dream realm experience strikes me as being more authentic than normal waking reality does. The dreamland always impresses me as more "real than real," but the experience is never confused for reality itself.

To be sure, dreaming of the ordinary kind feels very immediate and gripping when one is not aware of its true nature. Who hasn't suffered from night terrors? It's only upon awakening from the non-lucid dream that you realize it was all just make-believe. This is precisely the same case when endarkenment ceases to function. What you once took to be "real" now impresses less than stage props do. It's all empty. It was hard to fathom how I ever took all this to be real in the first place. But that's Maya for you. The illusion must be top notch if we are ever to buy into it.

The only thing that might in a sense be called "real" is the awareness that apprehends the unfolding show. That is ever present no matter what realm I inhabit. This awareness, as you know, has no qualities but is in a loose sense what I am, though be careful in taking that distinction too seriously, like some teachers do.

A lucid dream is entirely unreal yet, if I allow myself to play along, it can still certainly appear quite authentic. It's like suspending your disbelief for a moment while watching a 3-D movie. But to be clear, no matter the kind of dream, lucid or otherwise, always, always, always it is seen for what it is, a thought projection as you so rightly point out. The realm we inhabit seems to be thought manifested into form. There is no tree unless I "think" I see it.

Some physicists are playing around with the idea of reality as informational hologram. Sounds similar. Who knows, but it reminds me of the Bill Hicks quote, "We are all one consciousness experiencing itself subjectively. There's no such thing as death, life is only a dream, and we're the imagination of ourselves." So, in my final estimation, is dreaming real? Yes and no, depending on where identification lies. Somehow grace befell me, identification switched and the play revealed itself for what it was: chicanery through and through. But what an amazing "fabrication" it is. Life itself...well, I'll be darned...who would have "thunk" it, eh?

And can one still see it's a dream when faced with death or acts of violence in one's direct experience?

My first inclination is to say drop the self and find out the answer on your own. Then you will know, and it won't be a matter of speculation. But to answer you directly: Of course. It's a dream, silly. In a lucid dream, of what real consequence are these things you speak of?

Similarly, there is no difference when I am in the eyes wide open kind of dream state. What are these acts of violence or death you speak of? Whose death? Whose violence? From the viewpoint of distinction or separation then, sure, such experiences are perceived as abhorrent. Just like Frankenstein's monster is a terrible vision to apprehend until you awaken shaking your head in the morning and laugh at yourself for being so gullible. An apt biblical quote might be helpful to consider here: "One is in, but not of, the World." Strangely enough, though, a non-centred -- as opposed to the ordinary self-centred--kind of compassion wells up by its own accord once one awakens. How this may operate is left up to you to discover, but I can tell you that there is no lack of it.

And what are the implications?

"Implications?"...?

David, we have talked about this useless kind of speculation before. Who cares? Wake up and all this useless navel gazing will go away. The ego always wants to know the lay of the land before it enters unknown territory. Again and again you get sucked into the musings of a madman. Again, I admonish you to withhold the urge to engage in such distinction-making and conjecture. You know this yourself, otherwise you would not have asked, "Are such questions meaningful?" No, they are not! In fact, "meaning" has nothing to do with the search at hand. We aim to find true self/non-self, **NOT MEANING!** There will never be an end to this mind crap unless you see how inane and unreal such banality is. When questions like the following arise:

> Does it deny compassion for suffering? Is it a very different quality of compassion than when the dream is believed to be real? In what way is life real and in what way a dream? All a dream and at the same time real? One or the other? Both? Neither? Beyond the paradox of such dualities? Are these questions meaningful? They seem to be just arising in the moment with some curiosity.

Can you for Buddha's sake just pay them no heed? Please...with a cherry on top?

Trust me when I tell you that you will never find any answers. When the dream of you utterly ceases, such "curiosity" will no longer arise as all will be clear. You will find your self to be clear, brilliant luminosity itself. I ain't shittin' you here, my friend...I swear on the honor of my beloved samurai sword and all I hold dear that all I say is as truthful as any words allow. You will never discover yourself to be Reality itself while engaged in mind-centrism. You can take that one to the bank. So to sum up once again, how wonderful to hear about your latest revelations. These recent events make me feel that your future, you know, the one that doesn't really exist, is going to be very bright indeed.

On another front, find below a comprehensive (you might be inclined to say verbose) second part to conclude the initial letter I sent to you before departing on my hike. It continues the investigation into 'dying.' I appreciate the fact that you don't much enjoy my long-winded musing, but it is the length that arose, so there you have it. I think it is pretty good spiritual pointing and quite on topic, if that is any consolation.

Can you do me a favor? Can you get a librarian to help you print it out? Maybe copy and paste it into the program Notepad. Or save it to a portable thumb drive or SD card and bring it home to your computer. Can you do that please? With more time to read it, I hope the experience will be less daunting, rushed, or uncomfortable for you.

Of course, if you don't want to read any of it, that is fine as well. Understand that whatever you do read is not meant to harm you but, rather, to encourage you to peer more deeply into the void. You are quite aware by now that I do like to try to utilize the odd "Zen bitch slap" from time to time to help snap seekers out of their confusion, but it is intended solely for their benefit.

If you come across any, please accept such admonishments with the love and compassion from whence they originate. Sometimes this awakening thing requires a bit of tough love, but it wells up from the heart, I assure you.

One more thing: I see that these days you are resisting the urge to defend yourself while reading my prose. I encourage you to continue along such lines. It's the mark of a wise sage indeed that disdains notions of personal offence. But if you come across something that your heart knows to be unfounded then, by all means, let's discuss it. Similarly, I am totally open to clarification. It's the position taking of the ego I would prefer to avoid. Now, go get the librarian and get this darn thing printed off if you don't mind.
DJ

AND NOW FOR SOMETHING COMPLETLY DIFFERENT

If there is, in fact, no I or separate self, and it is only a mistaken idea, then why does that which doesn't exist have to die?

If...If? It seems using "if" is simply an honest reflection of reality for you at this time, isn't it? You simply don't know whether or not so-called "oneness" or abiding non-dual awareness is the way things really are, do you? I take it your present experience precludes this absolute kind of knowing. David lives out his life relying upon duality to inform himself of his existence, so of course you are dubious of non-self and, therefore, treat it as a point of speculation or conjecture. This explains your inclination to hedge the bet with the modifier "If." Good for you.

But I wonder why the urge to mention the above arises in the first place. If it is only a product of conceptual belief - and a very tenuous one, at that - why bother? Citing beliefs or disbeliefs seems pointless to me. The status quo for you has always been life with David at the centre and the concomitant suffering that results from such a more or less steady state, correct? Why proffer beliefs as if they had any relevance regarding Reality? Concepts in any form are empty symbols, mere pointers, devoid of reality itself and not to be confused with the alive, vibrant emptiness we truly are.

You might agree, then, that things need to radically change if suffering is to cease. I call this change a kind of dying, a death of the ego, if you will. Disintegration of self. You can call it something else if you prefer, but the thing that you presently take yourself to be has to walk off-stage after the final curtain call if the final reckoning is to occur. Sometimes I wonder if you are resisting this outcome. Perhaps your ego wants to persist. I'd lay a thousand bucks down that this is indeed the case. It's statements like the one above that clearly demonstrate confusion. Your clever ego exploits such non-clarity to continue to "bamboozle" itself.

On the flipside of duality, of course, there is nothing that needs to die, but a fat lot of good this will do you when you are still firmly in the grips of Maya. I think we presently recognize that David is very much a product of duality. Though, through this present investigation I have also come to learn that you have done very, very well in recognizing the many kinds of tricks Maya presents to sustain herself. This is wonderful and takes great guts and fortitude, indeed. To be sure, I never wish to downplay your growing spiritual maturity.

But, fundamentally, delusion still rules and that is why my words often raise your ire. Perhaps it is time for a change. Change that matters. Not the kind Obama promised but in the end never delivered. A real letting go that doesn't involve the ramblings of the deluded mind. Emancipation. "How about it?"

When I consider your question, "Why does that which doesn't exist have to die?", I have to ask you something. How is it that you take the "I," which in truth is "that which doesn't exist," to be something ontologically real in the first place? You propose that the "I" is not "really real." I am very skeptical about this kind of position taking.

Is it not the case that something is either "real" or it is not? A diamond is either authentic, or it isn't. To say a diamond is not "really real" makes no sense. It's either a diamond or another thing entirely. What does "really real" mean? Seems to me that small s self is, or it isn't. You identify with self, or you don't. To say that the self is not really real seems to me to be a ploy the ego utilizes to keep itself moving along quite nicely, thank you very much. Have you ever wondered if it is precisely this kind of conceptualization that allows the ego to sustain itself?

"Oh, I am not "really real," so anything that transpires is just groovy, isn't it?", it might say. "I mean isn't it...isn't it...???" Though, once again, pain, suffering, self-loathing, greed, and misery still endure. Can't you see what is wrong with this picture?

It's like calling Frankenstein's monster not "really real." Though an assortment of dead body parts, not really a human being at all, it sure created havoc, didn't it? For a moment it sure seemed to live, as do you. Then it ceased to exist. I agree that the notion of dying or not dying is ridiculous, for in truth nothing lives nor not lives. But I assure you this notion of a separate "I," just like the monster, must be well and thoroughly eradicated if peace is ever to be found.

You really do have to break out the torches and pitchforks (or better still laser-guided a-bombs) with great determination in order to subdue the beast. Cut its head clean off, using the power of presence, until it is quite evident that this once very laudable notion is now laughable in the extreme.

Stop playing around with ideas. Leave that for the kiddies goofing around in their sandbox. Really, really see through all this nonsense. What you are seeking is not another thought. Become it. Be it. You are it. Then this "if" thing will fall away along with everything else. When you ask the question," What is it that must die?", again, I say, "YOU." It's pretty obvious. You must die. Or, more pointedly, the belief in self must be completely eradicated. Not through force of will but by simply noting its inherent unreal nature. Sincerely routing out delusion is most helpful here, but in the end, grace must befall us all. At best all we can hope for is to make the conditions ripe for this to happen.

If you are authentic, then the "no-self" experience Bernadette Roberts speaks of will naturally become evident. Buddha's Anatta (non-self) must replace the dream of me, or the Zen "no mind" of emptiness becomes SELF-evident. In other words SELF realizes itself, and abiding non-dual awareness will come to replace your present self-centred paradigm. Awareness "awaring" itself must truly replace the narrative of "me."

I suggest that at this time you, to some degree or another, lack the eyes and ears to fully hear the TRUTH as it is being whispered to you. Though it is apparent to me that your "Spidey senses" are getting more acute day by day. I would not be at all surprised to find out very soon that this "whispering," such that it was, stopped for you entirely and then great shock proceeded to overwhelm you as you discovered that you had been "The Whisperer" all along. You will have come full circle, and that will be that.

I really understand your current frustration, David, and wish nothing but the best. What I am attempting to impart in this forum is not some version of "my truth." It's "our truth." It's THE TRUTH. I have the strong impression that you will soon discover that you have been mumbling to yourself all along. Trust me, any day now you'll see what a skilled ventriloquist you have been. Not as a fleeting awakening experience but as life itself. I truly believe that if anyone in Canada — hell, in the entire world — can awaken, it is you, David. Why? Why not? You truly are that guy. I know for a fact that right now there is less than a hair's breadth separating you from Reality as it truly is. I know you can smell it; sure you can, right? So let's get back to exploring this "dying" business so we can put it to rest. Or put you to rest. Whadya say?

There is simply no way to wiggle out of this one, David. You have to definitely come to terms with the fact that self must be dropped. This doesn't mean that the idea of self is simply entertained less. No. It's the most radical thing that will ever befall you. Reality itself breaks out like the big bang, and you are annihilated in the process. Foyan calls it "instant Zen." Consider Ramana's experience as an excellent case in point.

Remember how Ramana imagined what it would be like to die and then awakened in that moment to the pure void of Beingness itself, which neither came nor went. You, too, must hold out no hope of survival. It's not a temporary awakening experience; it is just wakefulness itself. No one ever gets out of this thing alive. To imagine that you can "have your cake and eat it too" is delusional. There is no chance that David gets to persist.

The ego perpetually devises strategies to believe otherwise, like the concept of reincarnation and soul survival. I must exist and, therefore, I must persist. Heaven, Pure Land, Valhalla, the new-agers' concept of transmigration of soul to a higher plain of existence, and—if you happen to dislike Muslims—the Hell you hope they will endure, are all indicators of this wishful kind of dreaming. Even when you supposedly fuck up, the deranged mind imagines you don't get to cease to exist. It's all very, very silly, isn't it?

You posed a good question when you asked, What does it really mean to die? I like it because it invites another question: What does it really mean to live? Talking about the why's and wherefores and how-to's of "dying" would be to engage in speculative contemplation at this point, but luckily you can examine something that is seemingly occurring to you presently. That would be David's so-called life. Do you have a life? I mean really? I state for the record (and I see it is the case that you are coming to the same conclusion) that you are nothing but a virtual symbolic representation of a "self-believed-in," so what truly is this life of yours then? Why do you take it to be ontologically real? How is this happening? Really, really take a close look and tell me.

Put aside the dying for now and take a closer look at the living thing. What is being lived, and who is doing it? I see emptiness with no distinctions or "other." I find the sense of self to be a fiction seemingly imbued with realism and vitality solely through the machinations of a self-referential mind-loop. You have told me how conditioning may help invigorate the pretense of a you. But there is nothing inherently real in that. Isn't it empty?

Take a look, and see what I mean. It seems that this conditioning is just part of the story believed in. Why do you consider yourself to be your thoughts? What are thoughts? Are they real? Are they truly "life" itself or just a symbolic figment of your own imagination? Does David have a life or, rather, does LIFE have a David? This is all it is, David. Just this. Really and truly this is it. Just this. Step back and see.

I discovered by and by how my whole "life" had been just a ruse or canard. Simulacra through and through. A past and future that did not exist save for a trick of the mind. One day I had an awakening experience some months before completely dropping the self and during it two very salient spiritual points arose.

One thing that became apparent (and I gather you just had a similar reckoning yourself) was how I was so thoroughly "entranced" (just like everyone else is I presume), living the dream of me through the cinema of that which ain't transpiring. Similarly, I realized that I had spent my entire life "phoning" the whole thing in. In truth I had never showed up a day for work. I hadn't actually been "living," save for the few odd moments I spontaneously became lucid every decade or so and in those rare cases I now see that there was not really anyone there to claim the experience anyhow. That realization was very astonishing.

It is this kind of direct experience, evidently born out of a desire to reorient identification away from self-deception, that really shocks one to the core, don't you agree?

Don't you also agree that that kind of experience clearly demonstrated that I, you, and, by abstraction the whole human race, were, in fact, engaged in some kind of play, movie, or dream, if you prefer, and we were all mere actors fumbling and stumbling about a set dressed with virtual props manifested from our own imaginations. Humanity is little more than an ocean of zombies, the walking dead perpetually entranced by a virtual reality comprised of a fictional past or future. I came to learn that I was something more akin to the Frankenstein's monster I mentioned previously than I was to an emancipated, sentient, living being. Existence itself is alive, vigorous, and naturally imbued with vitality. I discovered that I barely had a pulse. Thankfully, I was put out of my misery.

And that brings us back to the start of this investigation. You proposed months ago that we look at how it is that suffering can come to cease, how it is we can get off the "misery-go-round," as it were. The answer is you, the entity that labels itself as David, quite simply can't. But, to be sure, misery can be vanquished and is already presently non-existent, in fact. To my utter astonishment I discovered that there was no merry- nor misery-go-round (nor anything else for that matter) to begin with. Nothing was added unto me in order to experience this revelation. I didn't learn anything. I just gave up.

Yet many have described different kinds of intense experiences of ego death. Others have said the idea of the "I" only needs to be seen through.

You wonder if the "I" only needs to be seen through. Would that be akin to the alcoholic who sees through his addiction but continues to imbibe nevertheless? If transformation does not occur, then who is kidding whom? Can a distinction be made between "seeing through" and mere conceptualization? If there is no apparent transformation, then what does this seeing through business amount to? If fruits are not born, who cares? If suffering and craving still continue unabated, wouldn't it be good to continue to shine the spotlight (better still a billion-watt, coherent, monochromatic laser) of awareness on this fact rather than say, "It's been seen through; I get it. That's that. Time to settle back and relax"? If we consider Occam's razor, then what are we to conclude when an aspirant says that he or she has "seen through it all," yet suffering persists? Maybe the simplest answer truly is the correct one: They are still very much deluded. I can assure you that I never once concluded anything else but that I was well in the grips of delusion, firmly ensconced in the dream, right up until the very moment grace occurred. Then, I didn't have a clue what the hell was happening!

Further and further I must go until one day something points out that the journey of a thousand miles truly begins and ends with simply what is directly underfoot. And in that moment, in the eternal now, I laugh uproariously upon realizing that there never was a further, nor a journey nor anyone to take it.

Again I ask, do you really have a life? That's a matter best not left to the philosophers and their tiresome speculation. You can absolutely determine this for yourself right here and now.

I see through it but seem to have absolutely no control over the results of that seeing. There seem to be some other factors **(factors???...perhaps the play of Maya?**) that are at play here. And is it, in fact, a problem at all, or is that only an idea of the divided mind?

It is definitely not a problem. Are there really any problems at all? If you resist moving towards the mind to inform you otherwise, who can say, right? Yet David suffers, so problems must still persist in some guise or another.

Chapter 11 | September

No problems exist to the ineffable, but in duality there is indeed strife and identification with delusion. It's really exceedingly simple. There is either the divided mind...or not. No mind, no problem, no self. If there is position-taking and distinction-making going on, with the resulting suffering it engenders, then ipso facto divided mind must also be at work identifing with the so-called little me. Much as you may not like to hear it, my experience shows, as apparently does that of all "awakenists" I admire most, that awakened MIND is either the case or it isn't. You don't become more awake but, rather, you become less self-deluded. There is a great distinction to be made here. I assure you that you are either awake, or you are not. You differed with me on this point before, and I let it pass. Now I want to make myself clear.

I take it that you believe that you are becoming more spiritually advanced day by day, but you are not. Just ever less deluded. Being awake is not relative. It's digital. Either on or off, + or -, yes or no. Just like sleep is. You are either awake or something else. There are degrees of slumber, but awake is just that eyes wide open, clear minded, and lucid attention being paid to what is unfolding right in front of you.

I say bollocks to people who declare things like "She is the most spiritually awakened person I know." Rubbish. Reality, wakefulness, cannot be measured in degrees but confusion sure can. Did you know that the electron can only be found in one distinct energetic orbit around the nucleus, or another lesser or more highly energized one, but nowhere in between? It doesn't move in or out of orbits. It doesn't jump through the gaps in space between the possible orbits, though scientists sometimes lead us to believe otherwise by using such incorrect terminology as "quantum leap." In fact, when the electron spins in one orbit (and it really doesn't even rotate as a billiard ball would - which is what I learned in high school - but is really more of a field of potentiality) and then appears in another orbit, it does so as if by some means akin to teleportation. It doesn't move by increments. It is only here or there, but never anywhere in between. Never.

Reality works the same way. Digital. On/off. An aspirant is either deluded or she or he is not. You are either insane, or you are not. Who ever heard of a half-sane lunatic? A 50/50 schizophrenic? Or consider this little dialogue. "How's Audrey doing these days?" "Terrific, she is the most awake comatose patient I know."

No, it's not fucking terrific. All she does lying there with her festering bed sores is dribble and occasionally mumble an incoherent word or two. It's not bloody marvelous you fool: She's a vegetable!

WTF, but that is precisely how seekers view themselves when they believe they are becoming more spiritually advanced. I know this to be true as I certainly fell prey to this kind of deluded wishful thinking to some degree or another back in the day. Of course, through the benefit of hindsight I now see how truly confused I was. This explains my attempt to clue you in. Once the illness is acknowledged, treatment can commence. This is why I keep reiterating the "you are still entranced" point ad nauseam. That explains the Zen quote about "medicine" from a few letters back. Are you beginning to see the method to my "madness"?

I am not trying to belittle but, rather, empower you. I am pointing out that you are still dreaming, with the expectation that this realization will help you snap out of it. I once told you I was the best friend you ever had. Remember? That's because I shoot straight and am willing to tell you the difficult things that must be said, the kind of things we don't always appreciate right off the top, with no agenda other than wanting truth to reveal itself to itself.

When the spiritual "quantum leap" occurs (which I indicated is no leap at all), I don't mean to imply seekers become "not deluded." No indeed. Rather they become NOT. Either they are deluded…or NOT. Presumed self is "nirvanaed," and then all bets are off. The seeker passes away as if never having existed in the first place. That's because the seeker doesn't exist in the first place. I am adamant, David: The dream of you must cease entirely – YOU MUST DIE!

Truth is, David, you still have a "thinking problem." It's the morning after and you are only now sobering up. I put it to you that you are still "drunk." Therein lays the good news. Soon you will be shaking off your hangover. I think it is unavoidable at this point. Just as a drunk can never entirely avoid becoming lucid and clear-headed, so, too, you are going to become "clean and sober" sooner than you may think. Here's to the conclusion of this journey, the wondrousness and peace that awaits you. And if you got this far into this darn letter, an extra cheerio to boot.

☺

DJ

2 Sept. 2013
To: DJ

I knew after I wrote my last letter that you would call me out on my questions at the end. I knew they were just silly speculations that my mind was throwing up, although in the moment of their arising there seemed to be some sense of meaning in them. Right after sending the email, it was clear that the "answer" was, as Papaji used to say, to "just be quiet" and see what happens. Speculation is of no real value.

Will write more soon. I see you definitely followed my advice to keep your letters shorter!

David

3 Sept. 2013
To: David

"I see you definitely followed my advice to keep your letters shorter!"

Shorter...oops, sorry. This line of yours got me laughing. I really am terrible, aren't I?

About the speculation thing, I sorta figured you weren't so serious about it but just in case I included the reminder.

"Seeing what happens" sounds good. Quiet, now that's revolutionary. How are things going or not going these days? So there...how's that for a short reply? And you didn't think I had it in me.

Cheers,
DJ

6 Sept 2013
To: DJ

Hi DJ,

You ask how things are going...A sense of being "confronted" from many sides. Insecurity and turbulence...Will explain more later I expect.

Cheers, David

13 Sept. 2013
To: DJ

Hi DJ,

Things are still very intense and consuming my attention. No doubt at bottom due to identification. Burning, burning... Ahhhhhhhh!

13 Sept. 2013
To: David

Burning...burning...

Like I said before, when there is nothing left to burn, you have to set yourself on fire. Did you get around to reading the conclusion of "what dies"? What's causing turmoil of late? Sounds intense?

Cheers,

DJ

17 Sept. 2013
To: DJ

Yes, it must be a burning of myself, otherwise no real change.

Some big losses financially have been a trigger, with no way of knowing at this point when the bleeding will stop as it involves legal issues with no telling how much I will have to be responsible for. It's bringing up issues of survival and lack of support (for the "me") and a whole lot of anxiety. In addition, Meghan and I a couple of weeks ago ate a certain kind of brownie which turned out to be very strong, and during the experience I entered a space of seeing a profound emptiness of everything in a way that was kind of a shock to the mind. And then another experience of complete meaninglessness arrived. I could see that, if there was any taking of those experiences as a platform or ground for living, the mind could go into a deep depression. If there is no resistance, then, of course, no problem and the experience passes by, leaving no imprint except possibly a letting go of mental constructs of substance and meaning. But it does seem to have had a disturbing impact.

I think these triggers and some others not mentioned are just an aspect of a challenge to the self which is necessary, a part of the process of deconstruction of the self. I can sometimes see and feel the deeper benefit of this "dying," and then sometimes I just want to get the hell out of the whirlpool that seems to be sucking me down. It helps to ask, "Who is suffering this?" moment by moment.

It's clear that the "me" is the source of the conflict, but detaching by stepping back into the witness or pure awareness position appears to diminish the transformational power of directly being with the challenge to the ego's survival that is being activated by life. Awareness, presence, and fully experiencing without any avoidance strategies seems to be what is required. Pretty intense!

Hope things are well with you, David

17 Sept 2013
To: DJ

Just reread your recent letter on this subject and found it to be, in the light of my current experience, right on the money, profound, and prophetic, although I can't say that the full fruition of the prophecy has as yet come to pass.

Cheers,

David

19 Sept. 2013
To: David

Greetings David,

You said, "It's bringing up issues of survival and lack of support (for the "me") and a whole lot of anxiety."

That's terrible news. Sorry to hear that. What to say…?

You bring up the "survival" issue. Glad to see you spotted that one. That is one of the most difficult "triggers" to avoid. I really appreciate the dreadful place you are in. The survival instinct is "hardwired," so almost impossible to transcend. Let me tell you that if someone stuck my head in a bucket of water, I would fight like the dickens. While there is no fear of death here presently, the will to survive remains strong. We are creatures that are programmed to endure. The best news I can offer is that "this too shall pass," though at the moment it is not much of a consolation, I know.

In addition, Meghan and I, a couple of weeks ago, ate a certain kind of brownie which turned out to be very strong and during the experience I entered a space of seeing a profound emptiness of everything in a way that was kind of a shock to the mind. And then another experience of complete meaninglessness arrived.

Love to hear about this kind of development. "Shock to the mind": Now we're talking! More wonderful news. A few weeks back I had a strong intuition you were "snapping out of it." Please don't let this precious opportunity slip away. Presence, awareness, lucidity are more important now than ever. Do the things required to keep your life in order, but ignore your chattering monkey mind. It doesn't have the answers.

Strive to keep your heart open. During difficult times this is even more important. Behind all the seeming turmoil is a love beyond compare. The heart knows the way. Let it be your guide. Home is just over there...remember?

These penultimate experiences are "the real meal deal," I assure you. How exciting. I am intimately familiar with what you are going through. Trust me when I say all is well. All is really, really well. Take heart in consideration of all of your most admired sages and gurus. Every Buddha has been where you are now. I am sure they are all offering you encouragement at this point, as they are but manifestations of the ONE and this, in a sense, thrills at your pending liberation. Keep on softening. Relax (I know, I know, easy for me to say, as I am not presently going through all the shit you are...but nevertheless...)

I understand your present predicament and the fear and apprehension it must be causing you, but consider again those folks that most inspired you. They all managed to get through this terminal phase, myself included, unscathed. You don't lose your mind but, rather, find it. Keep the faith. Anyone who ever awakened never regretted the sacrifice called for. As you well know, it is "the thinker," or small self, that is not so sure about all this. Quite natural. Gets back to the survival thing.

Do I understand correctly that you have for all intents and purposes extracted yourself from the shabby (JK so loved to use this word, didn't he?) kiddies' sandbox of sugar-coated, fairy-tale spewing, dream-weaving spiritual rhetoric and now are bound for parts unknown? If this is not already clear, here is a spoiler alert. From here on in it is pretty much unexplored and—even more shocking—unexplorable territory. Few have ever tread the barren landscape where distinction never dared rear its head, but take heart: This is truly wonderful news. You have entered the penultimate phase, "the quickening," if you will.

From here on in things will probably start to feel ever more strange as self continues to evaporate. Loneliness and detachment may arise as well, as letting go proceeds. This will be tempered with bouts of great glee, humour, and profundity. Welcome it all, but at the same time resist the urge to identify with any of it. Otherwise, you may get lost in the strange viewpoint offered up in the book *The Haunted Universe*. It presents a dreadful nihilism any sane person would avoid at all costs. The problem is that this view is not the full story. The writer's destruction was not complete. Much identification remained. He was unaware that there was still further to go. The void is neither wonderful nor abhorrent. Only the thinking mind makes it thus. Don't contemplate meaning or consequences. Naturally, let yourself be swallowed up. I guarantee you that "all's well that ends well."

I think I mentioned before that, if carried out with great sincerity, one should be spiritually careful what they wish for, as it will inevitably come to pass. You know how it is that I am quite certain things are progressing well in your case? Well, it is like in a poker game when you catch a glimpse of your opponent's cards. You can make a huge bet, as the outcome is assured. Here's the exact "tell" I noted in this letter, though I could point out a few others that have arisen recently as well.

You said the recent state of affairs had a "disturbing impact." That is an authentic reaction if I ever saw one. Not often talked about in spiritual circles because it is not the greatest of selling points. Everybody loves to hear about the peace, love, and bliss. Who wants to be apprised of the blood and guts? Everyone seeks to be raised to lofty ethereal heights while no one wishes to get mired down in the shit and piss of the trenches. So when I hear you say you were "disturbed" I know this comes from real emancipation and in passing would like to offer the following gospel from Thomas as a bit of encouragement. Jesus said, "Those who seek should not stop seeking until they find. When they find, they will be disturbed. When they are disturbed, they will marvel (become astonished), and will reign over the ALL. And after they have reigned they will rest."

Sounds familiar, eh?

I could see that, if there was any taking of those experiences as a platform or ground for living, the mind could go into a deep depression. If there is no resistance then, of course, no problem and the experience passes by, leaving no imprint except possibly a letting go of mental constructs of substance and meaning. But it does seem to have had a disturbing impact... I can sometimes see and feel the deeper benefit of this "dying," and then sometimes I just want to get the hell out of the whirlpool that seems to be sucking me down.

This isn't namby-pamby, kiddy stuff being spoken of here. When I talk of unbelievably radical transformation that is precisely what I mean. Un-believable. Outside the realm of belief and thought. So, of course, "you" want to "get the hell out of Dodge." Who wouldn't? Don't. Stay put. You won't regret it. Sure, there might be a period of depression or a long dark night of the soul. If that is what is called for, then it shall come to pass. But pass it shall. That's an exceedingly small price to pay for what's on offer, don't you think?

If it's of any solace, my "long night" lasted just about that long. Within a day or two the depression and melancholy that arose over the decision to truly let self go (this decision preceded actual awakening by some months) was over and done with, and then it was time to move on. To avoid this "spell" is most detrimental. How about if you just let it happen and see what comes of it? Here is a wonderful little anecdote I just heard this week that nicely illustrates what I am pointing to. It concerns a bit of living Zen as told by E. M. from the Zen centre.

The Abbots podcast relates that he was some years into a very serious Zen practice. He describes himself as "macho" and very much into the stoicism of old school hard-core Zen practice. Great form, lots of control. Problem was he reached a point where he could no longer meditate without great struggle. It seems that for a nine- to twelve-month period he would almost invariably be tempted to fall into slumber within a minute or two of sitting on the cushion. What ensued was simply the struggle to remain conscious. His was a dead serious practice, so this state of affairs was intolerable. And then one day, one of those spiritual reckonings occurred that we all have. You know the kind. Something profound transpires that seemingly allows you to get to the next level of the journey. In his case he said "fuck it"… well, maybe not in that exact term, but that was the outcome nevertheless.

What happened was that he decided to stop the struggle against falling asleep. At the expense of great embarrassment, for after all nothing could be worse than having a Zen monk come crashing to the floor, he decided to see if that would indeed happen. If he were to be a laughing stock, then so be it. He closed his eyes and, as before, almost instantly became drowsy. But instead of resisting this urge he did nothing. Did he start snoring, fall to the floor? No. Most unexpected. But a greater shock awaited him. Suddenly, a new kind of awareness enveloped him. Rather than the single-pointed focus that usually ensued if meditation was going well, a new kind of holistic global awareness welled forth, taking him completely by surprise.

So, I guess the invitation here is instead of going with the normal "chase or embrace" instinct when a crisis or disturbing spiritual incident arises, how about do an experiment and just let things unfold as they will? Don't attempt to avoid or limit pain, discomfort, or things you find distasteful or weird. Here I am talking about spiritual pursuits, of course, not practical matters pertaining to relative reality. Of course, getting meat and potatoes on the table is important, so to speak...er... scratch that one, given your vegetarian bent. LOL. Try leaping before you look. I assure you, you will be pleasantly surprised. I know you are aware of this ideal or you would not have gotten this far. I am just stressing it, as now is the time to really "go for it," time to let it "all hang out."

"It helps to ask, Who is suffering this?, moment by moment, as it's clear that the "me" is the source of the conflict but detaching by stepping back into the witness or pure awareness position appears to diminish the transformational power of directly being with the challenge to the ego's survival that is being activated by life.

Yes, that is a very astute observation. Remaining in the thick of it is authentic. Like they say, the test of a man is not how he acts when times are good but, rather, when they are bad. Phony detachment is of no value just as you have so wisely observed.

Awareness, presence, and fully experiencing without any avoidance strategies seem to be what is required. Pretty intense!

What a thrill those words above give me. To see the truth of awakening unfolding...how marvelous! You hit the head on the nail (much better than nail on head) with that one. Your words directly echo what I was speaking about above. When I hear an animated Holmes proclaim to Watson, "The chase is afoot," I am left with a similar impression.

Those words bear repeating:

Awareness, presence, and fully experiencing without any avoidance strategies seem to be what is required.

The chase is afoot, old boy; the chase really is afoot.

"Pretty intense"? Yep... and this is but the prelude. Prepare to be astonished like never before.

All my love,

DJ

24 Sept. 2013
To: DJ

Hi DJ,

I very much enjoyed your last letter and expect to answer more fully soon. Your words accurately conceptualize much of what has been happening and your "enthusiasm" is delightful. Have been experiencing that sense of "fear" (if putting a label on it) that we spoke about which seems to have no discernable cause. Mostly in the solar plexus. It does look to be the primal fear of the thought-created sense of the separate self, the anxiety about the threat to the survival of something which in essence is unsubstantial and has no stability or ground within itself.

Bye for now, David

26 Sept. 2013
To: David

I am delighted to once again see another "tell" in your letter that surely indicates real spiritual awakening is in progress. It's the difference between talking about such matters and beholding actual transformation occurring right here and now. Here I am speaking about your line, "fear" (if putting a label on it) that we spoke about which seems to have no discernable cause. "Mostly in the solar plexus."

I was very interested to hear you mention this phenomenon before and am thrilled even more this time around. It's a sign rarely mentioned in spiritual circles which certainly can't be confused with anything else but legitimate reorientation. Of course, it is not strictly a prerequisite to enlightenment itself but a marvelous sign nonetheless.

Great news! Beingness is well and truly blooming in you like a patch of early spring flowers poking their heads out from the last vestiges of a late winter snowpack. Speaking of flowers, a biblical quote is brought to mind: "Consider the lilies of the field, how they grow: They neither toil nor spin." I would like to talk a little more in detail about this divine "gut ache" of yours. I don't recall ever explaining to you how it arose for me in the first place. First, I'll digress a bit and borrow Adya's "awakening in the head, heart and gut" analogy to explain how it arose here.

Perhaps you are unaware that Adya says the order is not fixed and could in fact progress in several ways, but for me it indeed followed precisely the usual prescribed order. Maybe it is similar in your case as well. First, I experienced awakening in the head so to speak. Seeing by way of a wisdom that was at times conceptual, at others more akin to direct experience, which guided me to realize how things really were or, more pointedly, were not.

This continued but was supplemented by an ever deepening and profound heart-centered opening. Call it *bhakti*, devotional reverence of the divine, tender heartedness, gratitude, love, whatever you wish, but it was a very powerful (and entirely novel) movement away from self. In retrospect it seems like a crucial piece of the puzzle naturally welled up if left to its own devices. Reverence was palpable at that time. In fact, by the end of the journey the "head" and the "heart" opening kind of balanced themselves out in equal measure. I am not implying that this is the way it should be, merely how it played out here. Your mileage may vary.

You may recall I mentioned that during the later stage of awakening, when great letting go into the Beingness of meditation was occurring many hours a day, I suffered extreme panic attacks which manifested in part as a strong constriction of the heart region. This fear resolved itself eventually as letting go proceeded. Then one day, the entire paradigm flipped with the dropping of self, and it was only then that I experienced the existential angst you are now speaking of. Not the least bit before that moment. Previously, like I said, letting go felt more akin to having a heart attack. Now this relic of emancipation felt like a jab to the mid-section. That "butterflies in the solar plexus" feeling remained with me for a long, long time as relaxing further and further into non-self continued. At that time my ego was mortally wounded but had not yet entirely expired. Just as it is said that patriotism is the last refuge of a scoundrel, so too in a loose sense perhaps, we can say that the gut is the last refuge of the ego.

I suggest you might use it as a convenient tool (but of course don't get too attached to it) to gauge how well the demolition project is proceeding. This "wakening" in the gut won't last forever. When it is gone for all intents and purposes so will you be, unless this is just a minor "glitch" in the system and next week you once again find yourself merrily (or more likely miserably) self-ing along quite nicely.

Doesn't it feel much like when one crests a huge peak on the roller coaster and then feels apprehension set in upon descent? It seems to be a visceral response in the stomach to the fear of extinction, doesn't it? It's the apprehension that wells up when you sense your pending annihilation. It's hard wired. Don't sweat it. It was of no consequence in my case as little identification remained at that time to consider it a bother. How about you? Eventually, it peters out of its own accord if authenticity prevails.

As an aside, I am curious if this kind of feeling arose for you prior to or during one of your ski runs down the mountainside, or is it entirely novel? Perhaps you momentarily sensed it as you flung yourself off a mountain top aiming for a championship winning time? And seeing as I have brought up the topic of devotion and the heart-centred approach, I was wondering if you would care to speak of this a bit. Was this ever an important part of your journey? Is it still ongoing or perhaps it is indistinguishable at this point? Some say ALL is love.

Cheers,
DJ

∞Chapter 12∞

October

2 Oct. 2013
To: DJ
Hello DJ,

    Your letter lays out your experiences in a way that is very much consistent with my own and as such I found it very interesting. Indeed, I did experience the fear of pending annihilation for minutes, even hours before pushing out of the starting gate in a ski race. It was a horrible feeling in the gut every time, and it seemed that I suffered more from it than others, but that's kind of hard to tell for sure.

Coupled with the prospect of physical injury or death, were the high stakes involved for the ego, which was in a full-on endeavor to prove itself worthy and lovable through the medium of success in the world of ski racing. My very identity and worth as a human being was at stake each time I stepped up to the gate. As you say, this present experience has the same quality to it. There also seems to be a pull to go into a low-grade depression, but so far I seem to be skirting around the edge of that rather than going right in. Resistance doesn't seem to be the way but more a letting be of the feelings and thoughts that arise and a seeing of the ego's maneuvers as it attempts to sustain its existence.

    I will write more about the heart aspect in my experience, but my daughter is here for a visit and I'm busy helping her with many practical things she needs to do while here and just hanging out together as it's a rare opportunity to spend time with her.

    Love, David

21 Oct. 2013
To: David

What's up? Still awaiting a reply to my question about your heart-centered practice. Haven't heard from you in weeks.

Still love to hear about it or anything else on your mind. Are you doing well these days?

DJ

22 Oct. 2013
To: DJ

Hi DJ,

Just spent the weekend at the K centre and will be back there again this coming weekend for a K retreat and then the following one for a Scott Kiloby retreat. I anticipate the Kiloby retreat will be interesting and there are already about thirty people signed up for it, which is not so interesting as the intimacy factor may be lowered due to so many people participating...But not necessarily, I guess, maybe...My participation at the centre seems to be more and more passionate in "confronting" the essential question of the self, and I think the dialogues are more intense and spirited than before—and more uncomfortable (see below). There are a few people willing to go into the question with some degree of depth.

The question of heart-centred practice seems at present to have lost its significance for me, but maybe there will be a greater urge to consider it at some point. What has been in the forefront of my experience lately is regular occasions of great discomfort and sometimes great insecurity and shakiness. The self is very uncomfortable in its own existence (or non-existence) and is sometimes in a sense of core instability and vulnerability as there is felt to be no solid ground upon which to stand. This shaking and insecurity is most pronounced after sexual activity involving the loss of life force through ejaculation.

The energy which normally holds the self together is felt to be lowered substantially and the whole ground of being (the separate Beingness of the self) is felt to be challenged and undermined in a fairly intense way. Even without that special circumstance there has been a heightened awareness of the core discomfort of the self-ing activity. For example, the other day having dinner with a friend and talking there was such an awareness of a self permeating or winding its way through everything I was saying, doing, and feeling. Nothing I could do to get away from it or change it.

A sense arose that this was real meditation, as far as that can exist within the limited context of a self being actively present. Anyway, these experiences are very raw and exposing - and challenging to be with. There seems to be no choice really about being with the experience, so in that sense it's not challenging or difficult to be with what's happening, but it is certainly not comfortable at all!

Then the shakiness partly subsides and there is often a feeling of the sense of Being having deepened or the knowing of Being having deepened. So far no sense of ultimate release. But I guess there are moments when the self-ing seems to give way to an authentic sense of presence which is grounded more in the heart or in a truer way of being.

I've signed up with Rob, Meghan, and a few others to be part of Adya's online course on "No self" which starts November 6. This should be right on topic, although I don't have a strong expectation that he will be saying anything I haven't already heard or that it will really help me in any significant way. I trust you know of what I speak. On the other hand, there can be openness to being surprised in whatever way and there does seem to be an interest in what will transpire.

You ask if I'm doing well these days, and I think you will see from my response above that the answer is no and yes, and I think you know what I mean. I'm reminded of Adya's response to a question, "Are we having fun yet?" He replied, "About as much fun as we can have while being burned at the stake." I'm sure we've shared that one before, but it seems to be a very truthy expression of how it is.

What's happening for you these days, if that question makes any sense?

Cheers,

David

29 Oct. 2013
To: David

"About as much fun as we can have while being burned at the stake"

That's a neat quote. Like we spoke about before, this part of the journey can be "disturbing" or unsettling but also quite thrilling and wondrous. I look back on it all quite fondly. The saying "This too will pass" springs to mind. How about, "There may be pain, but suffering is optional?" This statement has been quite true for me. I remember trying to explain this one to the New Thought ladies group in town. They talked about adversity and the ability to choose positive thoughts. I told them I didn't perceive any choice at all or any adversity as they saw it. Things just happened. It was the identification that followed which caused the suffering.

They said but surely I must choose not to be depressed about my physical problems, etc. I told them that there was no choice to be made about how identification unfolded. Unlike them, I had no "fence" to decide which side to be on. There were simply physical ailments and that was that. I asked them how it might be for any choice to arise regarding or disregarding misery or the like. There was simply disability and that was all. Truly suffering is entirely up to YOU. Of course, they didn't have a clue what I was going on about. Their mantra seemed to be "God is good, you are good, seek good thoughts."

I anticipate the Kiloby retreat will be interesting and there are already about 30 people signed up for it, which is not so interesting as the intimacy factor may be lowered by so many people.

True about the intimacy thing but with greater numbers perhaps also more likelihood somebody is actually sincerely interested in awakening in her/his lifetime. Do you think I am being too accusatory or cynical here? Like I said before, shutting off the auto-pilot is not all that difficult but few seem genuinely interested in doing so. I have heard - and suspect that there is truth in it - that in the general population one in a thousand people get on the spiritual path and of those you need a thousand seekers to amass before one actually awakens. Why so few?

Perhaps you would agree that the urge to cease dreaming is irrational and runs contrary to the survival instinct. Why bother, then? I haven't met as many seekers as you. How many have you met who actually care only about awakening? Is that even a reasonable question to ask, and what do I mean by it? How would one know if "someone only cares about awakening"? I guess you wouldn't unless you asked them. How about you, David, would you say you only care about awakening?

My participation at the centre seems to be more and more passionate in "confronting" the essential question of the self, and I think the dialogues are more intense and spirited....and a few people are willing to go into the question with some degree of depth.

..."Depth"...that sounds like fun. How else to bump into Spirit than with "spirited" pointing out. But I know you have to be careful lest you perturb Brother Harvey too much. "Manifesting abundance," i.e, filling retreats and drawing a K centre paycheck seems quite important to him, and I wonder if it comes at the expense of awakening. But that's not really my business is it? My business is to stay the course. Keep on track. No longer dream…

What's happening for you these days, if that question makes any sense?

I wrote to an abbot of a Zen centre, requesting the opportunity to come down for a visit. He seems sincere and his dharma talks are very practical. Largely prescriptive rather than descriptive (practical guidance rather than spiritual blah,blah)---just the way we like the truth served up. No response yet as I just sent it off.Cheers,

DJ

31 Oct. 2013
To: DJ

So maybe I'll be seeing you in this part of the world again (if you visit the Zen centre).

You speak of the disturbing or unsettling aspect of the journey (which I had focused on in my last letter) and also of the "thrilling and wondrous" aspect of it. I, too, can say that such experience has been appearing at times in the form of a sense of harmony and subtle well-being and a "knowing" or "not-knowing" that is actually so simple that it seems to be funny. Spontaneous laughter arises for no reason except the perception of the full emptiness of is-ness. This sense of harmony is definitely interesting as it feels like a reflection of the no-self state or no-state. It is not a creation of the self but a flavour of the underlying Is-ness. And there comes the sense that there is an unfolding (in "me") that is flowing by itself.

You wonder how many people really care only about awakening and if that is true for me. When I ask myself the question, I don't feel it can be answered so simply. It's a good question to keep in front of one, so to speak. It seems if I only cared about awakening, then I would be fully awake. The fact that I can't say I'm fully awake means that there are other things I'm holding onto at some level, even though I may not be fully aware of those attachments. In one sense the "I" doesn't want enlightenment at all - it's the last thing it wants - as it means (or appears to mean) the ending of itself. It wouldn't be honest to say I only want awakening. Which I are we talking about? If God or Life wants this body-mind organism to "awaken," then it will. Or maybe it's more mysterious than Life "wanting" anything. Asking and remaining with penetrating questions seems to be of value perhaps. Seeing whatever arises and negating all efforts or strategies of the mind seems to be of use, but also it's not a doing. The way it really is appears to be beyond the duality of doing and not doing.

What do you make of Rupert Spira's pointings? Have you explored them to any extent? I sometimes wonder if he is the latest expression in the evolution of consciousness as his approach seems so direct and to the point, somehow more direct than all other teachings I've come across. Essentially not different, perhaps, but in practical terms looking into what is, in a way others do not. Comments? I'll let you know what my experience of Scott Kiloby is this weekend.

Love,

David

∞ Chapter 13 ∞

November

5 Nov. 2013
To: David

The question of heart-centred practice seems at present to have lost its significance for me, but maybe there will be a greater urge to consider it at some point.

I asked because I was curious to see how the so-called "heart-centred" practice actually worked in your life given its seeming fundamental importance during my own journey. I recall the teacher at the Tibetan centre where I stayed doing meditation advising students to gaze up lovingly at the portrait of some Asian looking guy barely out of his teens, the revered Kagyu lineage Karmapa, in order to open up the heart centre. To each his own, I guess, but that suggestion invited mirth and outright derision from me. Among the litany of delusional suggestions this Western Rinpoche had brought forth, this was one of the most outlandish. I didn't know this Karmapa character from Adam. First and foremost, an upwelling of the heart has to be genuine. All I knew about this recently appointed Karmapa dude was that his figurehead position was politically contested. In fact, there were (still are) presently two of them, one propped up by the Chinese government, the other by a certain Tibetan faction. The whole thing stunk. I could never imagine having the slightest reverence for this clown, and here I was supposed to somehow develop a genuine tender-hearted opening around him. What nonsense! Here's the real deal for me.

TRUTH = BEAUTY = JOY

Focusing attention on something other than conceptual mind, moving away from egoic self-centredness, became a very natural part of the process. Unavoidable really. A seemingly necessary part of the journey.

I found that the thing engendered by this natural inclination to move away from self was feelings, rather than thoughts. An upwelling of the heart arises which can at times feel very intensely physical. Of course, a myriad of paths lead to realization, but I recall Castaneda asking, "Does your path have a heart?" That is a very good question. As I mentioned before, it seemed that in my case heart and wisdom mind eventually equaled out. So what did I do to foster this? Not much really as the "I" had not much of a role here. Simply put, wonder, appreciation and joy were evoked by listening to or seeing things that somehow triggered an emotional response. The result could be laughter or tears or a combination of both simultaneously. The triggers were usually "profoundly mundane" in nature. Vintage Monty Python comedy skits, electronic dream/trance music, bits of well-loved classic movies. For example, the conclusion of Alastair Sim's "Scrooge," where he awakens from the dream (what a great allegory that is), moved me to tears time and time again. Viewing Johnny Cash's video "I Hurt Myself Today" had a similar affect. Sobbing was often the result of letting go into Bhakti. It wasn't really the experience of revisiting comedic routines or indulging in poignant nostalgia that moved me so. That was simply the catalyst. What was happening then? Hard to say. THAT it was happening was most evident.

It got to the point that I could watch a You Tube video of something like a wingsuit base jumper hurling himself off a mountain side and be moved to tears of joy and wonder. Such beauty. Some kind of intangible, inexpressible quality was being deeply felt. Beauty and wonder abounded. Like the saying goes, "I can't describe art, but I know it when I see it." With perceptual "filters" decreasing, with Huxley's "doors of perception" opening ever wider, life was becoming more and more wondrous. Heart-centred experiences brought about feelings of incredible amazement, joy and mirth. Celebrating the divine creativity of the human spirit was the thing, not dispassionately gazing at religious icons or crappy portraits.

Here is a YouTube link I just discovered this week that if viewed back in the day, would have surely elicited such a response I am pointing to here. Still I am quite enthralled to see such wonder and "beauty." Check it out. Perhaps you can see what I mean. I hope you have good earphones because this video is a feast for ears as well as eyes. Something stirs in/out me when I have this kind of experience. Words fail. Perhaps life celebrates itself for a moment.

Mont-Blanc speed flying
https://www.youtube.com/watch?v=t8W0m3NpjcA

What have been in the forefront of my experience lately is regular occasions of great discomfort and sometimes great insecurity and shakiness.

This "shakiness" business is another great sign awakening is stirring. If you relax and soften you will notice it disappear... as will you. Same, same. The topic of orgasm is quite an interesting one. Something I investigated previously. Consider that ejaculation, as well as a yawn or a sneeze, are occasions when the body-mind complex drops spontaneously into Beingness for a moment. I wonder if your orgasm naturally intensifies the letting go process for a short time, much like an entheogen might. Just a bit of conjecture to add to your own.

I remember the first time "I" fell into the void completely. I had been metaphorically circling the rim for weeks in great fear and one evening, during my final meditation of the day, I finally took the leap. Great surprise hauled me back almost immediately. An unbearable "electric" shock coursed throughout my body. It felt like an orgasm but ramped up by several factors. The divine "climax." What a show stopper that was. Quite unbearable. Humans are not capable of enduring such pleasure. The French call orgasm "La petite mort," the little death. Like true nirvana, both imply cessation of self.

I checked the latest findings awhile back regarding the brain and ejaculation, and it turns out that the region of the brain responsible for creating the impression of "self" gets momentarily shut down when we orgasm. A "small death" indeed. For a moment no-self prevails.

So there you have it. We are being "Nirvanaed" during the act of copulation, but no one is ever the wiser. When self disappears by other means like through meditation, the response in the body-mind complex seems to be similar, i.e., an intense feeling of bliss and joy. In my case, the first brief encounter with cessation created unbearable pleasure with some kind of energetic electrical excitation coursing throughout the whole body. It reminds me of the descriptions of a kundalini awakening.

To quote Blake, "Energy is eternal delight"; or consider Alan Watts' appraisal, "The force of liberation will blow the world to pieces. It's too strong a current." Maybe not surprisingly then, this kind of earth-shattering experience was a one off for me. Too extreme. The very next time self was sufficiently eroded such that the void was entered or nirvikalpa Samadhi produced, there was no repeat of the "unbearable lightness of being." Watts once said, "It's terribly important to see beyond ecstasy." And I guess this is a case in point here.

Thereafter, there might be occasions of joy, but it was never again stupendous. It doesn't seem like such a leap from orgasm to the "small death" to liberation does it? I posit the experience differs in degrees but not kind. We could add a certain entheogen in here as well. I am suggesting all foster varying degrees of cessation. Next time you experience sexual release, see if you can remain as pure awareness itself and see what the outcome of that might be. Could be illuminating.

Finally, I am wondering how your retreat went. Also I got signed up for the Adya web event. Asked him a question already.

Love,

DJ

6 Nov. 2013
To: DJ

Hello DJ,

The movie of the ski flying is "awesome" (ha, ha). But seriously, it did arouse "the heart" in an appreciation of beauty and joy. Kind of mysterious how certain appearances awaken these responses in the being. Something larger and transcendent of egoic consciousness.

At the recent Scott Kiloby retreat I had an experience that I'll try to describe (if that's the right word) of "no-self" seemingly accessed by doing a one on one inquiry with Scott within the group setting. The issue I presented to him was an existential fear of ego death which began at age eight when I began to contemplate physical death and what might lie beyond. What would be when I was no longer here? The unknowability of it awakened a sense of negative emptiness in my gut and solar plexus that has been with me ever since, only retreating into the background at times to re-emerge and significantly affect my experience of myself and "my" life. Anyway, after being guided through a process of looking to see where this me that is afraid to dissolve is to be found - which took about half an hour - we reached a point of apparent completion and let it rest.

The next day, I became aware that in the midst of whatever was arising in my experience there was no sense of a self mixed in with it. Even though at times anxiety was coming up, there was no self in the experience and, therefore, no concern about the anxiety or whatever was arising. It was remarkably different from my normal experience!

This no-self sense lasted throughout the day. Then when I spoke with Meghan that night after returning home, I suddenly found myself super sensitive and emotionally reactive to a perceived sense of being shut out (when she was tired and wanting some down time for herself). I was amazed that the no-self experience so rapidly changed to a triggered self experience. It seems that there was a heightened sensitivity which in the absence of a self came with a sense of "truth = beauty = joy," but in the presence of a self became emotionally painful and reactive. Obviously, there was still a "me" in the picture. Or was there really? That invited some more inquiry on my own and seemed to end up in a deeper sense of resting as awareness. Now the feeling is hard to describe and is more a sense of just being.

All pretty interesting to an explorer of inner space—as we are. Interesting in itself, it seems, and not so much because of any attainment experienced or "progress" being made. Whatever...

There is a resonance with your talk about the heart. The heart has for sure been a very significant element in my own journey. Hilarious about Karmapa. I may respond further to the rest of your letter.

Love,

David

6 Nov. 2013
To: DJ

Hi,

I received this in an email the other day and thought it was pretty good!

Cheers,

David

Subject: EQUALITY TEST

http://www.upworthy.com/2-monkeys-were-paid-unequally-see-what-happens-next?g=3

8 Nov. 2013
To: David

David, here are a few thoughts regarding your current "calamity" (UG Krishnamurti's quaint term, not mine) vis-a'-vis the Kiloby retreat.

Back in the day Kiloby was one of my favorites. A great inspiration and role model for those interested in investigating what it was really like to awaken. He oozed sincerity. I am pleased to hear how helpful he was. Regarding your experience,

> "....there was no sense of a self mixed in with it..... It was remarkably different from my normal experience!,"

I am always keen to hear descriptions of non-self. Adya's current four-week online course on no-self is a case in point though, as you point out, the first episode was not particularly revelatory or prescriptive in actuality. Let's wait and see.

At this point I expect you have come to see how eventually you leave all teachers and teachings behind you. Perhaps that is what partially informs your reaction to what Adya said. Also, I think we have pretty much covered anything Adya might bring up. We will see if this is so as he continues.

David, regarding the above quote, would you care to elaborate on what this lack of self felt/feels like... or feels not like. You said it differs from normal experience. Are you referring here to so-called normal waking reality, or the meditative state, or all states/experience? What did your opening with Kiloby feel like?

> This no-self sense lasted throughout the day. Then when I spoke with Meghan that night after returning home, I suddenly found myself super sensitive and emotionally reactive.

One thing I noticed early on when non-dual awareness began "heating up" was that with the filters/barriers the self normally employs to protect itself largely degraded, one could be quite reactive when the occasion arose. By this I mean that self normally carries with it all kinds of defensive mechanisms/measures to safeguard the ego from offence and emotional harm. One is hardened and inured to emotionally charged situations through a dampening effect.

You might imagine that no-self would make you less likely to take offence or be reactive, but in fact this may not always be so. I found I was more sensitive to everything around me as there were no longer any barriers to protect apparent selfhood. Everything was pretty full on. Emotions/sensitivity can be enhanced as you transition to LIFE itself. Don't worry. The cool thing is that you will find supposed slights and affronts falling away very rapidly. They are not so "sticky" like they once were. You might get PO'd in the moment, but almost as quickly, it is all forgotten. As you keep relaxing into it, you will find the inclination to just let things be as they are. It will naturally become harder and harder to get a rise out of you. If someone is not inclined to talk to you that is just how it is. It has nothing to do with "you." How they respond to you is their own business.

Case in point. I planned to go on that long summer hike I mentioned to you with another guy. We spent weeks planning, acquiring gear and grub, etc. Come the day of striking out, he is a no-show. Wouldn't even answer his door despite my walking all the way twice to his place to find out what the heck was going on; so I go off alone. We are still friends. Most would have been enraged and never spoken to the "fool" again. But things can't possibly work that way anymore here. He wasn't going to accompany me and that was that. Why argue with reality? I was surprised by my lack of annoyance. Of course, there were repercussions as I now don't take that guy to be reliable. That's karma. Simply the law of cause and effect. There were sensible repercussions but not ego driven ones. Get angry? That's a mug's game.

It seems that there was a heightened sensitivity which in the absence of a self came with a sense of "truth = beauty = joy," but in the presence of a self became emotionally painful and reactive. Obviously, there was still a "me" in the picture.

Yes, I gather a semblance of a "me" persists and will probably do so for some time as it degrades. But more to the point, a "not me" is replacing the old paradigm. As I see it, the gap, or supposed gap, between self and not self is shrinking. This will unfold as it will. Don't try to second guess it. It's all proceeding marvellously. The best you can do is remain as awareness. As I said previously, resistance is futile. One day soon you will come to intimately know this truth for yourself. You'll get tired of the whole thing. It takes a lot of energy to endure the "now you see me, now you don't" charade. These state changes are tiresome, aren't they? I eventually found it all a bit of a bore and apparently gave up or gave in.

Or was there really? That invited some more inquiry on my own and seemed to end up in a deeper sense of resting as awareness. Now the feeling is hard to describe and is more a sense of just being.

Is the present state of affairs of "just being" or "resting as awareness" the same thing as the "no-self" experience you had with Kiloby? "Are YOU resting as awareness or rather is there just awareness itself." In either case what is this like? Can anything be said to be happening while "just being"? If nothing is happening, how would you know this? If something is happening, surely it must be happening to "you," correct? What do you make of this? You said the day after the Kiloby investigation there was "no sense of self" mixed in. Does this "mixed in" refer to happenings? Just what the heck is going on here?

Love, DJ

PS: You asked me about my impressions of Rupert Spira. Very favourable. Like Kiloby, a great inspiration. I discovered him in 2009 and was fortunate to snag a first edition of his book. Your question inspired me to check out his latest videos to see how things were these days. Still top-rate pointers I conclude. I would never hesitate in the slightest to recommend him to a serious seeker. Here is a quote from his latest I thought you might like. He hit the mark with that one.

"If you want to learn to live without fear, you first have to learn to live with it."
R. Spira

9 Nov. 2013
To: DJ

Hi,

Probably a short reply today. I'll attempt to describe in more detail the "no-self" experience with Scott K. There was a feeling of lightness and clarity in my sense of being. A kind of hole in the middle of experiencing, but not an empty hole as much as an emptiness pervading everything. A definite sense that everything was just happening but happening to no one: Nothing insinuating itself into the experiencing. Of course, it wasn't a sense of something lacking but on the contrary a sense of nothing lacking combined with a clear sense of freedom. Very ordinary in the sense of nothing dramatic about it, but extraordinary in the sense of being different from the normal mode of knowing myself. A sense of freshness and aliveness.

I very much resonate with your descriptions of how it was for you with the "heating up" of non-dual awareness and just read some Rupert Spira this morning saying very similar things about it. That certainly bears out my experience. I've been shocked sometimes lately at the states of consciousness I've suddenly found happening (found myself manifesting) where I seem to have fallen into a layer of conditioned psyche which is certainly not loving and harmonious but over which I seem to have no control and within which I am unable to pretend, even if I want to, that I'm feeling otherwise, i.e., normal and rational, a "good guy," and so on.

It's a real sense of having no room to exercise choice or free will concerning my state. It's a great opportunity to contemplate at that point and a serious inquiry does bring a shift in the experience without any "doing" on my part. The essential ingredient in these cases seems to be just the willingness to be fully present with what's happening, and that's no small feat! Being aware presence does have a significant action and, as you say, it is most powerful and of a different quality when there is no "me" (or less me) mixed in with it.

I always found UG's expression very interesting, radical, and sometimes funny. "The Calamity" is perhaps the most memorable of his descriptions.

Cheers, David

15 Nov. 2013
To: DJ

Good day, DJ,

So, what did you make of the second online Adya talk regarding no-self. For me it was a little more interesting than the first one (but still not much "new"). To focus on the "negative" for a moment, one thing I didn't appreciate was the mixing up of definitions of "self."

He opened by defining self as the unseeable witness or seer of everything. So far, so good. I was surprised that he spoke of self as Mooji and others do from the Hindu background, with a capital S as Self, given his Zen background. Buddha and Buddhists, as far as I know, never speak of Self in that way. But that was clear enough, if he wanted to use that terminology.

Then he went on to speak of self in a few other ways throughout the talk, giving it limited qualities and dividing it into lower self and higher self, again something that wouldn't appear in the Zen tradition as far as I know. Sometimes he was referring to self as ego, sometimes as divine ego, and so on. It all seemed very mixed up. And again, in his exercise for week 2, he was mixing his ideas of self in a very unclear way. In one way I was quite unimpressed by this and even frustrated, but then that's only the mind wanting everything to be neat and tidy and rational. Still, it seems surprising that logically it was so unclear - or so it appeared to me.

While experimenting with Adya's exercise from last week, seeing that all thought is only thought and doesn't refer to anything real beyond itself, an insight arose that (psychological) fear only relates to thought and is completely a product of thought. It's a simple and ordinary insight in a way, but in the moment it seemed to carry an impact, and that has remained as a flavour of peace, clarity, and suchness ever since. And actually, as I write, that insight seems to really cut through the whole mechanism of identification with thought and how thought creates meaning. That dovetails with the second week's exercise.Enough for now. Looking forward to hearing from you,

David

19 Nov. 2013
To: David

Hi David,

In your interesting missive you have in a fashion provided an example of the spiritual pull that leads us one way or the other: Direct experience versus matters of egoic conceptualization. Regarding spirituality, I tried to keep a lucid perspective by asking myself, *Is the TRUTH being served here?* Is the impulse to awaken in this lifetime front and centre, or is the ego up to its old tricks of obfuscation once again. Plain and simple, are my interests and actions (or lack thereof) more or less likely to cause self-ing to cease? Your letter wonderfully describes just such an example as it unfolded, i.e., seeing through thought and fear. Terrific!

At the same time I wonder if you are not wandering off course a bit in the rest of your letter. Maya is really good at what it does and it often goes unnoticed. Let me elaborate by way of a couple of anecdotes.

Last night at supper I had a discussion with two housemates (boyfriend/girlfriend) around "sacred hunting practice," which arose since boyfriend wants to try his hand at bow-hunting a deer and these folks are of the "green" persuasion. Nice people who want a source of clean natural meat but are not so sure about the killing part. Long story short, we ended on the topic of baiting deer to enable a sure kill. She had never heard of such a practice. I explained it as being similar to shooting "rubber duckies in a bathtub."

Such inflammatory speech elicited the desired rise. "Oh that's not sacred, how despicable," she said. "Sure it is," I replied, and then used her logic against her. If the deer '"wants" to be taken (that's a fundamental premise to a sacred kill), then it will be found at the feeding site happily munching on deer chow, awaiting its demise.

Otherwise, it won't appear and the bowman will come up empty handed. "What's not sacred about that?" I asked. Her boyfriend seemed to not be too averse to this suggestion, as it was he who wanted the meat most and understood how difficult it would be to actually procure it, while she seemed more inclined to find strategies to assuage what I took to be a guilty conscience. Of course, this woman resisted my suggestion, as she couldn't imagine poor little "Bambi" being skewered in such an ignoble way. David, being the vegetarian that you are, I imagine you would have arisen to her defense if present or, even more likely, asked why the enterprise was necessary in the first place. Yet another viewpoint to add to the mix.

"Oh come on," I said, "it's all just storytelling anyhow. It's just stories. You tell yourself yours, I mine. She and her partner had recently finished an intensive by a guy who sells "expanding the box" (box…what box? seems to be the more salient question here, but anyhow…) self-help and part of his shtick is the line "It's all bullshit, all just stories." Previously, she told me she found the weekend workshop "inspirational" and liked the idea of life as "story." That was until put to the test, and then, of course, she wasn't so inclined to support that pointer after all. Pay lip service to it, yes, but in reality: no way. Her boyfriend echoed back to me my "just stories" line and at least did not overtly resist the sentiment outright. His girlfriend, though, was disturbed. After a pause, where I could see her mind begin to grasp the actual ramifications of what I was suggesting, (i.e., discounting all stories, which unfortunately included hers as well) she would have none of it. She glanced at her boyfriend and said, "Just stories…well sort of…" Her first inclination was to go along to get along, but that was replaced in a moment by a very certain…"BUT NOT REALLY." It was clear to me what she meant by her backtracking. I caught her in the perennial lie we tell ourselves. "Yes, it may be just storytelling as far as you jokers out there are concerned because you don't really have a good grasp on what is really going on, but I...well, that's a rather different case, isn't it? I have my finger directly on the pulse of reality, and we'd all be a lot better off if you could just acknowledge this fact."

Certainly she was more than willing to concede that "DJ" may be full of crap, but most assuredly SHE was not. From the vantage point of her reality tunnel her story was clearly not a story at all. "Not really." It was real and true and it counted, God damn it. "How dare anyone equate my unique, special, meaningful viewpoint for mere storytelling," she was thinking. And so it goes...

David, can you detect the hints of desperation there? She was only too happy to go along with the storytelling thing as long as it did not apply to her. After all, she has never been able to understand why all seven billion of us have gotten it so wrong for so long. But I am not singling out this woman, for she is just a case in point. Everybody seems to believe that if it were possible for all of humanity to see reality as they did, the world could not help but be a happier, better running, "proper" place to inhabit (hmmm...living on earth being described as in-"habit"...interesting).

When I say it's all stories, of course, I draw no distinctions here. All of us really are but players upon a stage, reciting lines fed to us by some unrecognized teleprompter. The story of me has no author, purpose, or meaning save for the imaginings of a deluded mind. This brings me to my next little "story."

It speaks to a position above where I said the story of "me," very much unlike the way we regard good old-fashioned moral fairy tales, is in truth inherently meaningless. I see Adya's second supplemental material addresses this issue very well. Adya puts it, and I have come to clearly see it as so myself (perhaps you as well...?), that the conditioned mind has a propensity to derive meaning where in fact there is none to be had. I don't mean incorrect conclusions are arrived at. Rather, all conclusions are spurious, a fiction of the mind.

Case in point. One day I was walking the few blocks from Meghan's place to my editor's house to finish up the final draft of the book and this topic of a Universe devoid of meaning came once again to mind. I was mulling over how abundantly clear and almost comical the drive to impart meaning into everything was. I always had a tender spot for my confused ego. It simply never realized that while things did indeed appear to happen, it was the secondary "spin," imparting meaning or purpose where there was none, that was the delusional bit. Very wacky.

Anyhow, so there I was about one block from the editor's house, smiling at how truly strange this altered state of consciousness really was and low and, behold, I spied two boisterous crows/ravens in a front yard. One was particularly animated and flapping about in front of a solitary meek looking pigeon. How odd. A very agitated black bird was cawing and pecking at the docile pigeon quite aggressively for what initially seemed to be no reason at all. BUT THERE MUST BE A REASON. Why? Why was this happening, I wondered? And so it was that the mean machine clicked on...

I had never seen such odd bird behavior before. "Curious, very curious" (or so my mind insisted); I thought that I must get to the bottom of this. I couldn't see any food about to cause such a strange display. Two crows, one clearly bullying a poor defenseless pigeon for no discernable reason. But why? Just then the pigeon took flight. Good. I was wondering why it hadn't done so sooner. The pigeon flew across the road to a neighboring front yard. The dark rabble-rouser went after it. More tussling ensued. Well, that proves it. Crows are belligerent birds, I always thought as much, and now I see that they are taken to bullying for no reason at all. Poor little pigeon. I like pigeons...much more cute and adorable than those nasty loud mouthed crows...who...who...now, what was I talking about...? Oh yah, awful crows and lovely pigeons which...And then, thank God, SILENCE and LUCIDITY.

Out of clarity a big, jolly belly laugh erupted. I hadn't laughed so hard in weeks. Incredible. The very thing I had just been cogitating over not a half block previously had just transpired for real. I had seen a few birds and somehow my mind had uncontrollably fabricated quite a tale around them. Meaning was derived and conclusions garnered, all nicely wrapped up in a tidy package, thank you very much. But it really wasn't so.

What had seemed to play out hadn't actually been a live action diorama featuring the age old story of good versus evil. Crows are not belligerent bullies, pigeons meek and mild. I really don't know what, if anything at all, transpired on that lawn. Maybe there were signs of aggression, but for all I know that could have been play. Maybe that pigeon had been part of a flock that had attacked the poor crow in the past and now it was payback time. Do birds seek retribution... who knows? Maybe the Bird in Black was really the good guy here. If you investigate closely, perhaps you will see that there are no good or bad guys. The point is, Do you actually know anything? Does anything truly happen at all? Again, ask yourself, "Aren't I making it all up?"

Certainly the laugh indicated the recognition that there was no inherent meaning to any of my conclusions. There really was no possibility of any conclusion at all. How illuminating it was to be thinking about the mind's ability to manifest marvelous feats of mental prestidigitation (i.e., pulling meaning out of a great big nothing), for a moment to succumb to it, and then have clarity again and see it for what it really was: The ramblings of a conditioned mind that simply knew no better. Like I said, it struck me as an opportune comedic moment, if nothing else.

Heh, did you hear the one about the birds? Well it seems that two darkies and one whitey saunter into a bar and the barkeep says, "What'll you drink?" Of course, that's all it takes to get you off and running. From there the punch line can be anything you like, as you truly are making the whole fucking thing up. I hope you paid attention to what Adya said in this week's supplemental material.

See it for yourself and that will be enough to see very clearly indeed. Lines from it like the following stand out for me:

- We are living in a dream - literally!
- The story is not really happening.
- The narrative of "me" is the programming at work. The narrative is not really true.
- Notice that there is direct sensory experience...and then there is everything that you THINK about that experience, which follows. Shift attention to direct experience rather than your interpretation of it.
- When self disappears, the narrator disappears...and you are in the world of suchness... things simply as they are... extraordinary!

If you take Adya's words as direct invitations to find out for yourself, it can make all the difference. If not, it is yet more tired old sayings. If you directly see what he means, it will be abundantly clear to you that there never was a punchline to be had. You'll realize the answer to, "Who is it who makes the grass green?" or, "Who is it who makes the flag flutter? " Now on to what you wrote.

In kirtan, the heart-centered spiritual music of India, we find a kind of call and response going on, as I am sure you are well aware. Great stuff eh? So to use it as a metaphor, if my call and Adya's is to pay attention to fabricated "meaning," how thrilling to hear your response below. The old chap has already got it. In the final summation, call and response are not different. You said:

While experimenting with Adya's exercise from last week, seeing that all thought is only thought and doesn't refer to anything real beyond itself, an insight arose that (psychological) fear only relates to thought and is completely a product of thought.

What you have written above is the plain honest truth, and you know it, don't you? No one could dissuade you of this fact. How rare to hear such truthiness. A guru says "all thoughts are inherently empty" but to really grokk that with one's entire being is amazing, isn't it? In my experience the simplest insights have always been the profoundest. They are the ones that tend to stick and lead to transformation, self-immolation, grace, etc. In my journey Adya was the master of pointing out the obvious.

But just as common sense is not so common, so, too, in spiritual matters the obvious is rarely so readily apparent. That is until you have an "aha" moment and then you wonder how it was ever overlooked for so long. So you've seen the ephemeral nature of thought, eh? That's the clarity that arises when one sees for one's self. How is it, then, that everyone takes him or herself to be their thoughts, places such tremendous import on what they think?

I reckon that a solitary photon, said (and I find this quite astonishing) to have zero resting mass, would outweigh all the thoughts ever conceived in comparison. Experience shows that thoughts are less tangible or "weighty" than a sub-atomic particle said to weigh nothing at all. Thoughts are mirages, spectral will-o-the wisps. Like a rainbow they evaporate when closely inspected. Like the rainbow's trick of the light, they are nothing more than a trick of the mind. What are they? How much do they weigh? What colour? What do they feel like when grasped? I've searched long and hard and find no qualities I can ascribe to them. I and neuroscientists alike don't have a clue what they are and don't even know how they arise or from whence. Everybody is under the misguided impression that they can choose their thoughts, but the most cursory investigation proves we don't even have the power to make them. They spontaneously arise by their own accord. How is it, then, that this is what we take ourselves to be? What a joke.

It is apparent, if one cares but look, that everyone is somnambulistically munching away on tubs of hot buttered popcorn, seated amongst rows of Coca Cola-stained chairs, fully ensconced in the cinema of that which ain't transpiring. But David, it seems probable you have spied the emergency exit. I take it you have even nudged the escape portal open from time to time and "peered" out a bit. Shortly, I have full confidence, you will be astonished to realize the cinema does not even exist. Seeing that you are not your thoughts is a tremendously liberating insight, isn't it? Just tremendous, and I daresay a crucial one, too.

Kudos to you if this came via "good works"; otherwise, congratulations on having such a splendid spell of good luck. You know I once was lucky enough to be at a casino in Macau where the dice rolled favorably nine or ten times in a row. Astonishing good fortune. I recognize that you are on a similar "roll" right now. Get ready because a couple of goons are gonna soon grab you by your elbows and haul your ass outta the joint for good. Funny thing is, as they do so, you will have the biggest frickin' grin on your face, since for the first time in your life you won't have a care in the universe. Here's to breaking the bank!

If you recall, last time I included R. Spira's pointer, "To live without fear first you must live with it." Do you see what he is pointing to here? This reality exactly played itself out in my own journey. Fear arose and there was simply nothing to be done about it. I didn't try to avoid it, nor did I try to imagine how I might go about embracing it. The simplest and best thing was to do nothing at all. I'll be damned if it didn't just eventually fade away all by itself.

Trying to develop evasive strategies just prolongs the agony... and, more importantly, is entirely fruitless. I understand your newest insight is proving most helpful in this regard. Now it is time to "man up" and get that one way ticket to nowheresville once and for all. Take the leap. You might feel like you are jumping into a scary void, but what is actually transpiring? There you peacefully sit in your living room, utterly safe and secure on your couch as the BIG NOTHING slowly envelops you. You are not going anywhere, save for your thoughts. The unpleasantness, angst or horror is only imaginal. There is nothing to these thoughts. The leapless leap awaits. I'd like to say only time will tell, but I know you've seen through that one. There is only NOW; there is no place but HERE. Trust me when I say it ain't ever gonna unfold tomorrow.

As for Adya's conceptualizing...most, if not all, of the points you make I agree with, but to what "end"? All of us know you can't talk about this stuff and not fail. But is he failing eloquently? Who is to say? YOU? And who is that?

Certainly if we examine what he is saying, we should do so from the viewpoint of TRUTH. Does Truth have a point of view? I think such speculation is interesting, certainly at times I find it quite enjoyable, but I wonder if it ultimately serves the truth in the highest regard. Sure I would love to talk to you about such matters on a car trip to the K centre as we used to do, but in this forum let's stay on topic, shall we?

Are Adya's pointers helping you in your own practice? Sapere aude. I have some theories on what Adya is up to when he languages the material as he has done, but I will save that for another time. Furthermore, who knows what he really means? Language is symbolic, totally open to interpretation and speculation. I have no clue what the Buddha said. Let's stick with the facts, and that is, "What do you know right NOW"?

Chapter 13 | November

We can and should look at more important things in the last few remaining weeks allotted us. *Tempest fugit.* Take Adya's words for pointers as he intends them, not as fodder for debate. Like I said before, I could care less what the man says. You are your own authority. It's all up to you, baby. Are you emptiness or fullness? Are you self or non-self? Who cares what the advaitists or Zenists say? What say you, good sir? Or, what say you not?

Have you looked at any of Adya's Q and A sessions? Some of those are quite relevant and on topic. I find the range of questions quite interesting. And, as I alluded to above, I think that this week's supplemental material is bang on. As you are doing, keep your investigation focused on the straight forward simplest pointers. If it doesn't involve your own awakening, save it for another time. Who needs external validation? Again, I say, "Who cares what the Buddhists, Hindus, Scientologists and Proctologists have to say?" Fuck them all!

On second thought, better not ignore the sage advice of your proctologist, but screw the rest. The same, of course, can be said about my drivel. I throw out a lot of ideas in the hopes that you might investigate one or two of them wholeheartedly. So far I guess none have floated your boat, but no matter. One can never predict what will resonate for a person, so I fear my strategy has been to make up for this limitation by compensating through sheer volume and for that I do apologize. LOL. I reckon it's a lot like projectile vomiting. If you stand back far enough you are ensured a wide enough stream such that at least some of it makes it to the intended toilet bowl. Score!

Love, DJ

PS: Thanks for the link on primates "covetous" behavior. That was illuminating and hilarious. I went on to watch the whole Ted Talk by that scientist.

The Clothes Have No Emperor
22 Nov. 2013
To: DJ

Hi,

Just a quick message today. I found the Adya talk on Wednesday excellent. The way he opened with the exploration of the issue of dissolving of the self was completely in alignment with my experience as far as it goes. He was speaking my language in a way that I've rarely heard from any teachers: "I" felt totally met in what he said. (What is the "I" that felt met? is another question.) So that was a good start, and then the rest of the talk, including the way he spoke of the "human" aspect, continued to be so in tune with recent experiences it was almost uncanny.

Interesting to note at the same time that nothing he said was "new" to me or hard to comprehend. It seems we only resonate knowingly with what we already know in some way. Otherwise, we can resonate (you may take exception to the language here) with the energy or intuitive sense of what is being heard without necessarily comprehending it in terms of concepts and knowledge. I'll write more fully soon...Love, David

25 Nov. 2013
To: David

It seems we only resonate knowingly with what we already know in some way.

Yes, I concur, David. We resonate more fully with what we have already glimpsed or experienced; and at other times I found something would arise, a feeling, a sense of "recognition" that I "knew" intimately but seemingly had forgotten. It really felt that way, realizations so utterly apparent but seemingly put out of "mind" for a while. I like your use of the word "uncanny." I couldn't agree more. But I wonder if it is not more a case of TRUTH realizing itself rather than a "me" doing so.

Otherwise, we can resonate (you may take exception to the language here) with the energy or intuitive sense of what is being heard without necessarily comprehending it in terms of concepts and knowledge.

If this sentiment actually involves truthiness, you'll never hear a peep from me. If it's an intuition that emanates from some place or thing, or NO-THING, other than conceptual egoic mind, which if it is actual truthiness can't help but be the case, then I reckon things look bright.

The problem is hearing that small, quiet, unassuming voice. If you are not vigilant, the chattering monkey mind invariably drowns it out such that delusion passes for truth. I found Adya was particularly adept at pointing out how Maya keeps us transfixed in the dream state. But I also like to point out that Adya is fond of saying, "When I awoke, I awakened from all traditions. That, of course, included my own."

Love to hear more...,

DJ

The Clothes Have No Emperor

∞ Chapter 14 ∞

December

5 Dec. 2013
To: DJ

Hi DJ,

    Wrote my first blog (see below) in ages for the K-centre website and decided to send you a copy as my latest foray into the mystery. I hope I am honest in saying that I assign no value to it:

> For quite some time now I have not written anything and there has just been no urge to do so. This morning some curiosity arose as to this lack of motivation, along with the idea to write down something about how that curiosity would unfold. What can be said about truth, and what value is there in saying anything? Is it helpful for anyone else to read about my experiences and insights? Maybe, or maybe not. And what can be said about emptiness, the reality beyond concepts? All words and ideas fail. If words are spoken, they are spoken. If there is interest to listen, then there is interest. If there is interest in exploring or inquiring, then it will take place. Interest cannot be manufactured and the results of it seem to be unpredictable. Who is going to benefit from any of it? Who is there to not benefit, or to be concerned either way? Life is just unfolding. Further questioning and looking just continues to reveal that thought is not the instrument which can give any real answers. There is a sinking back into just simply being and effortlessly perceiving, the simplicity of which is more truly the "answer" than anything thought can produce. In the not-knowing, the knowing without anything to be known, without any object of knowledge, all seeking has come to an end in the fullness and wholeness of emptiness. What the mind sometimes labels as boring is revealed as a lovely kind of paradox:

A freshness without content. Then, whatever arises partakes of this quality of "freshness..."

That's about all for today, my friend. I hope all is well with you. Still living in the same place and working at the soup kitchen? Anything coming of your inquiries at the Zen centre?

  Cheers,
David

7 Dec. 2013
To: David

Hi,

I liked your last blog entry. I want to comment a bit on it and start wrapping this investigation up. I'll send that to you shortly, but first offer the following in answer to your question about the Zen opportunity I was seeking at the Zen centre.

Like in the game of Jeopardy, first see the Abbots answer...then my question will follow. Here is the Abbott's reply to my query email.

  Cheers,
  DJ

Hi DJ

Bwahahaha!

That was great! Quite a journey you had, indeed. I wonder if you know Ms ??? (name excised for privacy concerns) in those parts. She was a member of ours off and on, and I think she did some practice with Adyashanti as well.

If you are in town, please do contact me and let me know, and I will do what I can to arrange to have you visit for tea and practice with the Sangha here. So much more can be known in a day of practice than in hours of chatting. You will feel at home, or you won't.

Thanks for taking the time to write, and to share your story. I look forward to meeting you.

Be well,

E

And here then, David, was my original query letter to the Zen Abbot.

Hi E,

DJ here from charming BC, Canada. Pleasure to get your invitation awhile back to correspond. Sat with it for quite some time. Listened to your Oct. 8 podcast where you again invited folks to write and thus this email eventually manifested itself. These days a movement to act may arise but no apparent "actor" seems present to claim doer-ship, so these decisions evolve at their own pace. But I have already gotten ahead of "myself." Let me explain. Here's the brief back story:

Guy becomes middle aged. He spends decades half-heartedly conceptually inquiring into the nature of reality but doesn't progress very far in a pragmatic way. Then several upheavals befall him, causing the loss of pretty much everything he values and cherishes. His slate is pretty much wiped clean. Quite an op-

portunity arises. This newfound (though at the time not very welcomed) potential freedom eventually precipitates an "aha" moment. "Why not get off your ass and find out for yourself just what the fuck is really going on"? Resistance prevails, but eventual capitulation. So, ok, let's earnestly, and I do mean EARNESTLY, endeavor to discover the ultimate nature of reality instead of just playing the armchair mystic. "Awaken or bust" becomes my rallying cry. Find out if this spiritual thing is just one big scam or discover that enlightenment truly exists….or simply expire due to old age catching up with you and thus never find closure one way or another. Any of those outcomes would have been fine since at least I would have known something for myself. Conceptual philosophizing had run its course. *Sapere aude*, daring to know for oneself, became the overwhelming drive.

I had no immediate mentors to draw upon for this journey. Only a vague notion to uproot from Ontario, go west and try plant medicine, and then hopefully immerse myself in meditation. This was all foreign territory as I was entirely ignorant of the subject matter at hand.

Things came to pass as envisioned. A certain natural *entheogen* (revealing the Spirit/Divine within) was consumed many times until it worked its magic fully, and then it was time to move on.

Next, self-inquiry was embraced wholeheartedly. With the greatest sincerity I could muster, I took up prolonged "true" meditation practice, nine to ten hours a day, month after month, ensconced in a secluded Tibetan hermitage off Vancouver Island. I was fully dedicated to discovering my true nature, so never became a "real" monk (wasn't at all interested in adopting a new lifestyle; I wanted a resolution as quickly as possible) though oddly it seemed as if I was the only "true" monk there, as nobody else (teacher included) seemed particularly inclined to, or interested in, waking-up.

Found my real teacher, Adyashanti (fourteen-year American Zen guy, though no longer affiliated with that particular tradition per se) who provided several simple pointers to help me find my way home. I spent my time there mostly secluded in my room. This living space was a renovated bit of the back of a barn (THE original founding Greenpeace members built it back in the day) that gratefully afforded me the opportunity to be totally isolated from the main retreat centre. For the large part I independently did my own cooking, cleaning, work and meditation schedule. I sat silently as much as was useful. In the beginning, ten or more hours per day garnered great results. Later a few hours less were needed to provide optimum stillness. Everything was totally focused on awakening and then one day around a year later, through something I can only call "grace"—for I certainly had nothing to do with what transpired—the self simply fell away. The journey ended. Seeker and seeking stopped dead in its tracks in a moment out of time.

This "experienceless experience" was not totally unlike how my meditation had been at the time, but the Beingness engendered through silent sitting came and went, depending on whether or not I was on the cushion, and this transcendental happening was vastly different than that. With "self-ing" ended, coming to be "nirvanaed," or being "cessated", call it what you will, I can tell you that the feeling was not entirely different in kind but certainly varied tremendously in degrees of experience when compared to my normal meditation practice. What happened was unimaginable, literally. It would be impossible for the conceptual mind to ever conjure up such a thing in a million millennia, since this "thing" (which is not a thing at all) has nothing to do with thought in the slightest. And to think it was there all along.

The paradigm totally flipped. In a sense a new reality revealed itself. Or more exactly, the old one fell away to reveal nothing at all. Astonishing! A seamless indivisible mass of every thingness prevailed. So called "oneness" blossomed. Forget the Big Bang. Most astonishing of all is the "Big Bloom" which reveals Plotinus' *monad*, THE ALL, to itself. In a sense MIND turns inward and reveals itself to itself. "Holy fuck" pretty much sums it all up!

Though, to be clearer, it impressed more like emptiness than something I could point to and say, "Behold, here lies oneness." Of course, you would never get an argument out of me if you were drawn to label the ineffable as oneness itself. In truth all labels fail. Things didn't quite end there, though. After a day or so of non-dual awareness, a kind of subtle delusion re-exerted itself.

What transpired next was a several-months-long-period where a new and improved "spiritual ego" arose. This re-invented, re-imagined, and re-invigorated persona thought it was a pretty clever chap for figuring out this whole awakening thing. At that time Oneness, non-dual awareness, became a kind of cheap parlor trick that was called upon whenever the desire arose. Relax et voila: Foyan's instant Zen. But this Beingness was only a temporary state. It gave away once again to identification with small "s," new and improved, self.

Long story short, eventually abiding non-dual awareness stabilized itself as...as...as what...? ? ? Can't say. Emptiness so incredibly full, intimate, vibrant, wondrous, and alive that it still on occasion brings tears to my eyes. How jolly everything becomes when you stop thinking it ain't. I am referring to non-duality here, definitely not implying I strive to think "happy thoughts." Silence, spaciousness, awareness, peace and quiet. Life itself. Existence. Awareness awaring itself. I like the term "suchness" that you Zen guys throw around due to its inherent meaningless nature. I have found that it is impossible to contextualize or objectify who/what I am. Indeed, I am not a who/what. Indeed I am not. Or else, in a certain sense, what I am is simply that which is. But whatever that is, it seems much more akin to a verb than a noun. Existence is no longer objectified as it once was. These days it's more like the eternal now is Life-ing = Is-ing itself merrily along.

Perhaps I am pointing to the grand, unified, indivisible wholeness that remains when I am not engaged in the narrative of me. So just what does remain when I am not thinking about it? Who knows? Above all else, life defines itself these days as "don't know mind." Silence. You could say the gap between the thoughts, but that is misleading for thoughts are not excluded from what I am alluding to here. Emptiness truly is fullness and fullness truly is none other than emptiness, I can assure you.

What I am speaking of here is not the exclusion of thought (though the past and future no longer persistently arise as before) per se, but rather the narrative of me has simply lost its power to bamboozle. Auto pilot has been disengaged. At this point, more than four years on into this new way of being, the derelict "cinema of *that which ain't transpiring*" (i.e., the past and future where I use to solely hang out) lays abandoned and mouldering through disuse. In fact it is a stretch at this point to believe it even once existed. Dreaming has ceased, the dreamer has passed away, but it is not the end of anything. Is there really an alpha and omega? That question has been rendered irrelevant.

So why the urge to write? Not quite sure, but I'll make up a story. A while back in a podcast I recall hearing you say that you have no one around to talk to about such matters. Yep, I know the feeling well enough. I seem to be a "Wandering Whosit" these days. An *unsui*, cloud water monk, as you Zennists sometimes put it. I'd welcome the opportunity to come up to your neck of the woods to chat. Apparently these cloud water guys wandered around to "test" themselves as I am sure you are well aware. It's not quite like that here though. I would not outright reject that sentiment but meeting up feels more like an opportunity to "play." You could check me out, too, and if things seem simpatico I may even uproot from Nelson and wander on down your way. Maybe part of the reason I write is a hankering to join a community oriented towards actually waking-up. That certainly seems to be YOUR message of living Zen. Just like fine Japanese Gyokuro tea, "jade dew," that is a rarity indeed! Does meeting sound like something of interest to you?

Regarding Zen itself, there seems to be a fairly strong resonance with its outlooks and practices. As I said, my teacher used to be a Zen guy, so I have heard the core teachings before as well as I have been studying them myself. Layman Pang, Huang Po and Foyan are just about the most inspirational guys I have yet to bump into besides my dear teacher Adya (and, E., you are really growing on me these days as well).

I've experienced martial arts in several forms, including Judo and later Kendo; practiced in Tokyo, they were infused with Budo, which we both know is influenced greatly by the spirit of Zen.

Tea ceremony has been another avenue for me. A brief introduction to it was experienced while in Tokyo, but this past year I have begun to revisit it with a great passion. Quite wondrously I have found Tea to be Zen and Zen, tea.

I have to tell you that I listened to more than a few of your podcasts and many of them gave me quite a thrill! There was the recognition of TRUTH being spoken there. The way you articulate the dharma is on the whole very familiar to me and not unlike the way I might language great parts of it myself. One marvelous thing you do is keep bringing it back to waking up in this lifetime. It is rare to find a teacher so pragmatic in outlook, largely prescriptive rather than descriptive in approach. I reckon your wisdom is born from actual experience itself, isn't it? Not the typical dogmatic, philosophical and scriptural rhetoric most spiritual guides tend to serve up. In short, your podcasts and actions instill a sense of trust.

I realize one must be wary of projecting too much of our wishes and desires onto the guru, but, having grown up on a beef farm, I assure you I really know what crap smells like, and I haven't gotten the faintest whiff off of you yet. So, if you happen to be inclined, and have a suitable opening in your schedule, I would welcome the chance to meet. Any time is fine. This year, the New Year, whenever...

Be apprised that going from my place to yours is a greater undertaking than it might be for others as I am visually impaired. Legally blind, in fact, and on a fixed disability income. Well now, this email has already gone on too long, so I will conclude with just a little more lore you might find of interest.

I have two degrees, one in Agricultural Science and one in film studies. I once started the biggest organic garlic farm in Eastern Ontario from scratch, since at that time no garlic enterprises existed other than modest home gardens. Worked for years in Japan/Korea as an English teacher. Award-winning filmmaker. Last job was working for Corrections Canada until the eyes went bad. Am a survival/primitive life skills expert and am an ultra-lightweight backpacking enthusiast. Wrote a book which chronicled the first part of my spiritual journey, though I haven't been particularly moved to do all the things required to get it published. Presently rent driveway space for my camper at a vegetarian collective here in South Eastern, B.C. Still dabble in writing, and volunteer at the local Christian soup kitchen many days of the week. Life seems exceedingly uncontrived and simple.

Man, that was a hell of a lot to say about nothing at all. And that was the short version! It serves you right. That's what you get when you invite riff raff like me to shoot you a quick email. LOL.

Cheers,

"Layman" DJ

7 Dec. 2013
To: DJ

Chapter 14 | December

Hi DJ,

I enjoyed your letter to the Zenman. Since my last writing I have experienced a time of more or less intense rawness, the feeling of being exposed and emotionally sensitive. Like a layer of skin has been ripped off and the resulting sensitivity is painful. I'd have to say it is a deeper aspect of the "me," the self-image that feels vulnerable and exposed. It might be described as the discomfort of being an introverted personality in a mostly extraverted world, but that could be escaping the obvious fact that it seems to be a self that experiences this, or at least that gives it any meaning or importance. Having said that, it does seem unnecessary to give it any meaning. And yet it certainly is a "me" that is responsible for the experience, and without a me, it seems clear that the experience would most likely not arise. Is that true? What say you?

So, you're ready to wind down our conversation. What prompts you to do that (if anything can be said)? I can attempt a summary, although that may be difficult - or maybe not. How about an empty page? Just joking...I do feel our investigations have been worthwhile and am willing to continue if that seems called for in the future.

I think you could stay with me or Meghan for a week or so. We're going down to Costa Rica to visit my daughter on January 16 and returning February 6, so won't be in Victoria at that time. As it happens Pamela Wilson will be there at the retreat centre for at least part of that time. I could forward your letter to Josh if you give me the word and see if he'd be interested in meeting you. As for the K centre, I can mention it to Harvey and see what comes of it. We will be having meetings at K centre on the weekend of January 4 and 5, I believe, so we could perhaps do something then. I'll forward your letter to Harvey, again, if you say it's okay. How does all that sound?

David

10 Dec. 2013
To: David

... the discomfort of being an introverted personality in a mostly extraverted world...

Personality...? ? ? Who or what is that? I mean really, really, really...? ? ?

Yet it certainly is a "me" that is responsible for the experience and without a me it seems clear that the experience would most likely not arise. Is that true? What say you?

Yes, sure. Identification is the giveaway. If you still have angst and questions, be sure Maya prevails. Nirvana, freedom, is when questioner and questioning are knowingly seen to be irrelevant or pointless. This, suddenly in my case, more slowly in others, becomes utterly apparent. That is, no-self is discovered to be the TRUE way of the world.

Your question contains the very affirmation you are seeking. You must be well aware that Elvis is still in the building, or you wouldn't be asking. At this point we are no longer dealing with beliefs are we? I have full confidence that "You KNOW" and here I mean you are lucid enough to see that you are still dealing with duality. I have the fullest confidence you are orienting yourself away from delusion. Keep it up. Be persistent.

The David character at times seems terribly real and then later less so or not at all, correct? If you still experience an arising and falling away that's Maya at play. Your job is to be aware of this. If there is any "doing" to be had, then that would be it. Be vigilant to remain lucid at all times or, better yet, if possible rest as awareness itself. Observe the arising of David and then the falling away. As discussed previously, if pain arises, so be it, but resist the urge to invigorate it through identification. Just let things be as they are. You are experiencing the last vestiges of ego at play. I hesitate to say this, for in truth the ego does not really exist, so I don't want to overly animate it or give it undue credence, but I suggest it is, now that self is most desperate to persist. Just let it wind down by its own accord. It has nothing to do with YOU/TRUTH. It's great that you speak of feelings of "sensitivity and painfulness," for though there is still self at play, you are aware of this. I am afraid that is all to be done at this point. Awareness is the

Chapter 14 | December

antidote to dreaming. You have found the donkey, now get off of it. That is all.

> So, you're ready to wind down our conversation.
> What prompts you to do that (if anything can be said)?

Perhaps you have been so in the moment these days that you have forgotten that half a year back I encouraged you to continue this investigation by saying you had made it to the half-way point (or some such), so why not push on a bit further and continue to year's end? Remember? Here's a quote by me from almost precisely a year ago, Dec. 12, which started the whole ball rolling:

"This brings me to the topic for our first email inquiry. Can we start on Jan. 1 and continue for one year? Who knows, but we could try and see what transpires." Remember?

I suggested a fixed period as I wondered if it might not create a certain sense of urgency or finality and thus engender a greater sense of sincerity or truthfulness during our investigation. So, in that spirit I still think it would be a good idea to conclude this thing. Of course, we can still chat, but if there is a purpose to anything then I think this year has served us well, and it is now drawing to a close. Regarding this investigation and what I discovered, I certainly continued to appreciate how words fail but sure had fun trying to articulate that which is unspeakable. I think my ability to conceptualize this stuff improved but, again, to what end?

I had a lot of fun sharing with you and hope you had the same. I also hope I inspired you to continue to be aware of what is really going on and in that spirit think quietude will better serve you now than anything more this forum might offer. At this juncture the single greatest pointer I can offer is "give up." The mechanics of how that actually happens is still pretty much a mystery to me, but that it can and does happen is irrefutable.

> I can attempt a summary, although that may be difficult - or maybe not.

How about sit yourself down in a quiet spot and for the first time in your life be entirely truthful and see what transpires? Forget the bullshit. Be Truth Realized. Is that really too much to ask? Is the price really too dear? If it is, then just jot down a few words describing who/what you really are (damn there's that blank page again) and why you reckon this is not the case at all times. All times, of course, being the eternal. How is it possible to make such distinctions? Why do you still persist? Why do you keep insisting on playing "now you see me, now you don't"? How about an empty page?

That's a good start but still dualistic. Send me the page that distinction fears to tread upon. Send me the SUMMARY that eyes can't read but MIND recognizes instantly. Now that would be a treat to peruse.

Cheers,
DJ

12 Dec. 2013
To: David

Hi David,

In your recent letter you wrote for the K-blog you said, "There is a sinking back into just simply being and effortlessly perceiving, the simplicity of which is more truly the 'answer' than anything thought can produce."

Not really much of an answer is it, but therein lays the truth of the matter.

Can we take your statement, then, to be the answer to the question I posed at the very beginning of this investigation: "Regarding truth realization, can the right question ever be asked"?

Is there really ever a right question to be posed, or is the trick of the thing rather to exhaust all questions? It is only then that we discover no answer is ever forthcoming. When this is well and truly realized, nothing remains to be done, for one realizes that nothing ever can be done. There simply never was a doer in the first place. Then and only then do you find yourself to be the answer you were seeking all along. It's always been YOU, but somehow this fact was overlooked. This is the "sinking back into "Beingness" you are speaking of. Not as a concept, but as life itself. Not as correct spiritual talk but as truth realized.

At the beginning of this investigation I also wrote:

If one poses a "right" question then it follows that a "right" answer may eventually be forthcoming. If there is no correct answer ever to be had then the whole premise would be moot wouldn't it? Or would it? Could there be value in asking spiritual questions that never elicit any useful reply or even any reply whatsoever? The spiritually-driven ego seems to be forever holding out the possibility that tomorrow the right question will finally be posed and at long last ALL will be revealed. Perhaps tomorrow will never arrive. Ever.

In your latest writing you also said, "Life is just unfolding. Further questioning and looking just continues to reveal that thought is not the instrument which can give any real answers."

What a succinct and insightful observation echoing my writing above. Perhaps you have come to see that life is just "life-ing" itself along. No more than that. Everything just is. If this hasn't been realized yet, these words carry little significance. If it has, astonishment will be the result. It becomes utterly clear that there is no time but the eternal now. There is nothing left to discover at some point in the future, as tomorrow quite simply does not exist. Of greater importance is the fact that this "discovering business" has been a fool's errand. This is it, baby, and has always been such. As you say, there are no "real answers" to discover. Just relaxing as REALITY itself. And you are already THAT. And that THAT is most assuredly not that at all. There are no "that's." It's all you. Minus the David story of course.

Again I recall something you and I wrote at the beginning of this investigation:

> Talking about Truth seems to be a challenging endeavor. Some aspects can be clearly spoken of and then there is a point at which nothing can be accurately said: Words and concepts cannot reach the truth.

and

"This seems a good introduction for our correspondence about talking about the truth for the next year. Is it even possible? Why bother if it is not. You say words and concepts fail yet also say, "some aspects can be clearly spoken of." I wonder, what might these CLEAR aspects be?

Perhaps you would say at this juncture that it is abundantly (and paradoxically) clear that nothing is clear. In truth, when self-ing ceases, one discovers that they are clarity itself or, maybe more correctly, they are no longer un-clarity. Any- and I am being pointedly absolutist here- any and all thoughts, ideas, feelings, etc., have nothing to do with what we are trying to point to. You once said some aspects can be clearly spoken of. Perhaps you would now agree that this is decidedly not so at all. You were confusing the finger pointing to the moon with the moon itself. Yes, there are some helpful pointers that through better articulation seem to be clearer and more relevant than those that appear to be vague, murky, and less "truthful," but that is never the "no-thing" itself. What can clearly be said about no-thingness? How does one ever accurately describe emptiness? Nonsense.

In a sense that is what you are, and it is not open to objectification. So what can be said of it? What aspects are clear and others not so? Sounds like you were making a case for duality back then. No worries. The point is now you seem less inclined to do so and that is what waking up is all about. Distinction making naturally falls by the wayside, doesn't it?

Chapter 14 | December

In the final summation all pointers, questions and answers fold back upon themselves and implode. Time is rendered non-existent. Space dissolves. The ego never gets the satisfaction of finding the answer it so desperately sought, but there is no one left who cares. As you throw your last handful of cards upon the poker table and call it a night, the final reveal causes momentary shock as you realize that there was no mystery or uncertainty to the outcome at all. You held the winning hand all along. You always did. It can't not be the case. Not the cards, though, but you. You are the answer you have been seeking. In your current letter you ask," What can be said about truth?" That is one of the best questions you ever posed.

Of course, the answer to what can be said is: Nothing. Lots can be said about untruth, but the ineffable remains simply that. True nature is realized and that is enough. The questions cease. Stillness prevails. What more is required? If it's done, it's done. Only you will know this, and the revelation will be just as you say it is: "In the not-knowing, the knowing without anything to be known." But at some point it will never again be a mere concept. It will become embodiment. How marvelous to come across the answerless answer. Can the right question ever be posed? Who knows? Who cares? Does that question even compute? Does anything compute? That's liberation for you. You just don't know.

Finally, you said, "All seeking has come to an end in the fullness and wholeness of emptiness." I might be moved to say the same thing myself from time to time but surmise that there is one difference between our outlooks. I don't really believe my own bullshit. How about you? What is this "emptiness" you are speaking of? Emptiness as opposed to what? A full and whole content less nothingness—what clap trap. If you momentarily winced or took offence at this observation, be assured there is still a bull shitter lurking about and he answers to the name of David. As for me...

325

Sincerely,
Great Big Fool
DJ ☺

13 Dec. 2013
To: DJ

Hi,

    I enjoyed your letter very much and only winced perhaps a tiny bit. I'll try to write soon in response and with some kind of "summary." I think your own summary is very much on the mark, and there is no disagreement here. Occupied with events at the K Centre over the weekend...

Love,
David

13 Dec. 2013
To: David

    I'm glad you enjoyed it. Yes, please write a bit of truthiness in summary.

DJ

    PS I remember Richard Rose had some pretty sage advice when he used to encourage his students to set a goal, any old goal, and just stick to it. We managed to keep this one didn't we? Hooray!

DJ

20 Dec. 2013
To: DJ

    Okay, I will attempt a "summary" of our investigation from my side. I reread your summary and find it, as I said before, very much to the point and penetrating in its insights.

Chapter 14 | December

I think one of our starting questions was something like, "What can be shared and talked about in relation to truth and self-discovery, realization, or whatever we want to call it?" I would say that we've discovered that many things can be talked about. There is so much talk about these things going on all the time. But the thoughts and concepts about truth are all representations and not the actuality, not the direct experience. They are all creations of thought, whereas truth transcends thought, is prior to it or beyond it. Even saying that is dualistic, as you pointed out. (Emptiness in opposition to what?) Some representations are, however, more accurate and useful than others although, at the same time, so-called individuals may not agree on which pointers are the most accurate and useful. An important thing to see is that the pointers are not what is being pointed to.

It seems to me that an important aspect of our exploration has been the significance given to "truthiness" or speaking from where we really live, looking at and exposing the concepts that are actually significant in shaping our lives rather than speaking in abstractions and high-sounding spiritual concepts that are not being directly known in our own experience. In order for the investigation to have any real power and impact it has to include looking into what we are taking as real in our lives, and there must be an honesty about "where we are at." This keeps our inquiry authentic.

Seeing is different from thinking. Seeing involves honesty or truthfulness in the looking. Certain qualities seem to be important, such as the willingness to look and to see beyond the defensive reactions of the (imagined) self, steadfastness in staying with the process, and so on. How these qualities come to be active in an individual is mysterious and perhaps a question of "grace." Buddhists might disagree, but it seems that the whole thing is grace, as there is in fact no one here, no doer, to be responsible for the cultivation or arising of helpful character traits or capacities.

Upon closely examining the self, it is seen to be just like a rainbow. From a distance it appears to exist and be very real, but upon approaching it there is nothing solid to be found: It is an illusion, an appearance without substance even though, in the case of the rainbow, a very beautiful one. To see and experience this about the self, even to a small degree, can be very disconcerting as it overturns the basic assumptions by which I have lived "my" life. The process of facing the fact that "I" am an illusion is often felt as painful and upsetting. And yet there is no going back and there are also the moments and periods of joy and bliss in experiencing at least temporarily the freedom from the grip of the anxious, insecure "me" that habitually tries to shore up its illusory existence.

What is the point of it all? It seems to be the experiencing itself, life revealing itself to itself in all its variety which on the "spiritual journey" seems to take the shape of ever more subtle and profound knowings of life itself. And then there is the truth of simply being, the meaning beyond meaning. Consciousness experiencing itself in its expressions as this particular body-mind organism and even going beyond dualistic subject-object experiencing as we normally know it, beyond words and concepts to a non-objective knowing about which nothing can be said. And to come back to your statement near the beginning of your letter, nothing can ultimately be accurately said about anything, as the truth of anything cannot be captured in the representations. And beyond that is the fact that there is no "thing" to be spoken of.

Your imaginary friend in the inquiry, David

20 Dec. 2013
To: DJ

Your point about not believing our own bullshit is of great value in all of this, and I take it to heart. How often it can be remembered will be seen (hopefully)! It's a paradox that I was relating to Meghan just yesterday that "I" have a tendency to be a know-it-all and yet a contrasting awareness and feeling arises that any such positioning or posturing doesn't hold up as a real truth and is, therefore, not a coherent and genuinely harmonious expression of being, i.e., it's BS...

25 Dec. 2013
To: David

Hi David,

The subject line of your last message reads "final word?" I will add a concluding comment to compliment the part you wrote about not believing one's own BS. I consider the following to be the final punctuation point of our 12-month investigation, a final period mark that unambiguously wraps it all up.

Waking up has an intense sense of finality to it. Or perhaps it is the other way around. Perhaps finality has an intense sense of waking up to it. In whatever way that plays out, by whatever means or path one takes to arrive there, the seeker at long last is rendered speechless. Nothing remains to be said. Thoughts, self, time and space are all extinguished in the moment. Nothing endures but the eternal pause. In a paradoxical way, though, it is seen not to be an end point, for in truth one realizes that they are the eternal itself, the unmanifested, which you are well aware has no beginning or end to it. This is what you truly are and it has always been such. So utterly apparent once seen but previously so remote.

One laughs at how obvious it is and may wonder why his or her spiritual guide never pointed out such a simple thing to them before. You may feel utterly gobsmacked, as I did, and a bit foolish as well for being able to overlook such an obvious thing for so long. Amazement, mirth, profound wonder and unconditional love all mark the appearance of the divine period mark, the full stop. That's why my best advice is to "just give up."

But, of course, this has to be a natural inclination which often simply arises out of plain old frustration and fatigue. I certainly got tired of it all. All the untruth, position-taking, resistance, phony posturing and bull shit. Here's how it all ended for "the me." I don't believe I have ever shared my "final reckoning" in any detail with you before. Perhaps it will be of interest. I offer it up as "my" last word on the matter for, indeed, this occurrence marked the extinction of duality itself.

As I mentioned previously, there was a period of a few months, precipitated by a distinct incident which fomented the radical dropping of self, whereby I could subsequently bring "nothingness" to the fore by simply wishing it so. I referred to it previously as a "cheap parlor trick." I had indeed awoken out of self for a short spell but had again slipped back into delusion though now I had a new "super power" at my disposal. I was the character that astounded itself by causing the "big wide open" to break out faster than Clark Kent took to change uniforms. But this was not true abiding realization. Once back in delusion, though, this fact escaped me.

So there I was, still ensconced at the hermitage, quite merrily "doing" along as all human doings do, a guy who knew what awakening truly was (and to be sure I did, but the problem was it was not abiding but, rather, merely a state-bound phenomenon). And then an opportunity arose to take Lama Big Mucky Muck's two-week Mahamudra retreat. You had to qualify for this year-end special event by accumulating a certain number of other silent retreats under your belt. The year before I had received the initial invitation but someone subsequently decided I was still a neophyte and at the last minute I was duly uninvited. My feathers were a bit ruffled then, but a year hence everything had changed. Borrowing from Mafia terminology, now I was a "made man," a "wise guy" so to speak.

This Mahamudra event was touted as an opportunity to discover the direct path to enlightenment. Not needed in my case as I reckoned I was already there, but I saw it as a potential recipe book of sorts. Surely the Tibetan Buddhists had plumbed the depths of reality sufficiently enough over the course of several millennia to allow me the opportunity to cull the best of their clever pointers to share with interested seekers. I was expecting much more wheat than chaff, and I figured my new talent would allow me to easily discern the two. Now that I knew what this awakening thing was all about, how wonderful it would be to admire centuriesworth of accrued wisdom, I thought. I should have known better.

The western tulku leading this retreat centre had never presented as particularly wise or skillful in the past, so why should I have expected otherwise in this case? All my dealings with him suggested that he was a poor meditator with little to no direct experience of TRUTH realization. He never cited personal anecdotes nor seemed to understand anything spiritually relevant save for the most rudimentary aspects of the dharma as spelled out in his scriptural texts. He had spent the previous winter writing a fresh new treatise on Mahamudra especially for this upcoming event (the previous guide was truly dreadful) so I hoped at least here he could excel. How hard would it be for this titular guru to simply copy the work of past great master Mahamudra "chefs," I wondered, and in doing so compose a fabulous recipe book that would allow any interested parties who opened its pages the ability to serve up TRUTH feasts whenever the appetite longed for spiritually imbued gourmet fare? Again, my hopes had run much too high at this institution for the terminally confused. As things would transpire, this buffoon mightily failed once again.

What had promised to be a quintessential teaching manual turned out to be nothing more than a great recipe for everlasting delusion. Day after day this ignoramus served up "doing" after doing such that lifetimes worth of endeavor would have been required to wade through it all. And in the end Maya would have still ruled the day. Hour upon hour he overloaded the assembled seekers with outlandish nonstop philosophical rhetoric and dogmatic pronouncements and practices so far removed from common sense that only an imbecile could seriously entertain them. At one point it got so ridiculous that he invited us to leave if we didn't enjoy the message.

Most of the assembled seemed to lap it up. Couldn't they perceive the mushroom doctrine at play? Feed them crap and keep them in the dark. No one, teacher included, seemed the least bit interested in discerning the shit from the Shinola. How sad it all was. The longer it went on the wearier and more repulsed I became. After about three days of this onslaught, I could barely force myself to attend. Delusion upon delusion was the only thing being served up in the dank, moldering, underlit yurt that served as Dharma central. Still I continued to endure the banality of it all.

Around the seven-day mark a young friend, who was helping out at the hermitage and meditating a bit but not participating directly in the retreat, asked me how it was all going. "Well," I replied, "It's crap. It's all crap." Pressed further I added, "As far as the eye can see, its nothing but unadulterated bullshit." My chum and I laughed at the frank nature of my reply. What else to do but make light of a truly outrageous and absurd situation.

Then I offered him up an analogy. I said, "If we understand that ultimately all pointers are not the TRUTH itself, but for the sake of analogy take alive, eloquent and truthful pointers to be colorful jelly beans and the rest to be nonsense, then what I have found is that Adyashanti serves up boxcar loads of sweet jelly beans and on his great pile we find mixed in as well the occasional small fluffy stuffed teddy bear which represents a smattering of his less skillful pointers. Thus, sweet and tasty morsels are eminently easy to apprehend and grab hold of since they lie mostly unobscured by the fetters of untruth (the plushies)." Though Adya's pile was not entirely composed of the sought after jelly beans of wisdom, bumping into the occasional plush plaything wasn't all that bad either. That's the kind of pile I never hesitated to get myself mired in.

On the other hand, I explained, Lama Big Mucky Muck ignobly offered us a rank, stinking heap of fetid dung into which a few jelly beans lay deeply buried. Who should be forced to wade through all that crap in hopes of acquiring a sweety or two, I pointed out to my friend. And if the truth was ever momentarily apprehended, if one ever managed to snatch a bean or two from somewhere out of his revolting quagmire of rhetoric, still it carried a stench about it, for it remained apparent that it had originated from a goddamn shit pile!

Come day nine or ten it was clear that I had had enough. It was time to quit. I came to the meditation hall nursing the beginnings of a cold, just the sort of manifestation I needed to politely excuse myself from any further proceedings, but it was more than that simple kind of withdrawing I sought. I was really done. I recall sitting in front of that teacher and thinking "Man, how far off the mark you are. You are so full of it. And how about the" sheeple" lying about your feet? They are equally confused and full of crap too." And then a thought struck me like a Taser zap that sent me convulsing to my knees, perhaps the most liberating direct seeing of small "s" self I had ever had:

"And guess what... guess what Mister...yeah you, DJ, smarty pants: You are full of crap, too. The teacher, the assembled seekers, and you are not different. All is delusion. Nothing but bullshit from horizon to horizon." And I knew this was so. It was irrefutable. No more wiggle room remained to allow my gaze to shift. I saw like never before that I was full of crap too, just like anyone else. I was so fucking full of it!

And that was that. I/it was done. I was so fucking over it all. Done with the whole bloody affair. Kaput. I had well and truly had enough. Surrender with no conditions was the only outcome left to me. No more resistance or hope could henceforth ever be mustered. Just done...it was over. That's nirvana for you. That's true cessation. That's the kind of period mark that ends all further conversation. That's giving up. Nothing else will suffice. And that, my friend, brings this conversation to a full close. I ask you, David, is there really anything left to say? Really? Hopefully by now you have realized that there has never been any need to respond in the first place. You are the eternal pause. The end.

All is love. Love is all. Love ALL.
DJ

27 Dec. 2013
To: DJ

The Cloth... Have No Emperor

Dear DJ,

Here are my final, final words... for this year anyway.

I agree there is nothing that remains to be said. And yet the urge to speak arises and the sense that there is a possibility of expressing an ever deeper realizing of the truth beyond words, an even more final finality. It doesn't make any sense and yet it does... Oh well, what's the harm in trying. I can now confirm more truly than before it seems, from a deeper sense of direct experiencing, your statement that "I am the truth."

Your description of the experience with the tulku is hilarious and your letter does indeed wrap it all up. From my side, I wrote something in my journal the day before receiving your letter and am struck by some of the similarities between my insights and the ones you have expressed in your "summaries." So there arose an urge to share my writing with you, and I think I will also post it on the K centre website. So, here it is. I think it's interesting in that it speaks of the "means" or "method" as well as the "end" in a way that for me summarizes my exploration to this point.

During a dyad exercise a few days ago, while contemplating the question, "What am I?", a number of very interesting insights arose. The contemplation began with a seeing that an "I" thought would arise and then immediately another thought would assign a significance to the first thought, would give it meaning. The creation of the reality of an "I" was happening moment by moment through thought itself giving substance to the idea of a "me." Without this meaning given by thought the arising of a concept of "me" would have no significance.

The attention then naturally went to the looking at why thought was continuously doing this, being active in creating the "me" moment to moment. It was seen that thought was reacting habitually to avoid the void. Thought was aware (or was reacting to the awareness) that it is transient and dissolving into the unknown each moment. Thought was moving away from a perceived emptiness or not-knowing each moment

As this process was observed, there came a sense of falling back into the not-knowing aware space and a sense that this space was more truly "what I am" than anything thought could produce. The mind became very still and silent.

Staying in that still sense of being, there arose spontaneously a clear sense of timelessness and the word "eternity" presented itself as a description. Not eternity as never-ending time but as totally outside of time, in another dimension entirely. "I" was eternal, timeless Being. A sense of being was arising out of the Unknown. Somehow there then arose the perception that what I really am is not the limited "I" created by thought but that the roots of "my" being are grounded in the Source of everything, unbounded, Life itself. "I am That" became completely true: I cannot be other than the Totality, the Source of all. This was much more than an idea: It was a fact.

Then, in the effortless looking or seeing it became clear that even "I am That" was dualistic: "That," or Source, was being conceived as an object. It was being conceived out of the unknowable source and was in a sense grounded in that Source and at the same time the objectification of it was happening in thought and perception. When this was seen, the duality collapsed into a pure not-knowing. The "I" that had been the object of inquiry had dissolved. Laughter arose in this seeing that the natural culmination of the search for "who" or "what" I really am is the complete forgetting of myself. So much so that there is no knowing of a self or of there not being a self. There is nothing left to say about myself in that state of truth where the difference between "I" and Truth has dissolved. Thought can come up with approximations and descriptions of that which is beyond description and thus we have such proclamations as "I am That," "I am the Truth," "I am love, freedom, bliss, consciousness," and so on. These are beautiful expressions of what ultimately is beyond all expression.

And then comes the question, "Is it beyond, or is even that just another duality of thought?" The answer comes not in words but as a further falling away of division. In that or out of that or as that arose the perfume that might be called love.

What value is there in sharing these types of experiences with others? I don't know. Krishnamurti says it's like a flower opening to reveal its beauty to that which can perceive it and be moved by it. Life itself expressing itself within and as the play of duality and the melting away of the duality which never really existed.

Interestingly, since that experience and the writing about it there have been some fairly strong movements of such emotions as anger and sadness. Go figure!

Well, I think that does it. It has been a joy to engage with you in this exploration to end all explorations.

Love,

David

29 Dec. 2013
To: David

"Final, final words."...great words to end this investigation by. Very profound. Still a gap, though.

Look into this and see what I mean. Obviously, there has been movement in the right direction and this has been the case for some time, though I reckon still a bit further to go. You are still a bit "rare" in the centre. Not quite cooked yet. Come to the full stop and then rest.

DJ☺

Afterword

2 Aug. 2014
To: DJ

DJ suggested I might like to write something of an afterword concerning our experience of dialoguing for a year via emails. I am happy to address what was significant for me in the process. I want to comment on what changed or shifted as a result of our conversations and the inquiry inspired by them. Further, I'd like to discuss how is life different after the sharing we enjoyed. Writing about those issues sounds like a good idea, but as I sit down to write something about it, I realize that to say anything definitive about what life was like before – or even what it's like now – is not so easy. Perhaps that is something that can be said.   There just doesn't seem to be much interest in conceptualizing and verbalizing the past – what it was like a year or two ago – nor is there much interest in conceptualizing and verbalizing the "present" or more recent experience of the life. Perhaps this means that "I" am more in the present than I used to be, living more as Presence and less identified with the conceptual mind which creates past, present, and future – the time bound reality. The exercise of measuring the experience that is happening or that was happening doesn't seem very relevant, useful, or interesting.

Lately, life has been unfolding just as it has, sometimes flowing with ease, joy, and love and sometimes seemingly more difficult, challenging, and uncomfortable.   (I could say the same about the conversations with DJ. Sometimes easy going and enjoyable; sometimes a rocky road which produced reactions and emotions which were far from pleasant.) Throughout is an attentiveness to what is going on, to the quality of the experiencing and the way thought is creating and projecting my reality. There is a sustained interest in self inquiry, of which the conversations in this book were a valuable example. I deeply enjoy inquiring on my own, in the dyad format used at Enlightenment Intensive retreats, in group settings, and in whatever situations present themselves. Being aware and watchful as much as possible, which has become natural and spontaneous, keeps the consciousness open to ongoing insight, learning, and discovery. The sense of being a separate self seems to have thinned out significantly, which allows for a greater availability to the realms of pure being and the experiencing of beauty, wholeness, joy, love, contentment, and inherent meaning or significance. A lovely sense of peacefulness and aliveness in the heart often shows up. The conversations with DJ have been a quite one-pointed and concerted aspect of a varied and rich experiencing which, over the year, has included the various forms of inquiry mentioned, relationship, discussions with other friends, a few interesting experiments with powerful consciousness altering substances, listening to teachers, reading, and so forth. Some force from beyond "me" seems to be orchestrating a surrendering and letting go, and there is a sense as I contemplate and write this that there is an invitation from Wholeness to enter and merge with the beauty and ungraspable simplicity of Is-ness.

Has there been an awakening of the type that DJ speaks of, an abrupt break from the conventional dualistic consciousness, a radical shift from egoic consciousness to "enlightenment" or non-egoic consciousness? DJ may not agree, but for me at least at this point it doesn't seem that a definitive answer can be given to that question. It doesn't appear to be a case of "off" or "on", as DJ puts it. Of course, this may change, but as I write this, in this moment, the question itself just seems irrelevant. In this there is a beautiful sense of freedom and nothing is lacking. Perhaps DJ would not disagree with that. And yesterday he emailed me asking how life is treating me these days. (A leading question?) As I contemplated the question, there was an asking, "To whom does the question refer, who is the "me" that life would be treating?" There was a clear sense of the emptiness and non-findability of this supposed self, and again the freedom of this was felt. I imagined asking DJ the same question and sensed the emptiness of the entity who would have any response, the lack of any division between him, me, and life.

3 Aug. 2014
To: David

Dear David,

My reaction on reading your afterword is a recognition of : truthiness, aliveness, joy.

Could your summation be anything other than perfection? Somewhere in the book I wrote something along the lines of "...occasionally the wonder, love and joy can still bring me to my knees."

It's been awhile since that kind of experience has arisen, but after just finishing reading the last word of your last line I had a good long wonderful sob. I am in the library, as I don't yet have internet at the new place, but I could not care less that people could see the tears rolling down my cheeks.

Just wonderful. Thank you for those words that point to a profundity beyond compare. Thanks, my friend. Or just thanks. And thanks for being such a good sport while writing the book and during our many face-to-face conversations. Deep, deep gratitude. It's been about ten minutes now, and I'm still brushing away the tears.

Just wonderful...

Love,

DJ

www.ingramcontent.com/pod-product-compliance
Lightning Source LLC
Chambersburg PA
CBHW032059090426
42743CB00007B/179